D0787790

Comedy and the Woman Writer

Comedy and the Woman Writer

Woolf, Spark, and

Feminism

by Judy Little

Lincoln and London

University
of Nebraska
Press

Portions of Chapters 1, 2, 3, and 4
have previously been published,
in somewhat different form, as
"Satirizing the Norm: Comedy in
Women's Fiction," *Regionalism
and the Female Imagination* 2
(Fall 1977 and Winter 1977–78):
39–49; "*Jacob's Room* as Comedy:
Woolf's Parodic Bildungsroman,"
in *New Feminist Essays on
Virginia Woolf,* ed. Jane Marcus
(London: Macmillan; Lincoln:
University of Nebraska Press,
1981), pp. 105–24; "Festive
Comedy in Woolf's *Between the
Acts,*" *Women and Literature* 5
(Spring 1977): 26–37; and "Humor
and the Female Quest: Margaret
Drabble's *The Realms of Gold,*"
*Regionalism and the Female
Imagination* 4 (Fall 1978): 44–52.

The paper in this book meets the
guidelines for permanence and
durability of the Committee on
Production Guidelines for Book
Longevity of the Council on
Library Resources.

Library of Congress
Cataloging in Publication Data

Little, Judy, 1941-
Comedy and the woman writer.

Includes bibliographical
references and index.
1. English fiction – Women
authors – History and criticism.
2. English fiction – 20th
century – History and criticism.
3. Woolf, Virginia, 1882-1941 –
Style. 4. Spark, Muriel – Style.
5. Comic, The. 6. Feminism in
literature. I. Title.
PR830.W62L57 1983
823'.91'099287 82-19999
ISBN 0-8032-2859-7

For Frances L. Little and the memory of M. J. Little

Contents

Preface

This book began with an idea of Virginia Woolf's—that comedy written by women may be different from comedy written by men. The huge subject assumed a horizon or two as a result of several Modern Language Association special sessions on Virginia Woolf; during these discussions, papers by Margaret Comstock, Jane Marcus, and Beverly Schlack were particularly helpful to me. Two MLA special sessions on "Female Humor," generated by the energy and intelligence of Emily Toth, were extremely important in the development of the critical approach which I have taken in this study. These discussions about female humor helped me to ask the right questions. I began to define some answers as a result of a conference on "Women and Society" held in 1979 at St. Michael's College in Winooski, Vermont. At this conference Helen Trobian's paper "Feminism, Humor, and Religion" was especially stimulating because of the wide and overlapping implications it examined in its threefold subject. Finally, a rereading of the fiction that I planned to consider in my study confirmed my suspicion that the concept of a "norm" required an in-depth redefinition, particularly if a distinctively female comic perspective were to be identified. For this reason my first chapter needed to be more than a friendly greeting; it is substantive, providing the rationale and apparatus for my discussion.

A complete genealogy of this book would be as extensive as a Biblical series of "begats," but I do want to thank Eddie Epstein, whose reading of the manuscript at an early stage encouraged me to keep going, and Louise DeSalvo, whose perceptive criticism helped me to finish the book. Alan Cohn, our Humanities Librarian, has provided thorough and willing assistance. The English Department at Southern Illinois University has given generous financial support for copying and typing. The College of Liberal Arts has also extended financial assistance, as has the university by granting me a sabbatical leave. I wish especially to thank the typists who have worked on this book: Kay Parrish, Kim Grandys, Angie Spurlock, and Joy Starks. In addition thanks are due to Pauline Duke, the office supervisor who sees to it that the shuffle keeps going and that nothing gets lost in it. Most of all, I want to acknowledge the attentive encouragement given me by the late Virginia Faulkner of the University of Nebraska Press. She saw this book when it was no more than an idea, and her matter-of-fact belief in the book was a continuing support to my own belief in it.

Comedy and the Woman Writer

1

Ritual as Revolution:
Comedy and Women

As often as comedy has been awarded either firm or faint praise for its conservative and stabilizing qualities, it has also been suspected of subversive and revolutionary propensities. Both the praise and the suspicion are warranted. Subversive comic imagery may give us portrayals of the disillusioned and the oppressed as they mock the hypocritical or the tyrannous. The "outsider" is in this instance the hero, as Moll Flanders is, or Huckleberry Finn, or any picaresque hero. On the other hand the more conservative comic statements take the very opposite approach; they direct our laughter against the outsider, against the one who deviates from a norm of beauty or appropriate behavior. Both of these comic attitudes or approaches have been variously explained and defined as rooted in celebrations of human vitality, or linked to a satiric purpose, or released as wit from the psychological censor responsible for the civil utterance of sexual and aggressive impulses.[1] Although I will have occasion to draw upon these various attempts to define the comic, my primary concern in the present study is with the *kind* of comic imagery that is present in the work of Virginia Woolf, Muriel Spark, and some other writers. This imagery is usually that of festive license or of an important "passage" in life. Further, such imagery — imagery of revolt and inversion — is ordinarily not resolved in the fiction of these authors. In this respect the imagery differs from the license of traditional festive holidays, and certainly it differs from rounded-off comic fiction in which the hero is ultimately reintegrated into society. The comedy I am considering here is renegade comedy. It mocks the deepest possible norms, norms four thousand years old.

Such radical denials have a precedent in the context of comedy, but for the most part the overturning of accepted values has occurred within the carefully defined license of holiday celebrations. Comedy derives many of its characteristic motifs from the ritual practices belonging to "liminality." The word describes those threshold occasions in human experience which are marked by ordeal or celebration; these include initiations, weddings, or the arrival of a new season. In some societies these events give rise to practices which have become stock motifs of comedy: the blurring or reversing of sex identity, the inversion of the usual authority so that clowns mock kings, and a festive sense of community which celebrates a shared humanity rather than respecting the distinctions of class, prestige, and role. Such occasions are, in a stable society, surrounded by a context of order. The mocking is hedged with divinity and taboo; ultimately, the initiation, or other liminal event, is completed, and the festive license fades into the common day of social structure and orderly behavior. Comic literature, and tragic literature as well, often draw upon these liminal motifs. Comedy in which the liminal elements are never resolved, comedy which implies, or perhaps even advocates, a permanently inverted world, a radical reordering of social structures, a real rather than temporary and merely playful redefinition of sex identity, a relentless mocking of truths otherwise taken to be self-evident or even sacred — such comedy can well be called subversive, revolutionary, or renegade.

In a sense, all comedy might be said to mock some norms and to affirm others, but I want to emphasize that the comedy written by Woolf, Spark, and some other novelists mocks norms which have been considered stable values for millenia. Since comedy of this kind is intricately interlocked with everything else that is happening in the fictional medium, a rather substantial critical examination of all the novels written by Woolf and Spark is the best way to define and describe the comedy, and to show how it is functioning. Each of these two novelists is a major writer of her generation, and for that reason alone her complete opus deserves reassessment whenever scholarship or a critical model emerges that can illuminate her work. Following a close look at Woolf and Spark, I want to examine in the final chapter the appropriate novels of several other writers in whose work feminist comedy has emerged with vigor. In the fiction of these writers, such as Penelope Mortimer and Beryl Bainbridge, the comedy once again is a fairly extreme kind; the inversions continue as if all the year were playing holiday. The novels affirm — when they affirm anything — only a state of continuing liminality, betweenness, of being "between the acts," to use the title of Woolf's last novel. For these writers, in their most striking comic work, the basic comparison, or juxtaposition, which is essential in perceiving the comic, or in making the joke, is not usually the traditional one of instinct versus its civilized expression, or eccentricity versus a socially acceptable norm; instead, the deeply rooted norms themselves are the objects of attack. The other half of the comic juxtaposition, the affirmative half, varies with the author, but can be generally described as a reinterpretation of liminality itself, a hint of new motifs, new myths, often expressed in a distinctly female imagery.

Before turning to the novelists, I want to examine the social and literary implications of liminality, and then draw upon sociologists as well as literary critics to clarify the term *norm*; finally, in this introductory chapter, I will consider the issue of a women's tradition in literature, and especially in comic fiction.

Liminality describes a threshold (*limen*), a transition, a borderline area or condition. Strictly speaking, the word applies to the middle portion of each "rite of passage" as described by Arnold van Gennep. Rites which accompany major transitions in life — birth, initiation, weddings, death — have a tripartite structure of separation from society, transition or liminality, and finally reincorporation into society.[2] For instance, during the liminal phase of a ritual, individuals to be initiated have neither their old selves and old positions in society nor their new ones. The liminal phase of a rite characteristically emphasizes the annulled identity of the persons undergoing the rite and expresses sometimes their freedom from the usual norms of behavior. The anthropologist Victor Turner describes the features of the middle, or transition, phase of a rite of passage: "The intervening liminal phase is thus betwixt and between the categories of ordinary social life. Symbols and metaphors found in abundance in liminality represent various dangerous ambiguities of this ritual stage, since the classifications on which order normally depends are annulled and obscured — other symbols designate temporary antinomic liberation from behavioral norms and cognitive rules."[3] Since persons in the liminal stage are "betwixt and between," socially and psychologically, they are temporarily stripped of identity, role, even sexual identity. They are outside the usual behaviors. Each sex may, in some cultures, dress in the other's clothes at this time, or both may wear identical robes. The period of license, of freedom from behavioral norms, is also typical of seasonal rituals, and may express itself by means of "inversion" and "community." The jester will mock the king, the boy may pose as bishop, and lower-class persons may mock and playfully torment those normally in authority over them; further, the general merrymaking will express a sense of community in which all are united as equals, rather than bound by hierarchies of privilege and class.[4]

Certain features of liminality obviously translate readily into literary patterns, especially the patterns of quest and festive comedy. During rituals of initiation, Turner writes, "liminality is frequently likened to death, to being in the womb, to invisibility, to darkness, to bisexuality, to the wilderness, and to an eclipse of the sun or moon."[5] The paradigm of the hero's quest, which I will examine more closely a little later, incorporates these liminal motifs of death, a journey through wilderness or darkness, and often a journey into landscapes vaguely female or maternal in imagery. As Northrop Frye observes of literature, such archetypal imagery is likely to appear in the proximity of weddings, deaths, initiations, exorcisings, and occasions of seasonal celebration.[6] The archetypal quest pattern is in essence a rite of passage, and displays liminal motifs in common with those of initiation rituals. The imagery of seasonal liminality and the inversions of hierarchy make a large contribution to Shakespeare's plays, and C. L. Barber has aptly described its expression there as "festive comedy."[7] Further, and in a feminist context, Annette Kolodny has appropriately given the designation "inversion" to certain images in novels written by women, images which attack and sometimes parody such traditional modes of feminine fulfillment as pregnancy and large families.[8]

Liminal motifs do not always fall neatly into place within a literary context that affirms order or within a society that does so. Although the customary explanation of festivity offered by both the anthropologists and literary scholars is that it ultimately affirms the established social structure,[9] this interpretation has received some challenges. Ian Donaldson suggests, in his examination of the "world upside down" motif in English comic drama and fiction, that in the past the literary use of inversion has sometimes probed questions which are not entirely answered by a conventional happy ending of reestablished order; further, Rabelais could aim a sharp attack against medieval institutions, Mikhail Bakhtin argues, because this irreverent comic writer drew much of his material from folk festivals which had traditionally attacked prevailing social structures.[10] Anthropologists and sociologists have recently pointed to the liminal aspects of most religious or secular reform movements; these often proclaim the values of "equality," deny distinctions of class and prestige, deny the socially expected expressions of sex, and advocate a community of sharing rather than an organized structure of authority. Saint Francis, John Wesley, George Fox, modern Beats and Hippies — all manifested in various ways the liminal opposition to hierarchy and to worldly norms. Asceticism, voluntary poverty of a religious community, and the pacifist counterculture's adoption of sexually ambiguous clothing (a uniform of blue jeans for both sexes, for instance) can be described as liminal gestures, as symbolic statements of opposition to the prevailing order; these statements have in common with initiation rites, and with festivity, the elements of inversion, of annulled or blurred sex identity, and the rejection of class distinctions.[11]

Such manifestations of liminality are a potential threat to the established social structures. For this reason literature which uses liminal images can be called "political," and when I use the word *politics* or *political* in this study, I am using them in this thematic sense. Obviously, neither a festive celebration nor a novel is political in the sense in which a ballot is. Nevertheless, there is some indication that liminal images in a popular medium can have an effect on institutions. During the fifteenth and sixteenth centuries broadsides using the *topos* of the "world upside down" were extremely popular; these portrayed, for instance, a child feeding the mother, fish nesting in a tree, an ox slaughtering a man, a child beating the father, an army of women attacking a fortress, a woman bearing arms and standing beside her husband, who is spinning. David Kunzle argues that these popular publications made a large contribution to Lutheran propaganda against the pope and may have been associated also with the peasant revolt of 1525.[12] Further, the motif of the "woman on top," politically and domestically, a motif frequent in festive celebrations and in popular iconography, may have encouraged women to join in the riots of laborers in preindustrial Europe. Although the motif—a woman vigorously thrashing a kneeling man, for instance—was supposed to symbolize a quite reprehensible anarchy, the very existence of the idea in popular art, as Natalie Davis observes, may have rendered "the unruly option a more conceivable one."[13]

Liminality is the most ambiguous, the most potentially anarchic phase of ritual; it is also the most creative. When liminal elements are prominent in social movements, the result may be new institutions, new norms, new myths. While a traditional initiation rite will, after the liminal "death" and inversions, bring the individual to a "rebirth" and a new identity within the social structure, a social crisis may manifest liminal elements which do not finally become resolved into the former structures; instead, the liminal motifs themselves enter and change social institutions. Turner summarizes the potential reversals: "High status will have become low status and vice versa.... Institutionalized relationships will have become informal; social regularities will have become irregularities. New norms and rules may have been generated during attempts to redress conflict; old rules will have fallen into disrepute and have been abrogated. The bases of political support will have been altered."[14] Liminality tends to generate not only new norms, but also new myths, which may find expression in rituals, philosophy, and art. In fact, we can expect that such "exceptionally liminal thinkers" as poets, writers, and prophets will find new metaphors and archetypes—as Turner observes while he draws upon Shelley— since these are, after all, the "unacknowledged legislators."[15]

We can expect also, especially in a time of social change, that the work of writers who perceive themselves as "outsiders," as persons assigned to the threshold of a world that is not theirs, will manifest the distinctive features of inversion, mocked hierarchies, communal festivity, and redefinition of sex identity. If the work of such writers is comic, it will be comedy that mocks the norm radically, and perhaps generates hints and symbols of new myths. The novelists with whom this study is primarily concerned all perceive themselves to some extent as outsiders, though the term is Virginia Woolf's. Of the two she enunciates more directly her perception of the liminality of the woman writer. In an early review (1918) she considered the reasons that might have led women to become novelists: "The capacity to criticize the other sex had its share in deciding women to write novels, for indeed that particular vein of comedy has been but slightly worked, and promises great richness."[16] Later in her career, it was not only the "richness" of the opportunity for comedy that attracted Woolf's attention. By the time she wrote "Women and Fiction" (1929), she suggested that criticism offered by one sex about the other might substantially alter the prevailing notions of what is serious; a general inversion of values might result. The reason for this is that women's values are different from those of men: "Thus, when a woman comes to write a novel, she will find that she is perpetually wishing to alter the established values — to make serious what appears insignificant to a man, and trivial what is to him important."[17] As her work demonstrates, by "established values," Woolf implies basic attitudes, beliefs, and behavior, rather than the surface artificialities and eccentricities of a particular generation, for instance, although these eccentricities do also appear in her novels. In much of her most exciting and creative comedy she engages in a lyric and bemused mockery of venerable heroic (masculine) imagery.

Like Muriel Spark, Virginia Woolf mocks even the mythic patterns of male, or patriarchal, liminality. The long-standing, anciently derived pattern of the quest — a pattern whose heroic figures have been overwhelmingly male — contains elements that have analogues in the liminal phase of ritual. In stable societies, and certainly in long-enduring cultures, such as the one roughly designated as "Western," these liminal motifs dovetail safely and conventionally into an ultimate affirmation of a culture's deepest values, in this case patriarchal ones. It is only when liminality gets out of hand, so to speak, that its creative aspects, described by Turner, Davis, and others, begin to emerge as social reform and perhaps as major new cultural symbols. When Virginia Woolf, in her comic fiction, moves subtly against "established values," she moves against some of the most deeply established ones. She mocks the male hero even in his traditionally sacred archetypal landscape; in effect, by so doing she mocks the male-imaged pattern of the "hero with a thousand faces," or what Joseph Campbell calls "the norm of the monomyth."[18] Woolf, along with Spark, mocks many of the deeply established motifs which sociologists would say belong to our primary beliefs, especially when these beliefs concern sex identity and the roles of men and women.

The revolutionary laughter occasionally heard in the fiction of other women writers will further illustrate the point. The female warriors in Monique Wittig's novel *Les Guérillères* prepare themselves for battle (against men), or rest from it, by means of games which build their psychological muscles. In one of these games the women laugh ferociously at questions like the following: "Who must observe the three obediences and whose destiny is written in their anatomy?" Laughing, the women slap each other on the shoulders, and "some of the women, lips parted, spit blood."[19] A similarly violent and shocking laughter is described by Doris Lessing in *The Summer Before the Dark*. Although Kate Brown felt guilty about it, she and another London housewife used to indulge in "cow sessions": "They began improvising, telling anecdotes or describing situations, in which certain words were bound to come up: wife, husband, man, woman...they laughed and laughed. 'The father of my children,' one woman would say; 'the breadwinner,' said the other, and they shrieked like harpies."[20] The uncomfortable humor described here results from a very radical perception of the comic; Kate, her friend, and the mythical women in Wittig's book, are mocking the norm. The housewives "shrieked like harpies," the radically irreverent laughter besmirching the respectable, culturally sanctioned imagery of the male as conqueror, father, provider (breadwinner). In a similarly shocking episode of Virgil's epic, the female harpies dirty the meal prepared by the pious Aeneas, later the heroic father of his country. The women in Wittig's futuristic epic and in Lessing's novel of contemporary tension between the sexes are mocking conventions, values, and stabilities against which a comic writer traditionally would judge some odd deviation. It is one thing to find "manners" amusing, to "scourge" vices (as the satirist claims to do), or to mock the follies of lovers; it is a much more drastic act of the imagination to mock the very norms against which comedy, in a tradition centuries old, has judged the vices, the follies, the eccentricities. To suggest, without the protective context of a courtly revel or a Mardi Gras, that words such as *wife, husband, woman, father,* are funny—hilarious deviations from some unstated standard—is to make a real gesture against established values. If any norms and conventions are established, those listed by Lessing's Kate Brown and her companion certainly are. Or, they have been established until the very recent past, and still are established for a majority of both sexes in Europe, England, and the United States.

And yet some critics argue that our modern era — post-Newton, post-God, and even post-Einstein — has rendered even the established beliefs and behaviors relative and confusingly diverse; comedy, they assert, can no longer structure itself around the traditional idea of violating a norm. Critics, attempting to describe modern comedy, or modern fiction generally, have variously affirmed that for the novelist there is "nothing at the center," or perhaps only a variety of implied norms at the center.[21] Strictly speaking, true comedy is no longer possible, some argue, since there are no commonly held values.[22] Comedy, and the more virulent and topical satire, both used to thrive on the ridiculing of some recognizable "deviation"; if we can perceive a bent stick, there must be a straight stick somewhere, as Plato noted, and as literary critics maintain when discussing classical comedy. In the comedy of manners and in the drama of Jonson and Molière, the "satirical theory of comedy" follows classical principles, and the deviants are ridiculed for violating accepted norms.[23] Sociologists affirm, however, that these classic principles are still at work in life, whether or not they obtain in literature; ridiculing a deviant is still a means of social control — if the group is small enough. Even individuals, in order to shake off some doubt about behavior or attitude, will ridicule their own misgivings and laugh themselves back into the community of belief which their group of friends accepts.[24] In effect, sociology confirms the claims of satire, in a small, or very homogeneous, group.

The classic principles are still at work, but they nowadays just have more to work with; a modern, multicultural society will have more than one touchstone, more than one norm, for testing the comic or satiric comparison, and the resulting forms and meanings will be more complex and slippery. The critic's difficulties in describing or perhaps even in perceiving modern comedy become even more formidable when the norms under attack are so basic, so routine, that we don't even see them as norms. The norms — and they are often the subject of mocking for the writers here examined — are intimately accepted patterns of belief and behavior, patterns usually linked to the roles that we assign to each sex. Allowing always for some exceptions, such norms are analogous, in the social sphere, to the allotments of tasks and identities, with respect to the sexes, which characterize the heroic figures of the male quest myth.

Simone de Beauvoir has thoroughly examined this division of historical and mythological labor; the man is typically the hero, the subject, the representative of humanity, the winner and conqueror, while the woman is mother, background, landscape, temptress, or goal. She is so much an outsider that she is not human. She is "other"; she is "natural" or childlike or holy or evil, while the man is "man" (humanity).[25] These sex-associated norms have, with minor variations, survived substantially intact all the major revolutions which give chapter headings to history books and which do indeed indicate major social or intellectual changes: Copernican astronomy, Newtonian physics, the industrial revolution (though this did change the location—to the factory—of "women's work"), the Darwinian theory of evolution, and the "death of God." Human beings in the twentieth century may worry about the relativity of time, space, morals, and the habits of small particles, and they may well fear their own capacity for self-destruction, but their expectations with regard to the basic identity and behavior of each sex are still remarkably constant. In *Women in Love*, Birkin, the character who most nearly resembles Lawrence himself, explains that he hopes to make his love for a woman "the centre and core" of his life, "seeing there's no God."[26] The hero can lose God, but not the central emotional support of the male's world, a woman. This expectation, this right to seek such a center, is, to apply the words of Virginia Woolf, one of those "established values."

These values, or norms,[27] are in the first place what sociologists would call "institutions"; they are solidly entrenched and are very nearly "religions." Secondly, the norms that are often mocked by Woolf, Spark, Margaret Drabble, and others, arise from our earliest perceptions, from our "primary socialization." For this reason, these norms are closely tied to our sense of what makes life comfortable, secure, and even credible. They make up the core of civilization's structure for us. They represent a firm and reliable order, and can be contrasted with those dangerous or creative occasions of liminality when "the rules" are temporarily suspended. Such norms are the order that we expect to return to after the festive disorder.

The word *norm* has not settled into a single definition among sociologists, any more than among literary scholars. A sociologist's use of the word will vary with the particular experimental context, but the polarities of meaning for *norm* usually involve *belief* and *action*. In the following chapters, I will be looking at the social identity of characters as expressed through belief and action, especially when these things are used as comic material. The chief focus of my study will be on a deeper level, however. By *norm*, I mean especially "sex identity" (to which the social identity of occupation is usually related), and even "archetypal identity." I need to use this last concept, because the novelists here being studied often use archetypal images or patterns of action. In most of these novels the characters and the patterns of action are relatively "undisplaced," to use Northrop Frye's terminology; that is, the nearly allegorical patterns, the mythic images, associated with a character's identity or actions, are prominent and often contribute much to the meaning of the novel, and to its comic aspect. More often than not, the mythic imagery is itself mocked, inverted with regard to sex, or entirely reinvented.

Generally, when archetypal imagery occurs in a modern novel, the imagery implies a lost and noble glory, an ancient greatness in relation to which the pettiness of modern lives is mourned, as in *The Waste Land*, or benignly mocked, as in Joyce's *Ulysses*. Neither Eliot nor Joyce actually mocks the basic idea and value of, say, the Grail quest or the quest of Ulysses or Penelope's faithful waiting. Neither of these writers implies that our modern culture's lost intimacy with mythic imagery is good riddance. By contrast, Woolf and Spark often mock the archetypal imagery itself; they mock a character's archetypal identity — that is, the mythic, spiritual, and cultural norm which a character has accepted or is struggling with or is trying to reject. When these writers are not mocking the myths, they are radically altering them, especially with regard to the sex identity of the questing and conquering figures.

In other words, the norm being tested in the comic novels of Virginia Woolf and Muriel Spark is a very central one. We probably begin to learn it in infancy. It belongs to our primary socialization, to the values, the identity, and the beliefs which we learn in our earliest interactions with our parents, with those "significant others" who provide our first contact with society, who in fact constitute our first, small society. We have no choice about this first limited society to which we belong, this first world, as sociologists Berger and Luckmann point out: "The child does not internalize the world of his significant others as one of many possible worlds. He internalizes it as *the* world, the only existent and only conceivable world, the world *tout court*. It is for this reason that the world internalized in primary socialization is so much more firmly entrenched in consciousness than worlds internalized in secondary socialization."[28]

Secondary socialization gives us our education, provides us with the knowledge which we use in our adult occupations, and contributes to our sense of taste and personal style.[29] It contributes the more prominent aspects of our social identity. The world of primary socialization, however, is a more intimate one. Our emotions are firmly planted in it, and it apparently remains for us the root of all nostalgia. Berger and Luckmann say that we remember this primary world as the place where "everything is all right"; it remains the "home world, however far one may travel from it in later life into regions where one does not feel at home at all."[30] This world is not as amenable to change as the world of secondary socialization is; we may, for instance, change jobs. In another book, Peter Berger describes a continuum of identities, some of which are products of secondary socialization, others rooted in primary socialization. He suggests that a person could change fairly easily from a trash collector to a night watchman, but then he describes progressively more difficult transitions: "It is considerably more difficult to change from clergyman to military officer. It is very, very difficult to change from Negro to white. And it is almost impossible to change from man to woman." Even so, Berger notes, our sexual identities are to a great extent molded by society rather than by hormones or anatomy.[31] This fact is carefully documented by Eleanor Maccoby and Carol Jacklin, who have gathered and presented recent studies that confirm the large part played by society in the determining of sex identity.[32] The "society" that makes the most fundamental contribution toward sex identity is that very first society, the parents, the instructors in primary socialization.

The world of primary socialization has recently been scrutinized by Dorothy Dinnerstein in her book *The Mermaid and the Minotaur*. She emphasizes that the primary world is especially the world of the infant's relation to the mother—not to both parents.

Since the mother, or nurse, cannot constantly be feeding the child or giving it attention, the child experiences its first sense of betrayal at the hands of a woman. Dinnerstein argues that most of the ambivalence which human beings of both sexes feel towards woman — those ambivalences culturally documented in mythic symbols of woman as guide, fate, temptress, betrayer — are rooted in the very young child's earliest interactions with the mother.[33] On the other hand, the father is perceived as being outside the world of nature, flesh, mortality; he takes an active role in history. The male-female division of labor during infancy and childhood, Dinnerstein suggests, ultimately yields most of those mythic images which characterize our expectations regarding the sexes. Men adventure and conquer, being sure to depart from the female world in order to accomplish their ordeals and quests.[34] Dinnerstein thus implies that there are important links between myth and primary socialization.[35]

According to classical sociological theory, myth and socialization are indeed closely connected. The most extreme view is that of Emile Durkheim, who affirmed that human beings in effect worship society, religion and its symbols being merely an expression of social norms and institutions.[36] These norms include the behavior expected of each sex. In her book *Sex and Caste in America*, Carol Andreas links sex roles to the rigidly defined limits associated with "caste." She observes: "It is unlikely that the sexual caste system could survive in a society that did not manufacture an unimpeachable source of authority to justify its existence. The oldest such authority is religion."[37] And the more contemporary authorities, which Andreas goes on to describe, are Freudian psychoanalysis and the Madison Avenue advertiser. These latter-day institutions are authorities comparable in function to religion.[38] Following a similar line of thinking, Eva Figes argues that Christianity, in its medieval institutions especially, reflected the imagery and values most advantageous to the men of the patriarchal society for whom it was enunciated and projected; with the retreat of religious belief, a consumer society, wherein men achieve a secular immortality through control of capital and of women, became in effect the new religion.[39] Whether faith or consumerism inspires him, the man tends to have the controlling role, the woman the passive one.

And yet, limiting as the normative roles for each sex may seem, such carefully defined roles, by virtue of their strict dependability, have one very positive function; they have a stabilizing effect on a society or an individual during a crisis. At the death of a close relative, for instance, individuals will more easily recover from the loss if their community, or group of friends, holds in common a "symbolic universe" — an explanation or ritual, whether religious or humanistic.[40] Institutions, "normal" behavior, and myths are constantly warding off the intrusions of such disasters as wars, assassinations, and death, or an individual's disturbing nightmare. Berger and Luckmann observe: "All social reality is precarious. All societies are constructions in the face of chaos."[41] And against this chaos, marriage and family — or at least our ideas about these institutions — have loomed especially large as fortresses that can ward off the nonpersonal world of a bureaucratized politics and a competitive economy, against the "homeless" quality of life outside the family.[42] The conservative and even rigid nature of anything so institutionalized as sex roles, and the mythological imagery that expresses them, is understandable in the light of the dangerous social and psychological forces which "normality" holds at bay. Understandable too is the fact that the ritualistic or festive suspension of usual roles and rules is, on most occasions, an ultimate affirmation of the ordered world. Inversions of behavior, and threats to the ordinary social or even psychological order, are more comfortable if they merely release rather than wreck.

If the socially provided myths and institutions function in a sort of negative and defending capacity, as a protection from crises, they may also — to certain people in the society — give impetus to personal growth and self-discovery. The institutions and norms may thwart and limit an individual, or encourage a creative, fulfilled life. Berger sums up: "Just as society can be a flight from freedom or an occasion for it, society can bury our metaphysical quest or provide forms in which it can be pursued."[43] Society does not, however, encourage the "metaphysical quest" equally in men and women, as Beauvoir, Dinnerstein, and others have noted. The major and recurrent myths, the allegories of the soul's progress, the heroic monomyth, all testify to this inequity in the distribution, culturally, of "quest" roles among men and women. Traditionally men, not women, have been encouraged to see themselves as the hero who adventures into the privileged, institutionalized liminalities of self-discovery: knightly quest, ardent pilgrim in a divine comedy, Romantic hero in quest of classy sins, Sisyphus as absurd rebel— "Everyman" has usually been a man. This mythic, literary, and social inequity, with its psychological roots deep in early childhood, and in the primary socialization process, is the norm that is often mocked by Woolf and Spark.

Distinct from this norm, although at some point merging into it, are the "manners," which have weighed heavily in British fiction of the realistic and psychological tradition (for instance, in the novels of George Eliot and Henry James), and in comic fiction as well. Most critics, when they describe the objects of comic attack, wind up describing social features and personal behaviors which derive largely from secondary socialization. A "comedy of manners," whether we limit the term to English Restoration comic drama or expand its area of reference to include the comic fiction which revels in social behavior peculiar to a given era and class, nearly always is a comedy that derives material from elements of secondary socialization. A person's class, profession, eccentricity or obsession, dress, and mannerisms come in for much comic play.[44] The ruthless or fawning social climbers in Dickens' novels are characterized largely by reference to these features of social and economic life. Very often, a social eccentricity that becomes extreme or vicious will be satirized, while a deeper value will be affirmed. In Molière's *Misanthrope*, for instance, and in *Tartuffe*, villains and fools are mocked, but love is not; writing of these plays, Benjamin Lehmann observes: "Society is brilliantly satirized in the interest of something which is not satirized but approved—the love of a man and a woman."[45] Molière can assume that the relationship between the sexes is not going to change in any remarkable way, and that what is meant by *man* and *woman* is a constant, a trusted norm. Lehmann, in his remarks, states the two classic halves of the mechanism of satire: something is mocked, but in the name of something else which is affirmed as a norm.

From the pool of traits created by secondary socialization, I suggest, a classic comic writer draws something to attack; from the pool of primary socialization, the classic comic writer draws something to affirm—a norm. Of course these two categories are going to fade into each other. Secondary socialization usually builds on primary socialization; similarly, the manners of a society are the varied, frequently changing expressions of a deeper cultural myth which may be buried in literature, dream, or everyday assumption, but which the society implicitly accepts and approves.

In any given instance, in literature or in experience, it might be very difficult to identify just which trait or behavior belongs to secondary socialization and which to primary socialization. Nor would this be a useful exercise. The ever-changing manners as well as those centuries-spanning and more or less constant identities — man, woman, hero, breadwinner — both fuse into an individual's sense of self. My concern in this study is not to trace the fine dividing line between manner and norm, between secondary and primary socialization; this dividing line is not fine, actually, but a broad, blurred band. I am concerned, not with the middle, but with the polarities of the socialization phenomenon, and particularly with the comic capital which women writers have recently made from the imagery of primary socialization, imagery which for centuries has provided the norm. Such imagery has not been the object of comic attack except during festivities, other liminal occasions, or in the broadside cartoons, described earlier, which were popular in an era of social upheaval, an era not unlike ours in this respect.

By way of introducing the issue of a woman's tradition in literature, particularly comic literature, I want to emphasize that the monomythic norm — the varied quest myth described by Northrop Frye and Joseph Campbell — has allotted to women a peripheral role. In itself, this myth hardly gives women the rudiments of a tradition. The myth has been dominated by a male hero for the last 4,000 years or more. From Achilles to Dr. Strangelove, as Vivian Gornick has observed, the hero has been male, and if women enter the plot at all, they function as lures or guides for the hero. The female character "is only the catalyst for man's struggle with himself. It is never too certain that woman has any self at all."[46] The woman as a subject, as a hero, as a "self," is rendered especially problematic by Frye when he applies Jungian archetypes to the characters who conventionally appear in a "romance" plot (a quest plot which generally employs a stylized or allegorical characterization). Frye suggests that the hero (male) is a symbol for psychic energy ("libido") and the heroine, a symbol for the "anima," or unconscious self.[47] Jung himself, describing the Christ story and stories of similar god-heroes, writes: "All over the earth, in the most various forms, each with a different time-colouring, the saviour-hero appears as a fruit of the entry of libido into the maternal depths of the unconscious."[48] The woman is catalyst, landscape, or "maternal depths," but not herself the adventurer. In popular and secularized literature the allotment of sex roles reflects that of a culture's sacred documents. Considering the pattern of New Comedy, Frye observes: "The crudest of Plautine comedy-formulas has much the same *structure* as the central Christian myth itself, with its divine son appeasing the wrath of a father and redeeming what is at once a society and a bride."[49] In his later book, *The Secular Scripture*, Frye notes that characterization and behavior of the heroine in a romance necessarily conform to certain "social" facts of a "male-oriented society."[50] And even more recently, Charney remarks the important fact that New Comedy, from Plautus to the English Restoration, expresses the values of a male-dominated society; women characters play no decisive role in the drama, although some, like Congreve's Millimant, wax very witty as they reconcile themselves to marriage and maternity.[51] In more realistic literature, there have been spurts of interest in the female hero,[52] and there are some famous ones, Austen's Elizabeth Bennet and James's Isabel Archer, for instance.

Literature that moves away from realism and toward myth, however, literature that approaches the schematization and stylization of myth or archetype, tends to be dominated by a male hero. In this connection, Joseph Campbell describes what he terms the "miracle" of Greek and European contributions to the quest myth: the occidental world portrayed the hero as an individualized being, not merely an impersonal representative of the community. Even though this male individual was allowed a quest, others were denied; not everyone — whether socially, or symbolically through literature — could embark upon the course of spiritual rebirth, "as, for example, if the individual chanced to be a woman or a slave."[53] In Western culture for hundreds of years the early socialization of little boys has typically prepared them to see themselves as brave adventurers. Usually boys are given a more lavish respect and support than girls are, and a majority of mothers prefer sons to daughters.[54] Rather than being socialized for maturity and responsibility, Phyllis Chesler observes, girls are trained to become the supporting and self-sacrificing nourishers of the male enterprise;

religious imagery confirms this role dichotomy, giving us paintings and sculptures that "portray Madonnas comforting and worshiping their infant sons."[55] The monomythic norm of the Western world is bound to reflect the social fact that until very recently women were not perceived as having a quest that might serve as paradigm for a "tradition" in literature. Women had no life-adventure considered worthy of being used as a symbol for a divine adventure.

There is no reason, theoretically (though there are many social reasons, some of which we have already examined), why a pattern of events and images symbolizing a spiritual rebirth could not be expressed by a female hero. The Sumerian female god Inanna, for instance, descends into the underworld of death and is slain there; her body is hung from a stake for three days (cf. Christ hanging on the cross and then lying in the tomb three days) before she is restored to life by subsidiary friendly agents whom she had previously alerted to the hazards of her journey.[56] The more familiar story of Psyche, as Lee Edwards has shown, can be interpreted as a well-elaborated statement of liminal ordeals and of the heroic achievement representative of human, not merely male or female, aspiration and psychological growth.[57] As Gail Sheehy and Penelope Washbourn have given attention to the "passages" of women's experience, other scholars, such as Carol Christ and Annis Pratt, have enunciated the patterns of rebirth or quest in literature by women authors.[58] Using the Demeter myth, Grace Stewart discusses the character and quest of the woman artist in fiction.[59] Certainly one of the most famous and widespread myths of the ancient world is that of the Kore maiden, or the descent-and-ascent pattern of the combined stories of maid (Persephone, Kore) and mother (Demeter). Between them, the two gods, who were two aspects of one god,[60] cover just about the same territory, psychologically speaking, as does the Christ story. That is, there is a descent into the underworld and a separation of parent and child (by means of rape or of sacrificial death); then there is an ascent and a reunion of parent and child. In both stories the dying and rising god can be read as a symbol for the transformation, or rebirth, of the self; in fact, the Mysteries once celebrated at Eleusis evidently incorporated this meaning into the ritual, a meaning of personal regeneration which is akin to the symbolism of sacrifice and transformation found in the Mass.[61] Since several of the authors considered in this study do sometimes draw upon fragments of the Demeter-Kore myth, it will be examined in more detail as the context calls for it in the following chapters. Here it is important to emphasize that female imagery predominates in the myth; the story of a woman's adventure is in this myth the story of a divine adventure and of the regeneration of the self.

In the more familiar imagery, on the other hand, the story of the male's adventure is paramount. The female imagery which complements this adventure — that is, the imagery belonging to the male myth — is often a variation of the imagery of motherly protection. Some attempts to define a "woman's tradition" in literature draw on these patterns and archetypes complementing the male quest myth. For instance, the role of the woman as someone who spends her life taking care of others is a prominent theme in women's novels of the nineteenth century; Patricia Spacks finds the major female characters of Austen, Gaskell, Alcott, and Glasgow struggling against the restrictions of a domestic or supportive role and yet ultimately accepting this role as a woman's best source of fulfillment and of moral development.[62] In their book *The Madwoman in the Attic*, Sandra Gilbert and Susan Gubar perceptively document the subtle attacks which writers such as the Brontë sisters directed against the submissive roles expected of women. Many nineteenth-century women writers parodied certain pathologies linked to female socialization (anorexia, agoraphobia, amnesia); in fictional "re-visions" of their world, as Gilbert and Gubar observe, these writers emphasized strong female images of goddesses and rebirth, or sometimes asserted an identification with the rebellious figure of Satan.[63] One of Elaine Showalter's most interesting discoveries in *A Literature of Their Own* is an era of snappy comic criticism among women novelists whose protagonists direct much anger at the male-ordained female roles. These little-known writers, among whom Mary Braddon was prominent, flourished just after the era of the "feminine" novel, the novel of submission to women's supportive role. This brief comic tradition in women's literature is ultimately not very cheerful, however. The female protagonists described by Showalter protest in vain; that is, they are always punished.[64] Recently Emily Toth and other critics have clarified the character and point of the comic mode of protest among women authors of Canada and the United States.[65] In her discussion of con-

temporary American authors such as Didion, Shulman, and Bu-
chanan, Josephine Hendin finds a masochistic comedy which she
calls "she-wit."[66]

A self-destructive, masochistic comedy is not typical of British
women authors of the twentieth century. This is one consideration
among others (including the elemental consideration of space)
which argues for limiting the present study to British authors.[67]
Focussing on Woolf and Spark, each a major writer of her generation and each a writer with a preference for comedy, I find very little that can be categorized as masochistic, desperate, or cynical.
The comedy is sometimes uncomfortable, however. The British
critic Siriol Hugh-Jones, in her brief survey of wit among England's literary women, calls attention to the disconcerting comedy
in the fiction of Penelope Mortimer and Muriel Spark. Hugh-Jones
observes that Mortimer's novels "can make you laugh heartily in a
terrified sort of way," and with Spark, the laughter "freezes in the
throat."[68] The unnerving quality of Spark's fiction, and some of
Mortimer's, results from the close-shave of comedy's razor. Spark,
and to some extent Mortimer, mock what another writer would allow to stand as a norm, as something in which everyone could still
trust and believe. More consistently and ferociously than Mortimer,
Muriel Spark insists on leaving her comic world stranded in the upside-down anti-order of liminality, and for this reason she, along
with Virginia Woolf, receives extended discussion in this study.
Several authors, such as Dorothy Richardson and Doris Lessing,
who have developed distinctly feminist themes in their novels are
not included here because their mode is not for the most part comic.[69] Lessing and Richardson, as Annis Pratt observes, like the earlier novelists Fanny Burney and Ann Radcliffe, do battle with the
norms of a patriarchal society, with "stingy fathers, brutal broth-
ers, violent seducers, flattering fiances, aunt toms, and false friends,
all of them acting in accordance with accepted sexist norms."[70]
Lessing's attack, however, is earnest and even solemn, though her
characters often talk about laughter. My particular interest is the
work of writers whose comedy sounds the depth of the images,
biases, and nostalgia which we acquire through primary socialization and which constitute those archetypal, long-standing, and venerable norms.

After Hugh-Jones muses upon the slender contribution of women authors to comic literature she observes: "The pity of it to me is that wit, satire, irony, a way of saying serious and indeed perhaps unpopular, controversial and dangerous things obliquely and to all appearances lightly, are the best possible methods for a woman who wishes to make some communication in this country."[71] These words, written in 1961, are not far from those of Virginia Woolf in 1929 when she suggested that women writers may discover that something trivial to them is important to men, and may want to alter the "established values." Woolf, Spark, and some other novelists to be examined in the final chapter all say some "dangerous things obliquely" — dangerous because the comic context is a liminal one in which inversions are not turned upright again; instead, the distorted quests or bizarre festivities persist in the transition phase and are not resolved into an orderly close that would reaffirm at least the traditional, most intimately learned, norms of primary socialization. For these writers, the liminal motifs of inversion, of blurred or unusual sex identity, of a classless community, of annulled normality, are given the kind of radical freeplay that allows comedy to live up to the very best of its bad reputation.

2

Virginia Woolf:
Myth and Manner
in the Early Novels

In her novels, Virginia Woolf makes good use of comedy for saying many "dangerous things obliquely," so obliquely that readers have often missed both the comedy and the "dangerous," or revolutionary, implications. For the most part she follows her own advice against using fiction as a vehicle for grievance and instead uses a subversive strategy of imagery and irony which is infrequently recognized as comic. The mockery in Woolf's novels is directed, with considerable tension and ambiguity, chiefly at those cultural images which derive from primary socialization. While she also makes comic capital out of manners, as British fiction traditionally does, Virginia Woolf's most devastating mockery is directed at archetypal imagery, a questing hero, a scapegoat, an Angel in the House or in the soul. Her fiction is profoundly irreverent, attacking many of those norms of family relationship, of sex identity and sex behavior, which are reflected in the narrative paradigms of Western literature, in scripture, "tragedy," and "comedy."

For the writer who sees some reason to work loose from the plot patterns of the past two or three millenia, for the "free" writer, Virginia Woolf remarks in "Modern Fiction" (1919), there would be "no plot, no comedy, no tragedy, no love interest or catastrophe in the accepted style."[1] The obliqueness of Woolf's comedy, and the subtlety of its social implications are linked to the experimental quality of her fiction generally, to her deliberate rejection of the "accepted style." Although Woolf's formal and stylistic experimentation has received considerable critical attention, the ramifications of the persistent and varied comedy in her novels, especially its social ramifications, usually receive only the briefest aside or are overlooked altogether.[2] Very recently critics have shown a greater sensitivity to Woolf's social comedy, and to her wit and humor. Maria DiBattista, discussing a selection of Woolf's novels in relation to British literary tradition, emphasizes Woolf's antecedents in that tradition, including comic writers such as Sterne and Meredith; the essentially conservative model of comedy which DiBattista uses tends to throw light on the more benign aspects of comedy in Woolf's fiction.[3] On the other hand, Margaret Comstock, who examines biographical as well as literary linkages between Meredith and Woolf, points to the radical and political elements in Woolf's feminist comedy.[4] Feminism is indeed a major presence in the comedy of this writer, who was at least moderately active in organizations dedicated to suffrage and to other concerns of women. Although she found the rhetoric at a suffrage rally distasteful, full of "indisputable platitudes,"[5] her feminist tracts, *A Room of One's Own* (1929) and *Three Guineas* (1937), demonstrate that politics and wit can reinforce each other. Virginia Woolf did not think that passionate politics and good novels were compatible, however, and she accused Charlotte Brontë of having muddled the two in *Jane Eyre*.[6] Nevertheless, a very thorough and depth-sounding political comedy — a liminal comedy of unresolved, reversed, or radically questioned, values and roles — emerges in Woolf's mature novels.

The inward and mythic characters of this author may not seem earthy and active enough to carry much sociological weight, and many critics have accused Woolf of having little or no concern for human beings as social, industrialized, war-ravaged, modern people.[7] Woolf's concern in her novels is with the mythic paradigm behind the mores and institutions; she examines the psychological "quest," the mode of spiritual growth, that Victorian and twentieth-century institutions allow, or forbid, to men and women, lovers, businessmen, visionary soldiers, and others. She examines the imagery and ritual of various modern festivities, of those liminal and renewing occasions, such as dinners, parties, and pageants. Her social criticism is perhaps too radical to be obvious; nevertheless, her laughter touches the deepest nerves of Western culture.

Although Virginia Woolf did not write a "theory" of comedy, her essays and criticism contain intriguing remarks about the subject. She persistently probes the distinction between a fiction of externals and a fiction of consciousness, between the "materialists," as she called Bennett and Galsworthy, and those who, like the Russian writers so popular among the English in the early twentieth century, portrayed the "soul." As she writes in her famous essay, "Mr. Bennett and Mrs. Brown" (1924), the typical English novelist would portray a hypothetical character's eccentricities, giving us "Mrs. Brown" in all her particularity, "her oddities and mannerisms; her buttons and wrinkles; her ribbons and warts." The French writer would focus, Woolf says, on the more general qualities of human nature, and the Russian author would probe the soul and the large questions it asks of life (*CE*, 1:325).[8] If British fiction "in the accepted style" concentrates on dress, habit, and the particularity of social mores and manners, British comedy in the accepted style uses much the same materials, Woolf implies. In an early essay, "Modes and Manners of the Nineteenth Century" (1910), she questions the assumed links between manners and character, and affirms that people are not necessarily or adequately expressed by clothes and social gestures, though these elements are the traditional materials of the satirist.[9]

These are also the materials which inspired Woolf's own comic jibes at acquaintances, and the materials of previous English comic writers whom she admired. Her sense of the comic, which pervades her letters and which delighted her friends, expresses itself in exuberant and often malicious attention to eccentricity, to literary and intellectual posturings — to the "manners," in other words, of her Victorian relatives, her Bloomsbury friends, or her peripheral social acquaintances. She was, as her brother-in-law Clive Bell recalled, "a born and infectious mocker."[10] Comedy in the accepted style, deftly employed by Austen or Peacock, received Woolf's admiring critical response. Reviewing a biography of Sterne in 1909, she noted Sterne's comic thrusts at great wigs, solemn faces, and deceit generally (*CE*, 3:90). She admired the seventeenth-century letter-writer Dorothy Osborne for pouring "a fine raillery over the pomps and ceremonies of existence" and for choosing William Temple for a husband rather than men who styled their lives after certain exaggerated fashions of the time, the pompous justice, the town gallant, or the travelled monsieur (*CE*, 3:62-63). Woolf's own practice as a comic writer is sometimes quite close to that of Austen and Sterne. In *The Voyage Out* many of the hotel guests at Santa Marina are stock comic figures, as Avrom Fleishman and others have pointed out; these bored British tourists have a history among English satirists.[11] The characters represent comic protrusions of a society which identifies certain things as reasonable and good, and other things as peculiar or grotesque. The "little atheist," Charles Tansley, in *To the Lighthouse* receives similar treatment, and so does the "admirable" Hugh Whitbread in *Mrs. Dalloway.*

Suppose, however, that a society's notion of what is reasonable and good changes, or that a woman's view of reason and goodness develops differently, as Woolf says it does, from a man's ideas on these matters. Different traditions yield different notions of what is funny. Woolf points to the advantages of a solid norm for comedy. Such a standard permits the keen comic observations of the French letter-writer Madame de Sévigné: "She is always referring her impressions to a standard — hence the incisiveness, the depth, and comedy that make those spontaneous statements so illuminating" (*CE*, 3:69). In an essay on Oliver Goldsmith, Woolf observes that "one advantage of having a settled code of morals is that you know exactly what to laugh at" (*CE*, 1:110). The earlier writers — Meredith, Wordsworth, Scott — had such a code. In "How It Strikes a Contemporary," Woolf describes the condition of the older English writers: "They have their judgment of conduct. They know the relations of human beings towards each other and towards the universe" (*CE*, 2:159).

But, as Virginia Woolf is famous for having announced, "in or about December, 1910, human character changed." With this change, all those relationships which seem to be so secure in the works of Goldsmith also underwent a metamorphosis. "All human relations have shifted — those between masters and servants, husbands and wives, parents and children. And when human relations change there is at the same time a change in religion, conduct, politics, and literature" (*CE*, 1:320-21). And in comedy as well. Among the changing modes of relationship one that particularly interested Woolf was the code that governed behavior between men and women. As we saw in the previous chapter, Woolf mused on the possibility that women novelists might find an especially rich vein of comedy by observing and criticizing men. Since both sexes are now literate and verbal, the distinctions between the two traditions of perception and experience will emerge in the literature that each sex writes. A woman will want "to alter the established values — to make serious what appears insignificant to a man, and trivial what is to him important" (*CE*, 2:146).

Virginia Woolf is specific about some of the values which, in her view, the sexes do not share. In a letter of January 1916 she refers to the war as "this preposterous masculine fiction," and she observes in *A Room of One's Own* that "the values of women differ very often from the values which have been made by the other sex"; hence, a critic will consider a book important if it deals with war but dismiss another book as insignificant "because it deals with the feelings of women in a drawing-room."[12] Avoiding overt political pleading or denunciation, Woolf approaches political issues at a more buried and basic level; she cuts the root and branch rather than the leaves, the myths instead of the manner. She frequently inverts conventional literary and social judgments about the relative values of war and parties, of the activities, roles, and spiritual commitments of each sex. The "feelings of women," their values and their culture, are juxtaposed, often in a spirit of impudent holiday, against the earnest heroism of men (and a few rigidly "heroic" women such as Miss Kilman) whether that heroism attempts war, fame, or martyrdom.

Particularly in her first five novels, the questing male scholar or lover is a source of amusement, either to the narrator or to a woman character. The ritual activities of women, on the other hand, are presented as liminal occasions for celebration, and even for some antimale flyting. Beginning with *Orlando*, however, and to some extent in *To the Lighthouse*, the mockery undercuts even female festivity, or at least its expression in the social rituals of dinners and parties.

For Virginia Woolf, the "two cultures" are not those of science and the humanities, but those of men and women. She tells women authors, in *A Room of One's Own*, that "we think back through our mothers," since the great male writers do not help a woman writer in any essential way.[13] Later in her career, Woolf makes an angry diary note about "my civilization" and the unpaid work women have done, within the male civilization, for the past two thousand years.[14] And in 1937, facing yet another world war perpetrated — as she felt — by men, in *Three Guineas* she urges women to join a society of pacifist, feminist "Outsiders." She identifies a women's tradition or civilization. More recent feminists have pointed to the existence in the nineteenth century of a female subculture or "a separate women's culture."[15] The female counterculture functions in Woolf's novels the way a counterculture usually functions in society; it mocks and inverts the society's established values, especially its codes of what is trivial and what is important, its institutionalized assignments regarding sex identity, life-work or life-quest, "heroism."

Virginia Woolf's perception, and expression, of liminality in her fiction did not occur in a vacuum. She lived and wrote in an era of disconcerting change. Her attitude towards her Victorian family, particularly after her mother's death in 1895, was one of resistance and rebellion. She has scorn for her stepbrother George Duckworth, a classic, nearly mythic Victorian hypocrite who sexually molested Virginia and her sister and then "jumped through hoops" of the social circus adroitly enough to gain ultimately a knighthood; a mere spectator to this "patriarchal machinery," Woolf experienced, she says, a "feeling which I later called the outsider's feeling."[16] She and Vanessa were misfits in their Victorian family. "By nature, both Vanessa and I were explorers, revolutionists, reformers."[17] When, after Leslie Stephen's death in 1904, his four youngest children set up house in Bloomsbury, their revolution gained a new autonomy and self-definition.

The Bloomsbury friends, drawn initially from Thoby Stephen's acquaintances at Cambridge, constituted a living counterculture. The radical position of the group was described by John Maynard Keynes: "We repudiated entirely customary morals, conventions and traditional wisdom. We were, that is to say, in the strict sense of the term, immoralists."[18] The expression of this repudiation assumed an ancient and festive form when Virginia and several friends successfully impersonated a delegation of Abyssinians, and requested and received a tour of the HMS *Dreadnought*. Virginia, disguised as an African man and speaking in a low, gruff voice, was in a liminal role analogous to that of a Boy Bishop, as she barely restrained her laughter, greeting the flag commander, her cousin William Fisher.[19] In this escapade, the elements of disguise, of sex-role reversal, and of impudent mockery of a respected institution such as the British navy, all expressed the festive and revolutionary import typical of liminal celebrations. A revolutionary in a Victorian household, then an active member of the lively counter-

culture that was Bloomsbury, Virginia Woolf was thoroughly im-
bued with both the attitudes and the ritualized forms of liminal protest and satire, of comedy that mocks the norm.

The Voyage Out and Night and Day

The comedy in Woolf's first two novels is not as radical as it becomes in her later work, but in both *The Voyage Out* and *Night and
Day* the major female character is suspicious not only of manner
but of the deeper, "normal" expectations with which society confronts her. By its title *The Voyage Out* adumbrates the unresolved
nature of the quest that is its principal subject matter; Rachel Vinrace voyages out, but does not return, finally, to life and to love.
Like the initiates of exotic cultures, Rachel leaves society and
enters the jungle for a liminal period that should lead her to an understanding and acceptance of her new role in society (for her, the
role of a mature and married woman). But Rachel violates the ritual
by not returning to society. She evidently contracts a fatal disease
in the jungle. Symbolically, she may have contracted an austere
judgment against the human rules for molding her identity. Like
the author of her story, Rachel resists the accepted style of comedy,
of tragedy, of the young woman's initiation-plot.

The comic elements in the novel evaluate on several levels the initiation effort, the adventurous attempt to become human. The artificial manners of the hotel guests — who have in general failed the
attempt by defining their social humanity too rigidly — come in for
traditional mockery. Rachel, given a more fully portrayed consciousness than that of the guests, gradually develops judgment
and a perceptive eye for the comic, qualities reminiscent of the her-
oines of Austen and Meredith. Finally, however, the comedy
sweeps beyond the human altogether as the cheerless laughter of
the jungle cries seems to attack human socialization itself and to
imply that the basic myths of initiation, love, and identity are mere
human artifice, ultimately presumptuous.

Rachel's introduction to a society different from her own very
limited one (her father and her aunts) begins as she meets the Dalloways aboard the ship. The Dalloways introduce Rachel not only to
the manner and conversation of high society but to passion, and
especially to a man's interpretation of what sexuality means to a

man and to a woman. As the ship lurches in the uneasy aftermath of the storm, Richard Dalloway suddenly embraces Rachel with fierce intensity, explaining in a choked voice, "You tempt me."[20] Rachel's excitement following this event includes exultation and wonder as well as her subsequent nightmare of being trapped in an oozing vault where a deformed animallike man gibbers. For Rachel, sexual feelings are linked to a sense of her own vulnerability and to the idea that a passionate man is one who may abruptly possess her. The oppressive dream imagery of fear and cavernous dead ends occurs later in the novel, as almost all critics observe, particularly during Rachel's fever. But to see the kiss as associated with a fatal timidity about life, relationships, and sex is to forget the ambiguity of Rachel's response to Richard Dalloway's sudden embrace.[21] After she leaves Richard, she looks at the distant seabirds riding the peaceful waves, and she becomes "peaceful too, at the same time possessed with a strange exultation. Life seemed to hold infinite possibilities she had never guessed at." She continues looking at the waves until she is "cold and absolutely calm again. Nevertheless something wonderful had happened" (76-77). The phrases "at the same time" and "nevertheless" are too important to disregard. She is upset by the circumstances of the experience, and because of her ignorance, is quite unprepared for Richard's behavior. She is not, on this occasion, expressing a coolness towards, and a rejection of, a formalized Edwardian social ritual for the introduction of the sexes to each other. She is responding to something more deep and ancient in Western culture, to the notion of a man as having the passionate right to dominate a "temptress" who is all the more tempting for being completely innocent, completely naive. Rachel's ambiguous feelings are a response, not to sensitive courtship or even to seduction, but to assault. It is remarkable that she finds in such circumstances any feelings of wonder and exultation at all; the fact that she does indicates a brave vigor and a readiness for self-discovery.

The otherwise miscellaneous episode of the Dalloways is hooked into the structure by means of Rachel's need to grow in self-knowledge and to achieve a discriminating judgment of people. She is "taken in" by the couple, as she admits to Helen soon after the Dalloways are set ashore. Responding to Rachel, Helen observes that "one has to make experiments" and that her young niece must learn to "discriminate" (82-83). Yet an understanding of people is only part of what Helen hopes for Rachel. Helen affirms: "So now you can go ahead and be a person on your own account." At this suggestion Rachel suddenly has a "vision of her own personality, of herself as a real everlasting thing, different from anything else, unmergeable, like the sea or the wind" (84). Rachel here sees the core of herself, and of her autonomy, as analogous to nonhuman, natural phenomena. It is from this remote and mystical core that she judges people's behavior and judges also society's assumption that the basic myth of her life will be engagement and marriage.

Maturing socially on the holiday island and under the tutelage of Helen Ambrose, Rachel makes few errors of judgment as serious as her complete rapture for the Dalloways. Indeed, she develops a sense of the comic which resembles that of the narrator. The narrator, for instance, had been comically euphemistic about Mr. Dalloway's losing an election: "Unable for a season, by one of the accidents of political life, to serve his country in Parliament, Mr. Dalloway was doing the best he could to serve it out of Parliament" (39). Sometimes the narrator introduces a diction which is more sophisticated than the natural speech of her characters would be, and this diction can penetrate comic ambiguities which the characters could not perceive in themselves. For instance, as Rachel and the others at Santa Marina emerge from the chapel, they are "greeted with curious respectful glances by the people who had not gone to church, although their clothing made it clear that they approved of Sunday to the very verge of going to church" (232). Like the narrator, Rachel contributes her own mocking criticism of pose and blind spots. She had evidently neither laughed nor thought much as she grew up among her aunts, nor did she find the Dalloways amusing as Helen did.

It is during the dance celebrating the engagement of Susan and Arthur that Rachel becomes detached enough to laugh at herself for the first time. After an ungratifying attempt, she and Hirst give up trying to waltz together, and Rachel dutifully tries to make commonplace conversation. Hirst is bored and irritated. He praises Helen's beauty and tactlessly comments on Rachel's lack of education and her "absurd life until now." Then, promising to improve her with his books, he rises with the remark, "I'm going to leave you now" (153-55). The scene is very reminiscent of the episode in *Pride and Prejudice* (vol. 1, chap. 3) in which Darcy makes blunt

statements, in Elizabeth's hearing, about her lack of beauty; he refuses to dance with a second-rate woman, and thus his "pride" gives
the impetus to Elizabeth's "prejudice" which it takes her many
thoughtful chapters to lose. Rachel also is immediately prejudiced
against Hirst; to herself she uses some of Helen's words on him:
"Damn that man . . . Damn his insolence" (155). But when she tries
to explain her anger to Terence, she thinks of the way Helen would
have mocked the situation and remarks, "I dare say I'm a fool"
(155). Rachel has never been able previously to say such a thing,
but Helen's buoyant sense of the ridiculous here passes to Rachel in
a moment of perception and spontaneity. Soon Rachel and Terence
are laughing at Hirst's brusque and insensitive ways:

> Rachel veered round suddenly and laughed out too. She saw
> that there was something ridiculous about Hirst, and perhaps
> about herself.
> "It's his way of making friends, I suppose," she laughed.
> "Well—I shall do my part. I shall begin—'Ugly in body, repul-
> sive in mind as you are, Mr. Hirst—'"
> "Hear, hear!" cried Hewet. "That's the way to treat
> him. . . ." (156)

Rachel is mocking both herself and Hirst. She stages a light-hearted
mimic revenge on Hirst and never treats him thereafter with the
seriousness that he nearly always thinks he deserves.

While the narrator mocks and judges her characters, and Rachel wards off the wounding egotism of Hirst, the jungle itself becomes the final judge and mocker of the vacationing human beings,
whether they are idling away this potentially liminal and renewing
season or, like Rachel and Hewet, voyaging thoughtfully along the
deep psychological and mythic course of self-discovery. The jungle
laughs at both manner and myth and provides the beyond-the-
human norm which reappears, usually as a more ineffable and mystical ultimate, in Woolf's later novels.

The presence of uncivilized nature—a presence which becomes especially real, all-encompassing, and even sinister, during
the trip up the Amazon—gives an ironic background even to the
norms of love and integrity by which Helen, Rachel, and Terence
have been judging the deviant or eccentric manners of the hotel
guests. The laughter in the jungle is cynically alien and harsh. One

morning as Rachel, Terence, and the others move quietly up the river, Terence feels that he and Rachel are being drawn on irresistibly; while he reads, "a bird gave a wild laugh, a monkey chuckled a malicious question" (267). During a walk into the jungle, as the lovers become immersed in their own happiness, the forest sounds merge in a sinister way with the voices of the other strollers who walk behind them and call from time to time. The "repetition of Hewet's name in short, dissevered syllables was to them the crack of a dry branch or the laughter of a bird" (283). Although the narration becomes indirect shortly after this, Rachel is apparently thrown to the ground by Helen, whose presence continues to be apparent above the waving grasses and above the two lovers (283-84).[22] The evidently sexual episode occurs just after, and is followed by, affirmations of love and happiness, but the implicit violence recalls Richard Dalloway's sudden embracing of Rachel. In the jungle it is as though Rachel is raped by passion itself, if the jungle is an image of passion, of the instinctive chemistry that takes its own way through human veins. The abrupt loss of independence — this episode implies — occurs at a deeper and more drastic level than that caused by Richard Dalloway's grabbing of a woman in a storm. The jungle and the impersonal surge of human feelings mock not just the artifice of the social ritual of courtship but the presumption that definitions of love and marriage can adequately protect the initiates, Rachel and Terence, from the overwhelming power of this particular life passage. The wild world seems to be laughing at the civilized one and mocking it for its presumptions of love, of names, of communication, and of tenderness.

Rachel herself is linked to the animal images and to the alien nature of the jungle world. Critics have pointed out the sea imagery which is invoked while Terence and Rachel walk in the forest. In their absorption in their happiness, they seem to be "walking at the bottom of the sea" (270). Later, at the Ambrose villa, when they are discussing their future relationship, Rachel and Terence struggle playfully; she is thrown onto the floor, but claims a victory by redefining herself, "I'm a mermaid! I can swim" (298).[23] Her triumph necessitates an ambiguous image, half human and half alien, a mermaid. Rachel is, more than anyone else, associated with the nonhuman world of nature, and she seems to cherish a reservation about human closeness, even with her fiancé, Terence.

Rachel's death is a final echo of the jungle's mockery, and to some extent an echo of Rachel's own capacity for mockery. The fact that her death happens in the same book that shows us her unwillingness to draw close to another human being suggests a symbolic connection between the event and the attitude. Louise DeSalvo's recent study of the novel's extant versions presents evidence that Rachel's social and sexual reserve, as well as her death, find their origins in Virginia Woolf's tense family relationships; as the novel evolved, Rachel's death became a logical extension of her sense of powerlessness with regard to men.[24] Other critics see Rachel as sexually restricted, and perhaps morally culpable for the incompatibility between her new sense of freedom and the social duty and opportunity for relationship.[25] Does Rachel, as well as the jungle itself, deny and mock even such "normal" and basic socialization myths as a young woman's "sexual awakening," her discovery of identity in a loved man, and her engagement to him? Rachel's story and the imagery of the jungle cries are perhaps Woolf's vehicle for attacking this basic myth, a myth that seemed to have destroyed her stepsister Stella, who married and then died three months later. Further, the classic notion that a woman's awakening to life and to her own identity is inevitably part of her awakening to love is the Sleeping Beauty/Snow White paradigm defined by a male-dominated culture. The story of a woman's passage to maturity, however, may differ in circumstances and values from the "story" defined for her by a man. Annis Pratt has pointed out, for instance, that the male hero in a Bildungsroman must subdue nature, while the female hero most characteristically identifies *with* nature. Typically, the woman does not give herself completely or eternally to a man, but to a loved landscape instead, to a green world in which she finds her identity. Few women in novels written by women ever say yes to a man with the total submission that Molly Bloom says it.[26] Rachel's death is an analogue, though not a result, of her reservations about the mannered behavior of social intercourse and even about the myth of love itself as defined by her society.

Rachel is like Septimus in *Mrs. Dalloway* in that she is unwilling to let others define the terms by which her life is to be ordered. Before he jumps from the window, Septimus thinks, "It was their idea of tragedy."[27] Rachel in effect says, "It is their idea of love." It is society's idea that she must answer the artificial notes congratulating her upon her engagement; it is society's idea that she must find herself by restricting her life and love to one man. Rachel's own ideas on these matters are images of autonomy, of a wildly free natural landscape. She sees her unmergeable self as similar to the "sea or the wind." Terence speculates that she is not in love with him, that she will always want something more than he can be. And Rachel, though she does not say it aloud, agrees. "It seemed to her now that what he was saying was perfectly true, and that she wanted many more things than the love of one human being — the sea, the sky" (302). Both Rachel's newly discovered passion and her sense of an "unmergeable" identity are often symbolized by vast natural imagery — the sea, the jungle, the wind, the sky, and the storm that sweeps across the island some hours after her death.

In *The Voyage Out* Rachel embarks on what seems to be a very typical liminality — initiation into maturity. Naive and untried, she leaves England. She learns to discriminate, and her sense of the comic evaluates the social posturing of those around her. Eventually, she leaves the vacation community of Santa Marina and travels deep into the primitive wildness of the nonhuman jungle. Psychologically she remains in liminality; she remains among the symbols of chaos and of freedom; she remains on the "margin" of the initiation passage and does not return. For her — as for other women in Woolf's novels — liminality, or the green world, is not a temporary, festive escape. It is a revolutionary country. It is a place from which to evaluate "civilization," the male civilization and its traditions which, as Woolf noted, differ considerably from those of women.

If Virginia Woolf's first novel is a voyage out, her second, *Night and Day* (1919), is a voyage back, at least in form. Katharine Hilbery, member of a tradition-respecting family that maintains a ceremonious attitude toward its famous Victorian forbears, at first accepts dutifully an engagement to the qualified but stuffy William Rodney; when she subsequently decides on the honesty and comfortable freedom of a life with Ralph Denham (whose family is less well off and less formal), she and her mother successfully oppose the pride and will of Mr. Hilbery, the "blocking" father figure. Katharine and Ralph apparently bring the "vision" from the liminal and "night" side of life back into the structure of an ordered community's "day" side. The form both releases — as it traditionally should

—a festive questioning of social conventions, and then gathers back the green world of magic and tempest into the steady structures of a community renewed, but not radically changed, by its glimpse of a brave new world.

The images of opposing forces in this novel, which was once entitled "Dreams and Realities," constitute a major part of the book's symbolic and psychological import, and critics have often discussed the several polarities in the work, pointing to the characters' efforts to reconcile night and day, femininity and masculinity, vision and fact, consciousness and convention.[28] The difficulty of resolving these polarities expresses itself in Katharine's complex psychological life, and in Ralph's also. Such complexity, as many critics observe, seems inappropriately stuffed into the rigid formalities of a comedy of manners.[29] And yet, since the traditional comic form does incorporate a rebellion into its structure, the ideological revolt of Katharine and Ralph receives in this novel a schematic framework that at least calls attention to the revolt. Theoretically the "night" side of consciousness, the liminal, upside-down world of life's great passages—in this case Katharine's successive engagements—do have a built-in place in traditional comic structure. They constitute the ordeals, the journeys, or the holiday revels. Indeed, Mrs. Hilbery (modeled after Virginia Woolf's Aunt Annie Ritchie, who was part of the Stephen household for many years) fits quite well into the pattern. She is the magician-fool who journeys to Shakespeare's tomb and carries away from it some symbolic greenery; this she bears home and offers her renewing vision, which brings the action to a satisfactory resolution. She is the magician or priest of the liminality in the novel, guiding and encouraging the chosen couple in their initiatory confrontations with the old order as represented by Katharine's father. As Josephine Schaefer says of Mrs. Hilbery, she "is humanity turned inside out and upside down until what matters most (love, poetry, music) become the only things that matter at all." And Margaret Comstock notes that Mrs. Hilbery "makes a new order by creating disorder."[30] She is a symbol of creative liminal inversion. But what the conservative comic form here gives with one hand, it takes away with the other. Submitting to the comic plot, the liminality must be, and is, resolved. Considered in the light of the novel's action, Katharine's only revolt is to get away with choosing her own husband instead of bending to her father's choice. The only person to escape into social change is Katharine's friend Mary Dachet, the suffragette, who suffers somewhat from the satire that the author directs at Mary's colleagues in the movement.

Just as Mary's actions take her outside the comic plot, so Katharine's moral and psychological growth continues above and beyond the demands of New Comedy. Much of the meditative self-searching in the novel plays with the favorite Shakespearean theme of lies masquerading as truths. This theme itself certainly has a traditional place in a comic plot, but the amount of psychological energy expended overloads the structural circuits. Among the band, Ralph is the major speaker for truth. He insists that honesty and freedom are possible, and he puts before Katharine the "terms for a friendship which should be perfectly sincere and perfectly straightforward."[31] Her acceptance of these "terms" leads Katharine to question the discrepancy between her private world of freedom and the public one of dishonesty. In an often quoted passage she considers the problem: "Why, she reflected, should there be this perpetual disparity between the thought and the action, between the life of solitude and the life of society, this astonishing precipice on one side of which the soul was active and in broad daylight, on the other side of which it was contemplative and dark as night? Was it not possible to step from one to the other, erect, and without essential change?" (358-59). The great difficulty which confronts both parties to this pact of friendship is that neither can move easily from the night world of contemplation—which is haunted by the loved one's "ghost"—to the day world in which they try to see each other as they really are. Both Katharine and Ralph are true to the terms of their friendship in that they are honest with each other; they admit their lapses into dream or self-absorption, and they try to overcome the lack of communication which threatens them when they succumb to their illusions.

The ambiguity of these illusions is sharply defined by Katharine when she accuses Ralph of seeing her through an exotically romantic atmosphere:

> "You call that, I suppose, being in love; as a matter of fact it's being in delusion. All romantic people are the same," she added. "My mother spends her life in making stories about the people

she's fond of. But I won't have you do it about me, if I can help it."

"You can't help it," he said.

"I warn you it's the source of all evil."

"And of all good," he added. (404-5)

Ralph, from the beginning of his acquaintance with Katharine, has been "making stories" about her, imagining her with darker hair, a taller build, a more exalted and infallible mind (17-18); inevitably this "ghost" often comes into conflict with Katharine's actions and her real, physical presence. Katharine, for her part, has for a long time entertained an idealized image of passion—a "magnanimous hero," a horseman, riding beside the sea or through the forests (107-8, 145, 205).

These illusions seem at first to inhibit honest communication between Katharine and Ralph. By the end of the novel, however, the internalized images of their relationship begin actually to aid in communication. When Katharine looks at Ralph's drawing of the little dot with flames around it, an image which is Ralph's inarticulate expression of his love for her, she says, "Yes, the world looks something like that to me too" (522). When Ralph urges her to tell him how she came to love him, she resists, saying that she would have to speak of ridiculous things—"something about flames—fires" (534). But this imagery of fire makes Ralph feel that he can step into her mind; the "illusion"—this creative and shared one—unites rather than separates them. Their creative use of the "night" side of consciousness actually helps them to understand each other. The moral status of illusion in this novel holds a position similar to the one it holds in Shakespeare's comedies; as Avrom Fleishman suggests, the interruption of usual life by romantic love results in a transformation by means of the illusions, and these "illusions are not mere errors but a means of access to certain realities unavailable to ordinary experience."[32] The novel's incorporation of several kinds of illusion allows us to go further; we can observe the circumstances which render the untruths "mere errors," and observe also those contexts which allow the illusion to be, as Ralph insists, "the source of all good." The Hilberys, proud descendents of the poet Richard Alardyce, tend to make up stories about him and about illustrious relatives. The false stories are maintained because they become traditions; the illusion is kept up for the sake of family pride only. The illusions which perpetuate the past are, in this novel, portrayed as potentially harmful, oppressive, or at best comic and innocuous. Yet those illusions that allow Katharine and Ralph to communicate with each other and to envision their future are seen as fruitful and life-giving. The trying-on of psychological disguises, the liminal fantasizing during this period of the marriage initiation, is a way of keeping the future fresh and open.

Both the "night" and the "day," both the private vision and the behavior of the pragmatic social self, are presented as illusions. The externally expressed rituals such as tea and the guided tour of the family relics tend to be the distinctive attributes of Katharine's society, its "manners," and these are the subject of subtle mockery. In contrast, the subjective illusions, the fantasies of Katharine and Ralph, tend to be recognizably archetypal: for Katharine, it is the heroic horseman and for Ralph, the vision of a tall, idealized Katharine. The lovers recognize that such imagery is romantic and false. Yet neither they nor the narrator counter this imagery with more than mild amusement, even though in her later novels Virginia Woolf elaborately and subtly mocks the dream manners of human beings, the mores of the "night" side of consciousness, the habits of the soul. With a few exceptions, the only symbols that are sometimes allowed a complete and lyric seriousness in Woolf's fiction are those that do not involve the image of a human being—a globe, a lighthouse, a painting. In *Night and Day*, for instance, the fiery halo, the orderly flames circling a dot, represent an almost mystical communication between the lovers. Such images seem to be a further expression of the "globe" which Katharine feels that she holds "for one brief moment." It is "the globe which we spend our lives in trying to shape, round, whole, and entire from the confusion of chaos" (533). Jungian analysts and critics would find in this image a mandala, a deep and cross-cultural symbol of the Self, of psychological wholeness.[33] At the level of mysticism, Woolf's mockery ceases, though it remains quite active among the classic, humanly imaged archetypes—the horseman, the magnanimous hero.

Jacob's Room

One of the more renowned literary permutations of the archetypal quest is the Bildungsroman, and in *Jacob's Room* (1922) Woolf
thoroughly teases this classic structure. Under the guise of narrat-
ing the story of a young Edwardian "inheritor of all the ages," she
writes the first of her novels demonstrating her resolve to be a
"free" writer — free to concentrate on consciousness and to dis-
pense as needed with transitions, chronology, and traditional plot.
Jacob's Room has no tragedy, comedy, or love interest "in the accepted style." And yet the paradigm of the "accepted style" — in
this case the Bildungsroman structure — hovers like an antique
frame that doesn't quite fit Jacob's actions or personality. Many of
the novel's peculiarities in form, point of view, and characterization
are linked to the element of parody, since the "form" derives partly
from a strategy of literary attack. The novel shows very clearly the
marks of a playful rebellion; it is held together by the shadowy
structure of the very thing it is against, the Bildungsroman.

The parodic mocking of the form generates some mocking of
subject as well. The Bildungsroman, when it concerns a capable
Edwardian male, must deal in part with the hero's experience of
British institutions of higher learning, for instance. In *Jacob's
Room* the traditional male growth pattern, full of great expectation,
falls like a tattered mantle around the shoulders of the indecisive
hero, heir of the ages. The musing and amused narrator mocks the
structure of her story; she mocks the conventions of the hero's
progress; and, by implication, she mocks the values behind those
conventions. Frequently calling attention to the fact that she is an
outsider observing Jacob's room and world, the narrator is a lyric
jester who seems to observe a world — the natural world of sea and
stars — that is in a state of continual celebration, though it has its
melancholy aspects also. Looking into Jacob's life from this profoundly liminal vantage point, the narrator finds his life curious,
funny, sad. A distinct though mild feminism often coincides with
the narrator's bemused wrenching of the traditional male growing-
up paradigm.

For most critics Woolf's rejection of traditional "realistic" style
in *Jacob's Room* is at least a thoroughly interesting experiment,
although some find weaknesses in Jacob's characterization.[34] Yet

Woolf deliberately aimed at a main character who would have an empty self, an identity prematurely vacated, not just because the "plot" leads him to inevitable death in World War I, but because his civilization — of manly "honor" and intellectual achievement — elicits no real commitment from him. The satire on the values and expectations typical of males in prewar England is adroitly realized in the comically attenuated structure of the novel, although few critics have looked favorably at the comedy in *Jacob's Room*. In fact, Phyllis Rose feels that the social satire on male honor cannot be made to coincide with Woolf's sophisticated style.[35] I would argue, on the contrary, that Woolf's style in this novel is quite flexible enough to accommodate the wide range of the narrator's consciousness, from lyric description to lyric mockery, a mockery reinforced by the loosely architectured life-novel form.

I have discussed elsewhere Woolf's manifold acquaintance with the form of the Bildungsroman among her contemporaries.[36] In *Jacob's Room* the famous conventions are introduced only to be mocked. Jacob walks through his archetypal story as though he doesn't see the traditions. He is an orphan, or partly an orphan, because his father has died; but nothing Dickensian is ever made of this, Jacob being neither better nor worse for the fact. As a young man he moves from the provinces to London, but the narrator mines no moral riches out of this circumstance. Tom Jones and Pip would have gone badly to seed, and would have emerged with a greater knowledge of humanity and of themselves. But Jacob is not corrupted, and his move to the city is not made into one of the signposts of the novel. Jacob's education is something that barely happens to him, yet all the scenery is there — all the scenery for the awakening of his mind and for his rebelling against stodgy traditions. Finally, Jacob receives no revelation, no "epiphany." Opportunity after opportunity is supplied by the author, but she deliberately makes Jacob look the other way, or she ignores the offered moment. Virginia Woolf drags in all the Bildungsroman scenery; then she lets Jacob walk aimlessly about as though the stage were bare. The effect is a remarkable tension that gives fictional embodiment to the pathos, and comedy, of Jacob's life — a life which becomes emblematic of all lives to the extent that they do not fit expected patterns. The mockery against the form, the puncturing of the paradigm, elaborates the narrator's assertion that "it is no use trying to sum people up."[37]

Jacob's university experience, for instance, never assumes the importance of a solemn milestone. Moved on some occasions to a fleeting appreciation of the atmosphere of Cambridge, Jacob must also tolerate caricature dons and oppressive luncheons. The comedy of some of the Cambridge episodes may indeed be, as Aileen Pippett suggested, Woolf's "mocking revenge upon the ancient institutions where she was never able to study."[38] The narrator of *Jacob's Room* is outside the male institutions through which she moves the hero. Even the hero, though sometimes stirred by his college experience, is oddly untransformed by it. He too is somewhat on the outside. Jacob's education neither crushes him nor ennobles him; it perhaps has not very much to do with him. Unlike Stephen Dedalus, Jacob apparently develops no potent and complex theory of art or philosophy. Nor does he meet a G. E. Moore.

To Jacob, Cambridge offers Huxtable, Sopwith, and Cowan, who are figures of inadequacy — inadequacy rather than destructiveness. These scholars do not display the thin-lipped, rigidly restrained asceticism of the priests in *A Portrait of the Artist as a Young Man*, for instance. We are not made to feel that Jacob must escape from the Huxtables and Sopwiths or risk injury to his soul. Jacob's orientation is not religious, so there is no solemn moment during which someone approaches him about a possible vocation. Both the narrator and Jacob have a casual though sensuous attitude toward intellectual endeavor; both seem to take lightly the notion of Jacob's being the heir of the ages. H. G. Wells, on the other hand, writes in *Joan and Peter* of the war's effect on young people, and he loads with irony the idea of inheritance. After Peter is badly wounded, his guardian Oswald reflects bitterly on the way the world has treated its "heir."[39] Wells' Peter and Woolf's Jacob are brutally deceived heirs, but the narrator in Wells' novel provides voluminous hortatory comment on the failures of British education and on the need for the young heirs to rebuild their world. In *Jacob's Room*, neither Jacob nor the narrator reaps any edification out of the notion of inherited responsibilities or opportunities. As Jacob comes to the window of his friend Simeon's room, the narrator observes his face; he looks satisfied, "indeed masterly; which expression

changed slightly as he stood there, the sound of the clock conveying
to him (it may be) a sense of old buildings and time; and himself the
inheritor; and then to-morrow; and friends; at the thought of whom,
in sheer confidence and pleasure, it seemed, he yawned and
stretched himself" (43). The narrator offers only tentative interpretations here, but Jacob's actions are described without ambiguity.
The notion of his being "an inheritor" is very much underplayed.

The two undergraduates continue their discussion, and one of
them mentions Julian the Apostate. The narrator is more interested
in the lyric atmosphere of midnight and wind than she is in observing which man spoke the name. Nevertheless, she definitely asserts
that Simeon is the one who says, "Somehow it seems to matter." Of
the two, he is evidently the more interested in the philosophical
ramifications of the emperor's backsliding. Jacob says, "Well, you
seem to have studied the subject." Then something in both Jacob's
consciousness and that of the narrator experiences the pleasure and
intimacy which pervade the room following this intellectual discussion:

> He appeared extraordinarily happy, as if his pleasure would
> brim and spill down the sides if Simeon spoke.
> Simeon said nothing. Jacob remained standing. But inti-
> macy — the room was full of it, still, deep, like a pool. Without
> need of movement or speech it rose softly and washed over
> everything, mollifying, kindling, and coating the mind with
> the lustre of pearl, so that if you talk of a light, of Cambridge
> burning, it's not languages only. It's Julian the Apostate. (44)

A discussion that might have been the springboard for Jacob's *non
serviam*, or for his defining of a "form" for his life, is instead enjoyed as a sensuous event — by Jacob and by the narrator. Jacob arrives at no great sense of purpose and identity, as Stephen Dedalus
does in his lengthy deliberations with Cranly. Jacob does not live up
to the responsibilities of the well-brought-up Western male hero; he
undertakes no ego-defining rebellion and no mythic quest. He tends
to enjoy his mind and the ideas that he "inherits" from the past; he
does not do anything so practical as tie together his own ego with
them.

A later image suggests that the heritage of the ages is to Jacob
a neutral pleasure, something to be enjoyed rather than shouldered

and carried onward as part of the white man's burden. After leaving Florinda at the Guy Fawkes party, Jacob and Timmy are in high spirits, quoting Greek and feeling generally exuberant: "They were boastful, triumphant; it seemed to both that they had read every book in the world; known every sin, passion, and joy. Civilizations stood round them like flowers ready for picking. Ages lapped at their feet like waves fit for sailing" (74). For Jacob, intellectual conversation is valuable because it creates intimacy between friends. Ages lap at his feet, beckoning this Cambridge sportsman to a pleasant pastime of sailing. His sense of being an heir is linked, in his own mind, to the fact that Florinda called him by his first name, and sat on his knee. "Thus did all good women in the days of the Greeks" (75). Jacob here stereotypes both Greece and Florinda. Like the female statues of the Erechtheum, Florinda is pedestalled, a feminine prop for the structure of ancient civilization as envisioned by Jacob Flanders. This recent Cambridge graduate, unlike the narrator, is only too ready to sum people up — especially women, and especially "the Greeks." Ironically, Jacob is disillusioned a little later when he sees Florinda "turning up Greek street upon another man's arm" (93).[40]

Once in a while, Jacob and his Cambridge friends do approach serious cerebral maneuvers, but the hint of youthful discovery or youthful rebellion is immediately plowed under by a context of shared laughter and sensuous enjoyment. The narrator's frequent shifts of distance contribute much to the short duration of any philosophical or rebellious musings. Moving back a little, she suggests that the story may be following a typical Bildungsroman pattern; she hints that Bonamy or Jacob may be resenting the fact of Keats' early death — perhaps her characters are about to raise clenched fists against God or the nature of things. But no, she moves in closer, and without any hedging tells us that Jacob, "who sat astride a chair and ate dates from a long box, burst out laughing" (42).

True, this method of narration, this inconsistency with regard to distance, is perhaps confusing. I'm not sure that it is necessarily an ineffective approach, however. Hafley is right when he says that while one narrator insists on the impossibility of knowing Jacob, another narrator does a good job of disproving this by moving easily into the minds of other characters.[41] There are two narrators, or one

narrator who insists on giving us a twofold vision of Jacob, a vision
that shows the conventional pattern which he "should" follow, and
almost simultaneously points out that he is not following it. This
method is an extended version of what Woolf does in "An Unwrit-
ten Novel." There, a narrator within the narrator's head invents an
elaborate story about a woman, "Minnie Marsh," who happens to
ride opposite in a train. But when the unknown woman leaves the
train, the frame-narrator must admit that the supposed "Minnie"
really seems happier and more at ease in the world than the story-
making imagination had envisioned. The frame-narrator must confront the mystery which results from the discrepancy between the
two portraits, the imaginary one and the one revealed briefly and in-
completely by the facts. A similar double-narrator prevails in
Jacob's Room. She is continually sketching the mythic pattern that
young men are "supposed" to follow; then she provides suddenly a
close-up of Jacob eating dates or finding in the cheap Florinda the
emblem of all things Greek.

Even when he is actually in Greece, Jacob—and the narrator
—are bemused by the disjunction of emblem and reality. He visits
the Acropolis, emblem of all things Greek, and as he sits down to
read, expects to be inspired:

> And laying the book on the ground he began, as if inspired
> by what he had read, to write a note upon the importance of his-
> tory—upon democracy—one of those scribbles upon which the
> work of a lifetime may be based; or again, it falls out of a book
> twenty years later, and one can't remember a word of it. It is a
> little painful. It had better be burnt.
> Jacob wrote; began to draw a straight nose.... (149-50)

At this point democracy and the straight nose are interrupted by
women on tour. The comedy is doubled and tripled. First Jacob in-
terrupts himself by turning from democracy to a straight nose;
then the sightseeing women interrupt the drawing of the nose. To
be fair to Jacob, we would have to point out that the narrator may
be responsible for the comic thoughts about juvenilia on democracy; she doesn't say definitely that Jacob himself writes such a
"painful" note. She moves in closer, however, and we do see Jacob
drawing a straight nose. His meditations on history are probably
not those of a future Gibbon or a Clive Bell. Jacob curses the women

for interrupting him, but the comedy of the scene began earlier; he
had interrupted himself.

The narrator continues the parodic portrait of a British youth's
disillusionment with Athens:

> "It is those damned women," said Jacob, without any trace
> of bitterness, but rather with sadness and disappointment that
> what might have been should never be.
>
> (This violent disillusionment is generally to be expected in
> young men in the prime of life, sound of wind and limb, who
> will soon become fathers of families and directors of banks.)
> (150)

Jacob's disillusionment here hardly deserves the adjective "violent" which the narrator ironically applies, looking ahead to the pro-
saic destiny which—were it not for the war—ordinarily awaits
young men like Jacob; they become "fathers of families and direc-
tors of banks," not great historians and thinkers. Jacob's "disappointment that what might have been should never be" approaches
cliché in its phrasing; it is parodic.

The narrator puts the cap on this comic scene by letting us see
Jacob as he looks at the sculptures of the Erechtheum:

> Jacob strolled over to the Erechtheum and looked rather fur-
> tively at the goddess on the left-hand side holding the roof on
> her head. She reminded him of Sandra Wentworth Williams.
> He looked at her, then looked away. He looked at her, then
> looked away. He was extraordinarily moved, and with the bat-
> tered Greek nose in his head, with Sandra in his head, with all
> sorts of things in his head, off he started to walk right up to the
> top of Mount Hymettus, alone, in the heat. (151)

This is farcical ("He looked at her, then looked away. He looked at
her, then looked away."). Jacob's stagey double take lets all the air
out of the potentially epiphanic balloon. And, instead of the idealized "straight" nose he had been drawing, his head is full of the
"battered Greek nose" which he somehow associates with his new
infatuation, Sandra, who is travelling with her husband. What a
descent from Bonamy's prediction that Jacob would fall in love
with "some Greek woman with a straight nose" (139). For Jacob, no
bird-girl stands symbolically on a beach; if she did, he would prob-

ably notice her crooked nose instead of rising to the occasion with a lyrical definition of his identity and his vocation.

Jacob's apparently climactic opportunity for love and insight is his nighttime visit to the Acropolis with Sandra. Woolf doesn't describe it. The narrator's reflections indicate that she has deliberately turned away from this event. As Jacob and Sandra climb, the narrator's perspective widens, giving us Paris, Constantinople, London, and Betty Flanders, who sighs "like one who realizes, but would fain ward off a little longer — oh, a little longer! — the oppression of eternity" (160). Meanwhile Jacob and Sandra have vanished from the narrator's view. "There was the Acropolis; but had they reached it?" The answer to the narrator's question may be "yes," in the sense that Jacob may have actually reached the Acropolis with Sandra. From what we know of Jacob, however, "no" would be the answer to the more symbolic aspect of the narrator's question. It is doubtful that he reached the "Acropolis" of symbolic insight. Later, back in London, he is essentially unchanged and still suffering from his unmanageable passions. He draws a sketch of the Parthenon in the dust in Hyde Park and reads a letter from Sandra about her memory "of something said or attempted, some moment in the dark on the road to the Acropolis which (such was her creed) mattered for ever" (169). Moments belong to Sandra's creed, not to Jacob's. He overlooks them or distorts them; she, on the other hand, makes moments, contrives them.

Some sort of "moment" of insight is present even in Woolf's early novels. The newly engaged Katharine Hilbery, as we saw, held "for one brief moment the globe which we spend our lives in trying to shape, round, whole, and entire from the confusion of chaos." In *Jacob's Room*, however, the narrator goes out of her way to undercut such occasions. She troubles to point out the "dirty curtain" of the hotel window in Olympia where Sandra stands contemplating the burdened peasants as they return for the evening: "She seemed to have grasped something. She would write it down. And moving to the table where her husband sat reading she leant her chin in her hands and thought of the peasants, of suffering, of her own beauty, of the inevitable compromise, and of how she would write it down" (140-41). Her sentimental musings self-consciously place her own beauty in the middle of the picture. She says, "Everything seems to mean so much"; then she notices her own reflection in a mirror, and she thinks, "I am very beautiful" (141). After the big occasion of her visit to the Acropolis with Jacob, she reflects on their relationship, bringing back again "the soul of the moment": " 'What for? What for?' Sandra would say, putting the book back, and strolling to the looking-glass and pressing her hair" (160-61). Sandra cannot look deeply into herself; she can look only *at* herself.

The narrator, not Jacob or Sandra, has the imaginative and lyrical responses to Greece and to the English landscape. She gives us the illuminating meditation on the "exaltation" of young people such as Fanny Elmer and Nick Bramham, whose restless energy, if it were any more intense, would blow them "like foam into the air"; if we had such continual ecstasy, "the stars would shine through us" (119-20). And the narrator has the moments of insight; she is, in her own right, a distinct and important character, as recent critics have observed.[42] It is she who describes the spectacular and melancholy beauty of the Cornish coast as Timmy and Jacob sail close to it; it is she who imaginatively elaborates on the sense of peace, of "wisdom and piety," that settles on the sunny cottages and fields of the coast: "It wore an extraordinary look of piety and peace, as if old men smoked by the door, and girls stood, hands on hips, at the well, and horses stood; as if the end of the world had come, and cabbage fields and stone walls, and coast-guard stations, and, above all, the white sand bays with the waves breaking unseen by any one, rose to heaven in a kind of ecstasy" (47). This vision of "the end of the world" is the real norm of Woolf's comedy, here and in the rest of her fiction. From this mystic remove the narrator in *Jacob's Room* mocks the manners and the myths that have shaped Jacob's life, or are supposed to have shaped it. She satirizes Jacob's "socialization," which seems in his case—like a faulty vaccination—not to have "taken."

By parodying the Bildungsroman as a form, Virginia Woolf builds a comic tension between the stubborn mystery of Jacob on the one hand, and on the other the goals of love, fame, and the Western identity that he is supposed to be pursuing. In other words, she teases the pattern of male liminality, the male passage, through love and travel, to respectable adulthood. The real self of Jacob, and by implication the identity of any human being, retains a stubborn mystery that is resistant to Edwardian manner and even to the mythic life-passage patterns on which the manners of a particular age are based.

Mrs. Dalloway

Like the narrator of *Jacob's Room*, Clarissa Dalloway is convinced that there is a mystery at the heart of each person. She is amused, and sometimes angered, if anyone tries "forcing" the "soul," tries to fasten down a rigid destructive definition of "human nature." By many critics, Clarissa would not be considered a trustworthy judge of human beings; she is seen as cold, sexless, and artificial, an empty-headed socialite.[43] But Virginia Woolf, and Clarissa as well, seem to agree with the critics about the limitations of the major character's sensibility. After finishing *Mrs. Dalloway* (1925), Woolf was concerned that Clarissa might be "too glittering and tinsely."[44] Clarissa and her social world are themselves one of the objects of satire in the novel. Woolf wrote that she hoped to "criticise the social system," a phrase that could mean either the criticism of the artificial life of society people in general, or, as Alex Zwerdling argues, the criticism of the stoical postwar upper-class attitude which takes care to exclude sensitive outsiders like the suicide Septimus Smith.[45] Woolf's attitude toward the society women of her acquaintance, such as Kitty Maxse and Lady Ottoline Morrell, was ambiguous,[46] and something of this ambiguity is present in Clarissa's character.

Clarissa is troubled by the compromises she has made in her life. During the time span of the novel's surface "plot," the day in which Clarissa prepares for her party that evening, she thinks often of her past decisions and of her present life as hostess, an obligatory role for the wife of Richard Dalloway, M.P. She recognizes that her marriage to Richard and her constant social life have perhaps tarnished her heart; something has been "defaced, obscured in her own life, let drop every day in corruption, lies, chatter." And yet Clarissa does recognize the value of what she has preserved, salvaged from people like the psychiatrist Sir William Bradshaw, a man capable of "forcing your soul" (203), whose inept, insensitive response contributed much to the death of Septimus. Clarissa knows that she still retains the energy and happiness of her love for her girlhood friend Sally Seton (who has succumbed to egotistical motherhood), and Clarissa recognizes also that her friendly marriage to Richard has preserved her privacy and independence, her "self-respect—something, after all, priceless" (132). The lies and corruption of her decision to marry Richard, though she loved Peter Walsh, have given her in compensation the continuing opportunity to bring people together in her parties, her "offering" to life, given "for no reason whatever," an "offering for the sake of offering, perhaps" (134, 135). Her parties, as one critic has observed, are an expression of creative artistry, a courageous celebration poised against war and against intrusive people, including Peter and the zealous Miss Kilman, who try to force the soul into a tight mold.[47] Clarissa's party, which is the focus and culmination of the novel's action, occurs as a gesture of celebration and communication in a society that tends to confine people to narrow and discrete psychological boxes. Jacob pretty well escaped the stereotypes with which his education would have restricted him; he escaped by ignoring the classic growth pattern for respectable young men. All of the characters in *Mrs. Dalloway*, however, have compromised to some extent with the culture that defines them. More than the others, Clarissa has retained the "treasure" of a private self, as recent critics are careful to emphasize.[48]

Her party, though it is incorporated into the prevailing social structure, and though the prime minister attends, is still a festive gesture, a liminal occasion. Men prevail in the warring world which destroyed the heart of Septimus, but Clarissa, a woman in an appropriately green dress, presides over her life-giving party. Several readers have pointed to Clarissa's creative and renewing abilities as a hostess, and to the quality of ritual and festivity which prevail at her party.[49] Indeed, this party provides some very typical overturnings of value, some festive put-downs of those who are, in society, rulers and definers of policy. We discover that the prime minister "looked so ordinary. You might have stood him behind a counter and bought biscuits—poor chap, all rigged up in gold lace" (189). And as Clarissa moves through the little private room where the prime minister had been talking to Lady Bruton, their fossil imprints still dent the chair cushions and provide a quiet mockery of power and status. "The chairs still kept the impress of the Prime Minister and Lady Bruton, she turned deferentially, he sitting foursquare, authoritatively" (202). Clarissa's party is a traditional "festive" event—that is, it is contained in, and it resolves into, the larger structure of respect for order and power in which one most certainly does not note the expressive contours of a prime minister's bottom. The brief festivity of Clarissa's party is only a release; it is hardly a congregation of revolutionaries.

In their own meditations, however, both Clarissa and the narrator offer an intermittent choral critique of a society that expects people to conform to its definitions of love, war, and "human nature." This mocking and flyting—perhaps because no prime minister can overhear an unspoken attack—is more free and irreverent. In her own consciousness, Clarissa does not have to behave like a hostess, and the narrator certainly does not. Clarissa herself is of course satirized by occasional mock-heroic imagery, as several critics have pointed out,[50] and Clarissa, though anxious about the stiffly pious Miss Kilman's influence on Elizabeth Dalloway, manages to turn her laughter on this possessive and domineering tutor (139). The most irreverent mockery, however, a mockery that cuts at the images received from the primary socialization process of most people living in the Western world, is the subtle attack on Peter as the great lover with a glamorous grievance and the alarmingly comic, deflating account of Septimus as he commits suicide.

Peter himself admits that Clarissa's rejection of him was wise, that "it would not have been a success, their marriage" (171), but he still feels quite justified in ruining his life because of this thirty-year-long heartbreak. He is the paradigm of the nearly religious Victorian Lover, and perhaps of the Arch-Western Lover. In idealizing and remaining faithful—after his fashion—to Clarissa, he is responding to the lofty concepts of John Ruskin, who wrote, "In this rapturous obedience to the single love of his youth, is the sanctification of all man's strength, and the continuance of all his purposes."[51] Peter sustains the posture of an obedient excommunicant, unsanctified, lacking strength, his purposes certainly lacking continuance—all because the single love of his youth rejected him. This single love finds it amusing when he confesses to her, some hours before her party, that he is in love: " 'In love!' she said. That he at his age should be sucked under in his little bow-tie by that monster! And there's no flesh on his neck; his hands are red; and he's six months older than I am!" (50). This portrait of Peter is uncharitable, but it also is unspoken. And it is true: that is, "love," as expressed in Peter's life, is a monster both to the object of his possessive idealizing and to himself.

Clarissa is for Peter a prime example of Woman as Other, as love and God and country. Particularly interesting is Peter's tendency to see England as Clarissa. After their emotional interview, Peter walks about in London, feeling as ambiguous toward civilized life (after years in India) as he does toward Clarissa. Hearing St. Margaret's clock strike the time, he compares the church to Clarissa; both are a kind of "hostess," punctual, beautiful, and moving (55-56). He decides, after all, that British civilization is a fine achievement, and his thoughts indicate that he links it to his feelings for Clarissa: "There were moments when civilisation, even of this sort, seemed dear to him as a personal possession; moments of pride in England; in butlers; chow dogs; girls in their security. Ridiculous enough, still there it is, he thought" (61-62). The phrase "still there it is," which Peter here applies to England, is modified twice to apply to Clarissa. Peter thinks of how she stands in the doorway of a crowded room: "There she was, however; there she was" (84-85). The same choral phrase occurs at the end of the book, where Peter, in ecstasy, realizes that Clarissa has entered the room: "For there she was" (213). The nice irony carried by this repeated choral phrase is that Peter, though he criticizes Clarissa and London for their artificiality, is moved to ecstasy by them both. He is not free to judge either in a rational and fair manner, but instead is bound—almost duty-bound—to preserve an anguished, idealizing passion for both his country and his great love, self-consciously alienated as he is from both.

His self-glamorizing alienation is satirized in the well-known "solitary traveller" episode in which either Peter dreams he is a wanderer, a questor, or the narrator develops a mocking fantasy *about* someone like Peter while the real man sits on a park bench and dozes beside a nurse. In this comically grandiose vision, an adventurer contends with mythical landscapes in order to find solace in the arms of a feminized ideal: "The solitary traveller, haunter of lanes, disturber of ferns, and devastator of great hemlock plants, looking up suddenly, sees the giant figure at the end of the ride" (63). The rhetorical phrasing of the epithets, as though they were a citation for spectacular achievements (haunter of lanes, disturber of ferns), and the exotic fairytale context of the implied heroism (amid the ferns and hemlocks), are sufficient indication that the passage is satiric, though lyrical.[52]

The imagery, as the passage continues, develops a mythic vision of an all-consoling Great Mother. Writers have often described such a vision, but almost always with sympathy for the character who sees it, and with the implication that it is universal, an unavoidable part of "the human condition," a built-in quest that ennobles us all — especially those who are men. But Virginia Woolf teases this solitary traveller. His search is ambiguous, as Lucio Ruotolo has observed, and probably self-destructive: Peter wants to disappear into the giant female figure and "blow to nothingness with the rest" (64).[53] His visions tease him. No sooner does the traveller find "absolution" than the scattering visions "confound the piety of their aspect with a wild carouse" (64). They "murmur in his ear like sirens lolloping away on the green sea waves, or are dashed in his face like bunches of roses, or rise to the surface like pale faces which fishermen flounder through floods to embrace" (64). In his journey the searcher encounters no evil or ominous imagery, no Circe; his search is trivialized and mocked, and the visions are tossed in his face like roses. The alliteration, if nothing else, would keep the passage from being a serious ode to visionary love and adventure — faces, fishermen, flounder, floods.

The reason for the mockery is clearly stated; these visions "float up, pace beside, put their faces in front of, the actual thing; often overpowering the solitary traveller and taking away from him the sense of earth" (64). The visions obscure the actual thing, and the visionary tendency, at least as it expresses itself in Peter, is called an "infirmity"; the traveller imagines "an elderly woman who seems (so powerful is this infirmity) to seek, over the desert, a lost son; to search for a rider destroyed; to be the figure of the mother whose sons have been killed in the battles of the world" (65). Peremptorily, with comic brevity, Virginia Woolf has here summarized the plot of the hero with a thousand faces. To the solitary traveller comes a nebulous mother figure, an elderly Venus arriving to comfort the battle-scarred Aeneas, her son. There is more to the *Aeneid* than its plot, of course, but there is very little more to Peter than *his* "plot," his fantasy plot through which he consoles his ongoing immaturity. It is an "infirmity," the narrator says, for the traveller to escape into the realms of visionary goddess-mothers.

Further, Peter has never been "a rider destroyed" (the postured inversion makes the rhetoric subtly comic), nor a son killed in battle. He has not even been shell-shocked like Septimus.

Nevertheless, the experiences of the two men are parallel in some ways, and the parallels serve to reduce the heroic posturing of both. If Clarissa symbolizes the ideal for Peter, Isabel Pole holds a similar status in the mind of Septimus. Miss Pole wears a green dress just as Clarissa does at her party. Isabel Pole is the first love of Septimus. He goes to her lectures on Shakespeare, and she corrects his love poems without responding to the content. She in effect rejects him as Clarissa rejects Peter. Just as Peter sees Clarissa through a complex of images and institutions which he associates with England, so Septimus identifies Isabel Pole with an idealized England for which he goes to battle. An early volunteer, he "went to France to save an England which consisted almost entirely of Shakespeare's plays and Miss Isabel Pole in a green dress walking in a square" (95). Feeling that he has lied to Rezia, has married her without loving her, he thinks he has "outraged Miss Isabel Pole" (101). With regard to Septimus, Joan Bennett has observed that we are given a "sympathetic yet slightly mocking account of his intellectual aspirations and romantic notions."[54] Although Septimus' own consciousness gives us the painful disorientation of his madness, when the narrator fills in the flippant sketch of his life before the war, we see a self-centered young man with the precious ambition of seeking a glamorous future as a great poet: he "had gone to London leaving an absurd note behind him, such as great men have written, and the world has read later when the story of their struggles has become famous" (94). Septimus shares with Peter the tendency to think of himself in heroic terms; both men seem to be pleading that if only life and love had been a little kinder to them, had responded to their talents, they could have distinguished themselves in a manner worthy of great literature — worthy at least of their own memoirs. For Peter too, in his youth, had ambitions of becoming a writer (206).

Unlike Peter, Septimus resists the definition of "human nature" as advocated by his society, and by its doctors especially. Peter is content to wear his broken heart on his sleeve, his life being the emblem of a failed Ruskinian lover. Septimus, on the other hand, had tried to conform to society's expectations, but then he violently rejected the effort to be the tough manly hero. Although he was once proud of the fact that he did not cry at the death of his comrade Evans, Septimus manages to reclaim his soul; he worries, he feels and suffers, paradoxically, over his supposed lack of feeling. And in the last moments of his life he preserves — as Clarissa later suspects.— his diamond, his treasure, his integrity. He rejects the attempt by Holmes and Bradshaw to lock him up until he conforms to their notion of human nature.

Septimus' self-liberation from his earlier heroic ambitions is expressed in his sense of humor, or at least his sense of irony, as he prepares hastily to jump to his death. He recognizes his own absurdity at the moment of suicide. Dr. Holmes has pushed Rezia aside and is coming up the stairs to lock Septimus away from society. Septimus thinks of the gas fire, of razors, but there is not time for these. "There remained only the window, the large Bloomsbury lodging-house window; the tiresome, the troublesome, and rather melodramatic business of opening the window and throwing himself out" (164). A few seconds away from suicide, Septimus recognizes the melodrama of the great gesture. He no longer thinks of himself as "the scapegoat, the eternal sufferer," images which occurred to him earlier that day, during his hallucinatory walk in the park with Rezia (29). He is not hallucinating now. He no longer sees himself in grandiose terms — the great writer, the defender of Miss Pole and England, the suffering martyr. His suicide is, to him, merely a desperate, last-resort action, melodramatic and tiresome. Underscoring this perception, the narrator's description of the doctors and of Mrs. Filmer, the landlady, carefully skirts any implication of solemn tragedy; their reactions are almost farcical: "Dr. Holmes and Mrs. Filmer collided with each other. Mrs. Filmer flapped her apron and made [Rezia] hide her eyes in the bedroom" (164-65). The tragic tone that the scene might appear to deserve is deliberately avoided; Septimus does not perceive his suicide as a "big scene," and neither does the narrator.

The only people who see the event as a big scene are the insensitive Dr. Holmes and to some extent Mrs. Filmer. The doctor, who is in large part responsible for the scene, naturally executes his part with gusto. After all, Holmes and Bradshaw have written the play. Contemplating his suicide, Septimus had mused, "It was their idea of tragedy, not his or Rezia's (for she was with him). Holmes and

Bradshaw liked that sort of thing" (164). Holmes, the creator of suicide cries, "The coward!" He bustles around, mouthing clichés
about being brave and sparing the "poor young woman" (164-65).
The "tragedy" is something which Holmes and Bradshaw have
made. Septimus and the narrator refuse to see it in that light.

When Septimus says, "I'll give it you" (164), he is giving the
world of the Bradshaws back to the Bradshaws; unlike Jesus, Septimus is abandoning a world, not sacrificially renewing it. If he is a
Christ figure at all, he is a "comic Christ," as Hauck describes this
figure; the crucifixion of a comic Christ usually occurs in a context
of satire, the satire falling either on the society or on the Christ-
figure convention itself.[55] In *Mrs. Dalloway* the satire falls on both
the society and on the Christ-figure convention. In effect, one of the
most famous images of male liminality is mocked. Liminality *itself* is
not mocked; Woolf does not imply that men or women should abandon the process, or the stages, of psychological renewal. She does
refuse, in *Mrs. Dalloway*, to take seriously the archetype of a scapegoat. She mocks, as Septimus does, his society's "idea of tragedy."

The idea and practice of war is part of that tragedy; Septimus is
destroyed by the war, an idea of noble tragedy which his society
supports. His mock sacrifice is thus a judgment against both war
and rigid doctors. We observed earlier Woolf's assertion that a woman writer might find trivial what a male writer might see as serious; in *Mrs. Dalloway*, one of these serious patriarchal ideas is that
some concept of sacrifice is a way of making war seem a heroic and
renewing, though painful, necessity. Woolf does not accept this ancient, millenially respected paradigm of war as an ennobling ritual
of killing. In opposition to this ritual, Woolf, through Clarissa, presents the ritual of the party. In this connection, a recent critic has
observed that Clarissa's musings about roses and politics can be
seen as positive and creative rather than as frivolous: Clarissa
"loved her roses (didn't that help the Armenians?)" (133). Lee Edwards suggests that Woolf is offering solutions other than revolution and war—the usual paths to freedom and social change; instead, Edwards interprets, perhaps "the way of the hostess" should
be tried. "Could we learn to value joy as much as we now treasure
suffering . . .?"[56] The scapegoat war idea of tragedy is answered by
Clarissa's flowers and parties, by her idea of comedy, of hope and
communication. An appropriate accompaniment to this comedy is

the harsh satiric flyting, the severe rhetoric, with which the narrator attacks Sir William Bradshaw and the Goddesses of Conversion and Proportion. Many readers have felt that the portrait of Dr. Bradshaw is unfair and much too severe.[57] But Woolf is not attempting to give a "fair" portrait of Dr. Bradshaw. Her rhythmic, incantatory denunciation suggests a magical spell. She is not trying to describe Bradshaw; she is trying to get rid of him: "Naked, defenceless, the exhausted, the friendless received the impress of Sir William's will. He swooped; he devoured. He shut people up" (113). The syntactic units repeat themselves, and the cadence suggests ritual. Indeed, one of the traditional elements of comedy is the ritual of harsh rhetorical attack on the life-denying forces whose presence threatens the festive gaiety and the hope of fertility.[58]

Mrs. Dalloway concludes with Clarissa's party, her "offering," her festive gift of celebration. Bradshaw is of course present at the party; he belongs there, and in the novel, just as Malvolio belongs in *Twelfth Night*. The satire of a figure such as Malvolio is traditionally overdrawn and harsh; Bradshaw quite appropriately receives a similar treatment. The values that he represents, however, succumb at least temporarily to celebration. If Clarissa's "values" — flowers for Armenians and parties for doctors and politicians — do not seem political, the reason may be that they have not been used politically in Western culture, yet. They are liminal; they belong to play, to the other, tabooed side of the conventional, respected, traditional business of the world — wars and legislating.

To the Lighthouse

In *Mrs. Dalloway* the party is only for one evening, and the potentially radical notion of replacing political, tragic scapegoats with political flowers and parties, remains safely circumscribed by doctors and members of Parliament. With *To the Lighthouse*, however, we have another "voyage out," not just in Mr. Ramsay's boat trip to the lighthouse, but in the extended context of a vacation in the Hebrides. Mr. and Mrs. Ramsay, biographical portraits of Virginia Woolf's parents, are, in the vacation setting, like the English on Santa Marina, removed to some extent from the civilization that gave them their identity. Although one of Mr. Ramsay's students, Charles Tansley, is a guest at the summer home and is consulting

Mr. Ramsay about a dissertation, both of these intellectuals are removed from any traditional bookish context. Like Jacques and Touchstone, they are casuists in the wild, a circumstance not likely to confirm their scholarly identities. In this liminal setting Mrs. Ramsay is less removed than Mr. Ramsay from the identity-confirming activities of London life. She is still the hostess, still the angel-mother of the house. Like a madonna, she reads during the evening to her son James, both framed by a large window, an archetypal tableau which Lily is trying to paint from her easel on the lawn. And Mrs. Ramsay readily exercises her talent for arranging marriages when she secures the engagement of Paul Rayley and Minta Doyle. Nevertheless, both Mr. and Mrs. Ramsay are "on vacation" from their usual social world and, more significantly, from themselves.

Neither of the clusters of imagery and value—the cluster of masculine imagery associated with Mr. Ramsay and the cluster of feminine imagery associated with Mrs. Ramsay—receives an endorsement in the novel's action. Critics have often discussed these polarities in the novel, usually suggesting how the duality or conflict is then resolved, by Lily's androgynous personality, for instance, which can be seen as combining the complementary traits of Mr. and Mrs. Ramsay, or by the symbol of the lighthouse or of Lily's painting.[59] The fact that there are several novelistic candidates for the image of resolution points to the unsettled, unresolved quality of each major character's final outlook; in fact, there is no "final" outlook, no attitude or symbol or security, no certain and dependable relationship to others and especially to the unpredictable natural world of night, wind, death, and drownings. There is no norm here, and the profound liminality of landscape and attitude precludes, I believe, a conservative resolution to the comic elements, although Maria DiBattista, using the model of the family romance, has argued otherwise.[60] At the end of the novel the characters are still in the Hebrides, both actually and symbolically. They remain on Prospero's island, on the island of psychological tempest, but without his (and Mrs. Ramsay's) magical gift of resolving conflicts by a marriage or by other machination. True, Mr. Ramsay reaches the lighthouse, and Lily finishes her painting. But both the sailing trip and the amateur painting are merely human conjurations. They are smaller, more human symbols than the great idols of the first section, and in this lies their value and their "advance" over the statuesque myths that were mocked in the archetypal figures of Mr. Ramsay and Mrs. Ramsay. Apparently cut loose at last from his concept of himself as a heroic scholar-explorer among the Antarcticas of knowledge, Mr. Ramsay, munching bread and cheese, sails to the lighthouse and even praises his son for piloting the boat well. Similarly, Lily is free to have her own "vision," as she says, rather than chafing under the only vision which her idol, Mrs. Ramsay, could see for her: marriage. The polarities which are indeed in the novel and for which readers have sought resolutions are not so much resolved as reduced; in the progress of the book, they are reduced to human size.

The reductions begin in the first part of the novel, which contains the most powerful and yet subtle comedy. Sometimes the voice of the narrator, mingling with the thoughts of a character, directs the mockery at its traditional target, manners. We see the maiden painter Lily Briscoe, self-conscious and restrained while William Bankes eyes her canvas and praises her practical shoes for allowing "the toes their natural expansion."[61] Or we sense the vast embarrassment of the guests at the dinner table during a lapse in the conversation, which it is of course the obligation of the women to keep up. At such moments *To the Lighthouse* is indeed a "novel of manners," as Ralph Freedman notes, and its satire shows a "heritage" of Jane Austen.[62] On another level, however, the novel could well be called a comedy of myth, for the mocking voice frequently satirizes the archetypal fantasies of characters, or looks at a ritual occasion through mythic metaphors. In either case, the metaphors and the fantasies draw upon mythic imagery (not merely the external manner of an era), and this imagery is mocked. The effect is that of toppling an archetypal icon, something venerated for centuries.

Recent critics have noted in passing several of the comic episodes in *To the Lighthouse*. Many point to Mr. Ramsay's melodramatic recitation of "The Charge of the Light Brigade" as he strides over the lawn; and a favorite passage is his extended fantasy-effort to envision himself progressing through the alphabet of knowledge from A to Z, but sticking at Q, unable to push on to R though he keeps forcing himself, in imagination a Polar explorer, onward: "He would never reach R. On to R, once more. R—" (57).[63] What is the significance of this comedy? Does it extend beyond its deflating effect on Mr. Ramsay, Victorian and Edwardian scholar? The comedy is not, I believe, merely incidental to an otherwise "serious" novel about several characters who search for stability and identity in a world where Mrs. Ramsay dies, where the ten years intervening between vacations see Prue Ramsay die also and Andrew lose his life in the war. At its deepest level the comedy does from another angle what time, storms, war, and death do to the mythic values that provided an apparently sturdy and ancient order for those on the island in the first section of the novel. The comedy does, in a psychological way, what the peripherally described actions in "Time Passes" do. Woolf's comedy undercuts the power of the order-affirming images embodied by Mr. Ramsay and Mrs. Ramsay, the very ancient images, those given to us by our primary socialization (as distinct from the more external images and behaviors derived from secondary socialization, the gentlemanly conversational ploy, for instance, which prompts William Bankes to comment on Lily's shoes).

After this terrific battle with himself over his inability to reach R, let alone ever achieve Z, Mr. Ramsay tries to reconcile himself to a respectably middling achievement; he does so in images which underscore his enormous vanity, and which also underscore their own illusory fragility:

> Who then could blame the leader of that forlorn party which after all has climbed high enough to see the waste of the years and the perishing of stars, if before death stiffens his limbs beyond the power of movement he does a little consciously raise his numbed fingers to his brow, and square his shoulders, so that when the search party comes they will find him dead at his post, the fine figure of a soldier? Mr. Ramsay squared his shoulders and stood very upright by the urn. (59-60)

The imagery in this passage is ironically grandiose, giving Mr. Ramsay's vanity deliberate emphasis. The swelling verbal music works against him rather than for him. He envisions himself, evidently dying, yet "consciously" arranging his body so that it will freeze in a noble posture; the members of the search party will at least reap the "fine figure" of a hero for their pains.

People who have grown up within the last four thousand years have been trained not to laugh at figures like Mr. Ramsay. He has,

after all, spent his life doing what we are supposed to admire and respect; he has heroically aimed for the top of his profession, and he
has married a beautiful wife. He has translated into early-twentieth-
century manner a centuries-old myth of "man" voyaging out to
conquer the wastelands of the world. But the narrator is amused, at
Mr. Ramsay and at the mythic norm of masculine action.

As Mr. Ramsay, still rapt with visions of his own noble failures,
turns to look at his wife and son, the lyric irony undercuts the hero's
claiming and venerating of his prize, his beautiful wife:

> Who shall blame him? Who will not secretly rejoice when the
> hero puts his armour off, and halts by the window and gazes at
> his wife and son, who very distant at first, gradually come
> closer and closer, till lips and book and head are clearly before
> him, though still lovely and unfamiliar from the intensity of his
> isolation and the waste of ages and the perishing of the stars,
> and finally putting his pipe in his pocket and bending his mag-
> nificent head before her — who will blame him if he does hom-
> age to the beauty of the world? (60-61)

We find it hard to blame him, perhaps, until we remember that this
hero of life and love has some minutes before cursed his wife, the
"beauty of the world." "Damn you," he had said to her, crushing
her effort to hold open at least the possibility of a trip to the lighthouse which James had set his heart on (54). The long lyrical passage contrasts ironically with Mr. Ramsay's earlier brutality to his
wife. The reiteration of "Who will blame him?" begins, by its very
repetition, to cast blame, to question its own question, just as Mark
Antony's persistent linking of the word "honorable" to Brutus, begins at length to imply just the opposite. Yet in a sense — a patriarchal sense — Mr. Ramsay is blameless, since it is his privilege to
rule, or to give homage to, his wife, as he wishes. Probably Mr.
Ramsay, like Leslie Stephen, believes that modern couples retain
something of the "instinct" of striking (if a man) and being struck
(if a woman) — a process by which "the savage" acquired a wife, as
Stephen wrote in *The Science of Ethics*.[64] Being of such a bold and
archaic nature, Mr. Ramsay's heroism can lay claim to obedient
beauty, and the beauty of the world has no right to argue with him.

In addition to the ironic contrast of this passage with Mr. Ramsay's earlier behavior, lyrical sledgehammers of humor apply re-

strained taps everywhere. The vision of Mr. Ramsay in armor is comic; he truly is clanking about, mentally, in the heavy gear of Western chivalry. He has a tradition of knighthood behind him. The extravagant scope of the phrase, "the waste of ages and the perishing of the stars," gives a comically huge frame to the humble gesture of putting a pipe in a pocket. The adjective "magnificent" hovers uncertainly between Mr. Ramsay's consciousness and the narrator's voice, but either way, the gesture of "bending his magnificent head" is mocked. The narrator has been amused by Mr. Ramsay throughout his meditations, so if "magnificent" is her word, it is ironic; if it is Mr. Ramsay's own vision of himself, it is humorously quite consistent with the vanity of his self-conscious gestures as a hero. He has been thinking of staging his freezing body in an impressive posture, and now he bends his head, with the flattering knowledge of the dramatic effect that his handsome figure creates.

Likewise Mrs. Ramsay—whose prototype, Julia Stephen, was Leslie Stephen's "saint," as he said—is also mocked, especially the more destructive aspects of her archetypal capacity as Great Mother.[65] Mrs. Ramsay herself has brief lapses of confidence—as if she were questioning, not her capacity of moving on to R or all the way to Z, but the value and rightness of getting to Z at all. She has brief misgivings about the engagement she has worked so hard to accomplish (and which later results in an unhappy marriage). As she presides over the main course during her elaborate dinner, she has a "curious sense" that the serious business of matchmaking is founded on illusion and is in some ultimate sense comic:

> This will celebrate the occasion—a curious sense rising in her, at once freakish and tender, of celebrating a festival, as if two emotions were called up in her, one profound—for what could be more serious than the love of man for woman, what more commanding, more impressive, bearing in its bosom the seeds of death; at the same time these lovers, these people entering into illusion glittering eyed, must be danced round with mockery, decorated with garlands. (156)

This passage ventures to see as being joyfully laughable the centuries-old assumptions which even the agnostic Leslie Stephen and the agnostic Birkin (with Lawrence's voice) perceived as norms in a godless world: heterosexual love as salvation, and the woman as saint. Such comedy, by laughing at the roots rather than the leaves, and yet without nihilistic cynicism, implies an open sort of courage, a liminal recognition that the structures of human relationship are after all merely human structures, illusions.

These structures are swept away in the second section of the novel which is "all eyeless and featureless," as Virginia Woolf described it.[66] The adjective "eyeless" is particularly fitting for "Time Passes." During the intervening ten years, there are several normally important human events, deaths and wars among them. These events are appropriately given briefly in brackets because they occur in a destroyed world, a world which provides no context by which to *see* and evaluate such events. They are "featureless" as a consequence of their having been torn loose from the myths which would allow them to be interpreted, talked about, or even narrated and provided with a plot. Instead there are the bracketed intermittent fragments, several of which are cast in a mannered, teatime conversational mode: "Prue Ramsay died that summer in some illness connected with childbirth, which was indeed a tragedy people said. They said nobody deserved happiness more" (205).[67] The style here yields a grotesque effect, and implies that major human events — marriage, motherhood, death — are not only illusory but scarcely even noticeable in the ongoing rush of time. These reports of human suffering pass like mere blips across the screen of eternity.

Lily recognizes the featureless quality of a world without Mrs. Ramsay. As Lily eats breakfast in the Ramsay's summer home after ten years' absence, Nancy Ramsay bursts in to ask, "What does one send to the Lighthouse?" (226) Immediately Lily's perception of the question deepens into a general question about the dependability of any human project, any relationship: "She had no attachment here, she felt, no relations with it, anything might happen, and whatever did happen, a step outside, a voice calling ('It's not in the cupboard; it's on the landing,' some one cried), was a question, as if the link that usually bound things together had been cut, and they floated up here, down there, off, anyhow" (227). Lily's perceptions here reiterate the significance and effect of section 2, "Time Passes." The destruction that visited the Ramsay household and the world in the lapsed ten years has cut the social and psychological rituals that give shape to thought and to life. The person in whose actions these rituals seemed embodied, Mrs. Ramsay, is dead; symbolically, a myth is dead; a charm, a psychological fence, against chaos is gone. As we saw in Chapter 1, it is exactly this kind of drastic situation that myths, rituals, and taboos are designed to guard against. Without such rituals and psychological fences, "anything might happen."

The opportunity for a radical departure is present, and the characters respond in varied ways to the necessity of redesigning a world. The teenage children, Cam and James, have a pact of rebellion against their father, who has bullied them into making the lighthouse trip; they resolve to "resist tyranny." Whether they do or not is a little uncertain. As they arrive at the lighthouse, James and Cam feel drawn to their father in respect and love. By this time Mr. Ramsay seems to them to have changed. During the boat trip he was a "macho" of self-conscious grief, reciting poetry with gloomy emphasis, and taking a morbid interest in a famous drowning. Abruptly, and surprisingly (we are not given his thoughts so we don't know why or how it occurs), Mr. Ramsay loses his melancholy posturing. He seems to perceive the drowning, and by implication his own griefs, as natural, simple, as not benefiting much from overstated emotions; instead of bursting again into "The Castaway," he merely says "Ah" as the boat passes over the spot of the disaster (316). The collective consciousness of Cam and James supplies one interpretation of this "Ah"; the utterance seems to them "As if" Mr. Ramsay suddenly saw the straightforward nature of death and saw "the depths of the sea" as mere water (316). We are given no clear assurance that Mr. Ramsay has undergone any real change, although the critics who comment on the sentences introduced by "as if" interpret them as though they were Mr. Ramsay's thoughts.[68] Again, as the boat approaches the shore and Mr. Ramsay rises, James thinks his father looks "as if he were saying, 'There is no God'" (318). But neither James nor we know what Mr. Ramsay is thinking. His humanization is not accomplished by any psychological or symbolic maneuvers that we are allowed to perceive; we do not probe with his consciousness (as we did with Mrs. Ramsay's) a wedge-shaped core of darkness within him. Instead he is humanized by being allowed his mystery. The narrator now maintains a greater distance from him than she did in the first part of the novel; she allows James and Cam to speculate about his thoughts, and does not presume herself to know Mr. Ramsay.

Mrs. Ramsay also undergoes a change in the perceptions of others, especially and most significantly in Lily's perception. When Lily finishes her painting, Mrs. Ramsay is a memory, a psychological presence, and as such her power and status have changed. In most interpretations of Lily's painting and of the "vision" which Lily feels it has given her, the "female" qualities represented by Mrs. Ramsay (nourishment, intuition, vision) are seen as balanced at last by those qualities linked to Mr. Ramsay (the scientific, "masculine" view) so that Lily becomes the complete, the androgynous personality.[69] Lily does certainly experience a sense of fulfillment as she completes the painting, and since the painting itself is evidently not a masterpiece (Lily knows it will be hung in attics, or destroyed [320]) the fulfillment, the synthesis and balance, is really in Lily and not in the painting. Lily has said that she owed to Mrs. Ramsay the "revelation" of the human capacity to make a world out of chaos (250).[70] All morning during Lily's musings, she has associated Mrs. Ramsay with imagery that suggests Persephone or Demeter. In discussing this imagery scholars usually apply it to Mrs. Ramsay's character, to her associations with the Great Mother, with Demeter or Rhea.[71] Most important, however, is the fact that Lily's mind supplies us with many of these Kore images, of Mrs. Ramsay with a garland on her head (279), or letting a basket of flowers fall as she walks quickly away, perhaps accompanied by her dead children (308-9). Just after this last fantasy Lily begins to notice light behind the window of the house, and soon sees Mrs. Ramsay sitting there. Lily, in these fantasies and projections, no longer perceives Mrs. Ramsay as the formidable, controlling figure. Instead Mrs. Ramsay is, symbolically to Lily, a Kore figure or a Demeter, an emblem of death and rebirth, an emblem of the creative capacity to make a world. Like the Demeter or mother figure, Mrs. Ramsay sits quietly knitting, constructing, and making. Since it is in Lily's consciousness that these images occur, they can be understood as Lily's projection of, discovery of, her "Self," an archetype central, analysts say, to a woman's mature identity, and usually imaged as a Demeter figure.[72] What Lily sees is not the former Mrs. Ramsay in all her living complexity, nor is it Mrs. Ramsay's ghost. Lily has apparently matured beyond her fear and defensiveness regarding Mrs. Ramsay's power to control and manipulate; Lily now perceives her own ability to design her life and her world. What Lily sees is a projection of her inner self, in fact the "Self" archetype, and not Mrs. Ramsay. When Lily "sees" Mrs. Ramsay, she perceives the capacity to construct her own answer, her own, perhaps temporary, answers in a guideless and shelterless world bereft of myth. She says, "I have had my vision" (320) — not just "a" vision, but "my" vision, Lily's own.

Lily is, in some respects, a more successful Rachel Vinrace. Rachel wanted to preserve and explore her own "unmergeable" self, and Lily resists the "dilution" (159) of marriage. Lily stands, in Virginia Woolf's oeuvre, midway between Rachel, whose artistry on the piano led only to her own hypnotic comfort, and Miss La Trobe, the writer of the pageant in *Between the Acts*, who has no more self-consciousness about being her own person than Mr. Carmichael has about being himself. Removed from civilization, placed in a liminal context in which the manners of society, and more importantly the myths of Western culture, are mocked and tested, both Rachel and Lily experience nature's "jungle," where identity-confirming myths and norms are swept away. Both, but especially Lily, ultimately perceive such an event as an opportunity rather than as a disaster.

3

The Politics of Holiday: Woolf's Later Novels

In Virginia Woolf's novels the holiday context, removing characters as it does from the ordinary patterns of behavior, provides an opportunity for a profound and extreme kind of comedy, for a comedy of cultural mockery. Even the images which hold a prestigious place in the "secular scripture" are mocked by the holiday consciousness. When the overturning of ordinary conventions, the overturning typical of liminality, is defined in such an extreme context, when holiday is a contemplative blank, then almost anything is fair game for mockery. Rhoda in *The Waves* can speak of going through "the antics of the individual,"[1] i.e., of identity, of the ego. To the eyes that contemplate such an unmarked world almost anything is possible; as Lily Briscoe perceived, "anything might happen." If the norm is mysticism, the politics of holiday may become radical indeed.

The holiday experience is ultimately a mystical one for Woolf's characters, and perhaps for Woolf herself. In a very late memoir, she describes the vacations of her childhood, the family's annual sojourn on the coast in Cornwall; those early summers, full of waves thudding and light falling through window curtains, were "pure delight," and are perhaps linked to "art, or religion."[2] Many critics have pointed to passages in Woolf's diaries that certainly imply a psychological extremity of perception, and perhaps imply mystic contemplation. In February 1926, while she was working on *To the Lighthouse*, the novel that included material from the Cornwall summers of her childhood, Woolf described herself as a searcher and recorded a peculiar sort of answer, an "it," discovered during an evening walk:

I see the mountains in the sky: the great clouds; and the moon
which is risen over Persia; I have a great and astonishing sense
of something there, which is "it." It is not exactly beauty that I
mean. It is that the thing is in itself enough: satisfactory;
achieved. A sense of my own strangeness, walking on the earth
is there too: of the infinite oddity of the human position; trotting along Russell Square with the moon up there and those
mountain clouds.[3]

The ordinary human action of walking along the square becomes
suddenly an image of "oddity," once the ineffable "it" is enunciated
by a vision of the moon over Persia, a distant, exotic place with its
roots in prehistory. As time and space receive such tremendous expansion, the small human figure seems appropriately described by
the reductive, almost comic, "trotting."

Woolf's "mysticism," removed from the mystical tradition of
any defined faith, has been variously discussed as a perception of
form (the "it" being the presence of wholeness, of design) or as her
joy in the impersonal presence of the nonhuman world.[4] In November 1926, while she was revising *To the Lighthouse*, she recorded in
her diary intimations of future subjects which included "some semi-
mystic very profound life of a woman" (*AWD*, 102; 23 November
1926). Although the "life of a woman" became *Orlando* and the
"semi-mystic" book became *The Waves*, both books are distinctly
interior and psychological compared to the two that follow — *The
Years* and *Between the Acts* — which explore the more political
aspects of a renewed and, especially, a re-imaged concept of holiday.
The linking of mysticism and the feminine, in Woolf's statement, is
also significant because it foreshadows the linking in *Between the
Acts* of holiday and values that are usually considered part of a woman's "civilization" or tradition. The interior subject, the "semi-
mystic" life of a woman becomes in *Between the Acts* the more political vision of a semifestive life for human beings.

Orlando

The semimystic life of a woman, as it developed into *Orlando*
(1928), became a semipicaresque, semibiographical fantasy of the
life of a man, sixteen years old in the sixteenth century who retains

his youth for decades, becomes a woman late in the seventeenth century (but still occasionally wears men's clothes for excursions into London's rougher areas), marries under pressure from the nineteenth century, has a child, and finally in the twentieth century wins a prize for a poem that has been in progress for over three hundred years. In March 1927, Virginia Woolf saw the projected book as one in which even her own style would be satirized: "Everything mocked," she said (*AWD*, 105; 14 March 1927). A year later, as she finished the first draft, she called the book "a writer's holiday" (*AWD*, 124; 18 March 1928). It is in two senses a writer's holiday; it is a holiday for its author and for its main character, Orlando, who also is a writer and who mocks everything. Unlike Woolf, the character Orlando does not use her writing as a means of satire. Her slowly developing poem, "The Oak Tree," is apparently quite a serious work, but Orlando herself is a jester for all seasons, and Virginia Woolf's book is a burlesque of all genres — or at least, of many genres.

This holiday book is first of all a tribute to, and a caricature-biography of, Woolf's friend Vita Sackville-West; it draws upon the history of the Sackville family, its poets and diplomats, and it exaggerates the already large inventory of furnishings and staircases given in Vita's documentary book about the family home *Knole and the Sackvilles* (1922).[5] But *Orlando* is a mock-biography, the narrator complaining frequently that Orlando's life simply refuses to become manifest in the mere facts, though these are supposedly the biographer's medium. Instead of the realistic and fully developed characters of a "novel," those in Orlando tend towards caricature and even allegory in the latter part of the book; this mode of characterization suggests the romance form which, as Northrop Frye notes, is a more "revolutionary" form than the novel, because the characters are not so thoroughly enmeshed in the social fabric of a single, stable, realistically portrayed society.[6] Indeed the parodic history, the long time span of the action, sees its main character into and out of several revolutions and several distinct societies. In this respect *Orlando* demonstrates its affinity with the picaresque form, in which social institutions are attacked, the effect being, as Barbara Babcock notes, to remind us that norms are fictions and made by mere humans; further, the picaresque hero is never reintegrated into society, in contrast to the novelistic hero, who in classic works is so integrated.[7] Neither is Orlando integrated finally into society. She has a flexible and serviceable lack of commitment to the successively crumbling societies that she survives.

Although she tries to conform outwardly to each historical age and to the decorum and the codes expected of each sex, she becomes successively disillusioned with the values of each era and each sex. Finally shrugging off the last infirmity of noble mind, "gloire" (or "glawr" as her critic Nicholas Green pronounces it), Orlando recognizes that her imagination and its products are essentially a self-finding process. Ecstatically united with her "Captain self," allegorized in the irrepressible sea captain Marmaduke Bonthrop Shelmerdine, she evidently finds in him (herself) the "wild goose" of truth and imagination that she has been chasing. The end of the book is parodic mysticism: with the moonlit gleam of the jewels on her breast, Orlando guides Shelmerdine's plane towards her, and they are ecstatically united.

The androgynous Orlando is, appropriately, a vigorous counterculture of one. Her sexual versatility is an expression of a liminal androgyny, the symbolic sexual ambiguity characteristic of those undergoing ritual initiations and often typifying those who belong to revolutionary or countercultural movements. Orlando's famous and often discussed androgyny implies wholeness, completeness, as many have observed; it suggests also, as Avrom Fleishman has pointed out, a special power similar to that imputed to initiates who participate in the transvestite rituals in many cultures.[8] Orlando's androgyny further suggests the status of someone continually undergoing the liminal rituals of society, continually on the margins of life's major "stages" (to use Orlando's word), but never settling down into the conventions of any given society. Orlando remains in the liminal part of life's "passages"; indeed, the concept of a stable society in which such passages can be meaningful is itself mocked. Just when Orlando has undergone initiation into the first passionate love of his life, the planet itself (or at least England) undergoes a major passage; the Great Frost is followed by a great flood, Orlando sleeps for seven days, and when he wakes, both he and history seem to have entered a new era. The violent, lusty gather-ye-rosebuds society has disappeared; the disillusioned and gloomy Orlando meditates on poetry. Or, much later, in the nineteenth century, in the era of large families, Orlando finally marries and has one child. Just about this time, the century turns, and instead of the childbirth ritual being the defining stage of her life, she is a twentieth-century woman, and public recognition of her poetry becomes the ritual milestone. Each time Orlando enters, metaphorically, the anthropological forest in order to receive an identity that will accord with social ritual, the ritual changes. She emerges from the liminal state only to find that the conventions have changed; she thus remains in a state of perpetual initiation, frequently making rather half-hearted efforts to conform to rules that wear out before she can fulfill them. So Orlando remains on continual holiday, in a civilization that is itself in a state of continual holiday, forever overturning itself and exposing its rituals and rules as obviously ephemeral.

Orlando's psychological relation to the historical periods through which she passes is hard to define exactly. She and any given historical milieu seem to reflect each other, and yet most readers agree with Orlando (and with Orlando's servants, who enthusiastically recognize and admire either him or her) that the main character does not change in any essential way; only Orlando's social behavior varies from age to age. The major joke of the sex change is that it makes little real difference in Orlando's character; by implication, most expressions of sex differences are cultural and not biological.[9] The more Orlando changes, the more she stays the same. And yet the changes that she witnesses, and usually participates in, are major ones, not merely evolutions of manner but revolutions of basic norms and codes, those which, in the real, nonfictional world, are rooted in primary socialization; certainly the behavior of the sexes is so rooted. Orlando herself realizes this as she tries, on the ship, to adjust to the fact that sailors may drop off the rigging with excitement if she fails to keep her ankles covered. She realizes "for the first time, what, in other circumstances, she would have been taught as a child, that is to say, the sacred responsibilities of womanhood."[10] We may theorize that Orlando was nurtured (as a boy?), was socialized into the values of some remote historical period (perhaps among medieval gypsies?), but in a fantasy such as this book is, we can see a Utopian psychology in operation. Because Orlando arrives as an adult on the scene of each new era, she escapes normal childhood socialization; she escapes the limited vision of "home," of the one childhood world, domestically and socially, which usually gives human beings their primary values and loves.

Orlando's ancestral home perhaps symbolizes these prerational attachments, but even this home, this symbolic place of comfort, changes size and decor with each era and becomes emblematic of Orlando's capacity for change even at a basic level, at the level of what "home" means, of what psychological comfort and security mean. With an adult's judgment, not a child's dependent need, Orlando views each era, and is thus free to let go of illusion after illusion with a minimum of anguish and a maximum of growth and self-renewal.

Orlando's change of sex, important as it is, is only one of many changes; her discovery of the limited role allotted to women is only one of several major disillusionments. The feminist issues, prominent in this novel and in some ways parallel to those discussed in *A Room of One's Own*, are placed in the quite positive context of an ongoing process of personal and social evolution, an evolution which in this fantasy overturns stereotypical notions about sex roles as easily as stereotypical notions about the importance of personal fame or of social class. Because we have already seen her so readily and sensibly readjust to illusions about infatuation, fame, and class, we are carried buoyantly onward by the momentum of suspended disbelief — and the momentum of the narrator's detachment and humor — when Orlando passes through the oppressive nineteenth century unscathed, having paid her dues to the "spirit of the age" by acquiring a wedding ring; she feels, however, as though she is crossing a border and carrying contraband, for she is a woman and yet she has smuggled a writer's mind into the nineteenth century (239).

In each era, Orlando is taken in by, or provisionally accepts, some prominent value or presupposition and then discards it, or at least views it in a qualified light. And this value is not always linked to sex role. Orlando must confront and overcome a desire for fame, both as a man and as a woman. His most troublesome challenge, after his beloved Sasha betrays him, is his commitment to "la gloire" of poetry and to his identity as a literary, artistic lord, writing in aristocratic ease on his vast ancestral estate. When this grandiose view of himself is destroyed by Nick Green's sharp satire on him, Orlando resolves to write only for himself in the future. With chagrin, he tears up a scroll on which he had fancifully appointed himself "the first poet of his race, the first writer of his age, conferring eternal immortality upon his soul and granting his body a grave among laurels and the intangible banners of a people's reverence perpetually" (96). Orlando tears up his desire for fame as he tears up his presumptuous scroll with its aggressively redundant flourishes of Elizabethan style ("eternal immortality ... perpetually").

Later, during a sojourn among gypsies, the female Orlando begins to lose another illusion, another false claim to identity and to self-esteem: her aristocratic family's proud ancestry. To her humiliation, the old gypsy Rustum points out that his family goes back two or three thousand years, his ancestors having built the pyramids (135-36). Back in England, Orlando meditates among the renowned bones of the family vault and again considers Rustum's humbling revelation. She decides that she is "growing up"; "I am losing my illusions," she says, "perhaps to acquire new ones" (159). Her confidence about losing her great pride in her family's ancestry is a little premature, however, for she subsequently becomes rhapsodic about the grounds and grandeur of her huge home, and she decides Rustum was wrong (160).

In the nineteenth century—the century that launched a few women, such as the Brontës and George Eliot, into enduring fame—Orlando also gets her big break. Once again she confronts the illusion of fame. Orlando—like Lily Briscoe—suspects, without apology or malice, that she is less than a first-rate artist. She is not fooled when Sir Nicholas enthusiastically compares her work to that of Addison and Thomson (252), and in the twentieth century, when her poem wins a cash prize, she laughs philosophically at fame (280). The poem becomes for Orlando more important than the prize, and the original real oak tree is more important than the poem "The Oak Tree." Orlando at age thirty-six and on the very brink of "the present moment," on the brink of reality without the illusions and assumptions of mere history which would limit that reality, drives quickly towards her ancestral home, calling upon all her past selves as she drives and seeking especially the "Captain self, the Key self" (279). Arriving at the oak tree, she turns over her own history, recalling the illusions of fame and family: "What has praise and fame to do with poetry? What has seven editions (the book had already gone into no less) got to do with the value of it? Was not writing poetry a secret transaction, a voice answering a voice?" (292). Then she once again hears the gypsy Rustum's voice taunting her about her pride in possessions, in race, in family heritage (293). Illusions, and memories of illusions, fall from her as she waits on the dark hill expecting the "ecstasy" of Shelmerdine's approach. With her brilliant jewels to guide it, his plane arrives, and he leaps to the ground while a valedictory wild goose hovers in tableau over his head. Appropriately, as Orlando's voice answers her voice, as the Captain self (or his image) arrives, as the psychological *meaning* of her poetry writing shakes itself free from the trammels of fame, family, adolescent infatuation, and the womanly eighteenth-century coyness and shyness, the midnight stroke of the present moment arrives. Orlando's history ends once the complex self, to which history has contributed, no longer depends on any particular historical emphasis or value, code of behavior, or ambition for its reality and sufficiency. The "present moment" — something impossible to isolate except in fantasy — is a suitable symbol for the condition of a self who is free of the major illusions of many eras and the major illusions and stereotypes of both sexes.

This ending, this solution, really takes Orlando's biography beyond biography and history beyond history. It implies transcendence, an inward turning, mysticism; it implies something serious in a book that began as comic. In this regard Virginia Woolf herself had some misgivings. After completing the book, she wrote in her diary: "The truth is I expect I began it as a joke and went on with it seriously. Hence it lacks some unity" (*AWD*, 128; 31 May 1928). Critics tend to agree with Woolf's perception of a change in tone as the concluding events are narrated. Jean Alexander asserts that satire is abandoned as Orlando moves towards the "exploration of the religious unknown in life," a direction that Woolf continues to pursue in *The Waves*.[11] And Woolf indicated by a marginal note in her diary that she came to regard *Orlando* as "leading to *The Waves*" (*AWD*, 105; 14 March 1927).[12] It is true that Orlando's finding of her self, her Captain self, is narrated in a kind of rhapsodic lyricism, but Woolf does not abandon comedy; a goose is not the most solemn image for truth, for some large discovery. The hints of comedy, even in the final events of the book, keep Orlando's vital and creative self where it has always been — in the liminal regions just outside of any congealed and solemn definition of what human society is, of what the sexes are, or of what a self is. The extravagant ecstasy of holiday prevails.

The Waves

Woolf's recognized experimental achievement, *The Waves* (1931), covers much of the same psychological territory as her most distinctly and obviously comic novel, *Orlando*, although *The Waves* certainly does not come to mind when one thinks of comic novels. Both are spiritual fantasies, *The Waves* defining the luminous, remotely intimate, contemplative norm by virtue of which Orlando can find "everything mocked." From the perspective of the hushed, unconscious, yet blankly alert landscapes of *The Waves*, and from Bernard's perspective when he sees the "world" without a "self," all criteria for identity are, potentially and theoretically, comic, since they are as false, transient, and illusory as the passing and mocked historical selves, and the mocked historical and social orders, of *Orlando*. Like Orlando, Bernard perceives on the waters of imagination a fish or fin which might be the truth for him if he could catch it. Orlando, during her vehemently meditative drive home, speaks with mixed metaphors of trying to catch the goose of truth, or the "great fish" of truth, by using "words like nets" (282), and Bernard seeks the meaning of the fin that turns in "a waste of water" (134). Both are using imagery sketched briefly by Virginia Woolf before either novel was written. In the autumn of 1926, as she finished *To the Lighthouse*, Woolf described an exciting yet frightening "mystical" kind of "solitude": "It is not oneself but something in the universe that one's left with." She tries an image and writes: "One sees a fin passing far out. What image can I reach to convey what I mean?" (*AWD*, 101; 30 September 1926).[13] Woolf uses this image to imply a glimpse of a truth that lies behind or beyond, though evidently involved in, the phenomena of identity, behind the social and psychological constructions that make up a self. While *Orlando* most often notes the comic and blundering attempts to net this fish, *The Waves* observes the awesome, luminous sightings of the solitary fin and the close approaches of the characters to the empty wave that creates and re-creates the shape of the shore and the shape of the human personality. In *The Waves*

Virginia Woolf defines directly the norm which was suggested in-
directly in *Orlando* and which is implied in all her novels —
mysticism.

To indicate a point of view in which an observant consciousness is suspended just below or beyond words, just beyond the
idioms used in speaking and thinking, Woolf sustains a hypnotic
style no matter which character's thoughts are being imaged and
translated by the narrator. The narrator is a kind of seer perhaps,
and probably to be identified with the woman writing in a garden,
the woman whom Bernard and Susan come upon in their own imagination, in Bernard's fantasy about "Elvedon." This figure, much
more prominent in the earlier drafts, as Robert Richardson has noted, seems to be a persona of the central consciousness, probably of
the author herself.[14] The point of view is that of a seer, and the prose
by which the seer speaks has appropriately been called choral, vatic, sacerdotal.[15] Naturally such a style does not indicate the individual idiom and personality of each speaker, or thinker, and the style
is a large contributor to the peculiar characterization, but Virginia
Woolf did not want to give fully developed personalities in *The
Waves;* the characterization, she said as she was working on the
novel, "should be done boldly, almost as caricature" (*AWD*, 157; 9
April 1930). As Edwin Muir wrote in his review of the novel, for the
people in the book "character is merely a costume." In effect, as
James Hafley observes, this eliminates manners, the codes of social
relationship from which the novel traditionally takes its shape and
character.[16] For the same reasons, the opportunities for comedy are
limited; and yet Hermione Lee has found Jinny enunciating the
comic (perceiving that the casual Percival is "not dressed" for dinner), and Bernard supplying a satiric fantasy-description of the efficient, British Percival peremptorily solving an "Oriental problem,"
that of setting the overturned cart on its wheels again.[17] Not often,
but occasionally through the luminous solemnity of contemplation,
and especially in Bernard's mind, there arises an ascetic kind of humor, ascetic because it is stripped down to the bare "sequences," or
"phrases" by which the characters attempt to control chaos or to
net the fin of truth.

Percival, easy-going and comfortable in the world, laughs at
the "sequence," at the story that Bernard as a boy tries to tell his
schoolmates, who then take Percival's laughter as a cue for their

own (27-28). Yet they had pleaded with Bernard to tell a story. Neville had said (or thought): "Let him describe what we have all seen so that it becomes a sequence. Bernard says there is always a story. I am a story. Louis is a story" (27). In spite of their laughter, each of them wants to be a story, to become a life and a self that has some shape, some meaning. Except for Rhoda, each designs or accepts a social definition; each is conscious of those social categories of status or of sexual identity to which Orlando would temporally commit herself and then reject as illusion. The attractive Jinny perseveres well into middle age with a gallant hedonism, finding ready lovers whose presence reassures her that her "story" about her life — her identity — is true and nourishing for her. Susan remains loyal, even under some middle-aged disillusionment, to the self she had defined by a rather possessive motherhood and by the earthy quiet and fruitfulness of the country. ("I am glutted with natural happiness" [123]; "Yet sometimes I am sick of natural happiness" [136].) Bernard also settles into a conventional life of marriage and family, though he is not so obsessive about it as Susan, and he never ceases to suspect that there is some meaning or reality just beyond any given "story" of any given life, even his own life and self. Neville, a fearful and sickly child, was perhaps emotionally stunted by overhearing a conversation about a dead man. "He was found with his throat cut. The apple-tree leaves became fixed in the sky; the moon glared; I was unable to lift my foot up the stair" (17).[18] But against this potential psychological chaos Neville defines a story for himself, writing poetry, finding new male lovers, and he achieves some fame as an author. The situation of Louis defines most clearly the sociology of identity. An Australian, speaking with an accent, he feels powerless and insecure, but he becomes a hero of capitalism apparently, and sends his ships all over the world. He defines, or rather his unconscious as verbalized by the narrator defines precisely, the relationship between identity and the daily social relationships which reinforce one's "story" of oneself.

But if I do not nail these impressions to the board and out of the many men in me make one; exist here and now and not in streaks and patches, like scattered snow wreaths on far mountains; and ask Miss Johnson [his secretary] as I pass through the office about the movies and take my cup of tea and accept

also my favourite biscuit, then I shall fall like snow and be wast-
ed. (121).

Percival may laugh, but the secretary does not laugh; she supports
Louis's myth about himself. Each character recognizes at some
point, as Orlando also did, that one's life story, one's particular
brand of self, is a necessary and nourishing illusion. Only Rhoda
fails to find, or be satisfied with, such an illusion. She says of herself,
"I have no face" (158). Her suicide underlines the psychological
hazards of life without a "sequence," of life in a world in which stories, sequences, patterns, are perceived as arbitrary, even laughable.

In *The Waves* Percival represents a mythos, a narrative or "sequence" that gives shape to a culture and to individuals within the
culture. In a sense he is a "god" (97). Virginia Woolf's character
Percival, a mock grail-hero,[19] himself mocks the very notion of
story, of legend, of the presumptive heroism required to phrase a
meaning for one's life. Although Percival rejects or shrugs off any
verbal assurance or meaning, he yet provides assurance and meaning simply by his presence. He does this most obviously at the dinner which the friends all share before his departure for India. For
Rhoda and Louis, Percival's presence inspires thoughts of savage
festivity; in their minds are images of flames leaping as naked men
dance, of "leopard skins and the bleeding limbs which they have
torn from the living body," of violets being thrown (100). Such
imagery, typical of several rituals described in *The Golden Bough*,[20]
links Percival to the sacrificed god-kings of ancient festivals and
places the civilized meal at Hampton Court in a tradition of communal religious celebration. Percival, like the ancient victim-god,
does indeed unite everyone in a common focus on himself. Mrs.
Ramsay did this also, but we were allowed into her mind and could
see her deliberate effort, her human and social machinations as well
as her symbolic effect on people. The fact that we are never allowed
into Percival's mind underscores his symbolic presence in the book.
While the six others try to to design an identity, a story, Percival *is* a
story, a mythos; he is a cultural hypothesis about life. At the first
dinner he symbolizes the social presence of myth. When the six
gather again years later, and after Percival's death, their greater
difficulty in achieving a moment of release from their own nervous

and prickly egos suggests the importance of an accepted cultural myth and the psychological hazards and tensions of life without such a myth. Nevertheless the moment of peace and unity, even at the second dinner, is achieved. The implication is perhaps that a continuing community of friends is itself at least as important and powerful as any cultural myth that may once have contributed to its unity.

Among the six friends, Bernard is the only one who manages, outside the communal context of a dinner, to sacrifice ego to a moment of clarity and to survive and grow as a result of that insight. (Though Rhoda also penetrates to a reality bare of self, she collapses into it.) Significantly, it is Bernard who most often mocks himself and his stories and who most often places Percival in a comic perspective. Bernard, although (or because) he often tries out new poses, new life stories, for himself, seems to have expected less from these stories, and from Percival also. Bernard represents a point of view that recognizes the "sequence" of an individual life or of a cultural myth as an *image* primarily, as only a glimpse of the truth, as a fin and not the whole fish, certainly not the whole sea with all its contending waves. In the last section of the novel, as Bernard tries "to sum up" his experience and that of his friends, he recalls, with both mockery and tenderness, some of his former poses. He recalls that as a student he affected to be Hamlet, then Shelley, then a Dostoevskian hero. Bernard "was for a whole term, incredibly, Napoleon; but was Byron chiefly. For many weeks at a time it was my part to stride into rooms and fling gloves and coat on the back of chairs, scowling slightly" (171). And even more frequently, it was Bernard's part to pose as his own biographer, offering parodic snippets of biographical prose to describe his life; Bernard says, "But 'joined to the sensibility of a woman' (I am here quoting my own biographer) 'Bernard posessed the logical sobriety of a man'" (55). Even a moment of insight into his androgynous character Bernard subjects to the scrutiny of mockery, of stiff biographical prose. He is wary of any discovery or definition, since it probably, if it can be put into words and recorded in his phrase book, stops short of the truth. Like Jacob, Bernard once saw himself as an "inheritor," and like Louis, Bernard respects tradition, but he is not nervously obsessive about it. He does not revere the trappings of power and tradition, though he respects them; the idea that he and his family are

"inheritors" is "so grandiose as to be absurd" (183). To Bernard the
biography of a culture, like the biography of an individual, can provide only a limited angle on the whole truth.

As well as supplying a distanced, ironic view of himself, Bernard also provides, along with Neville, a nonreverential view of
Percival. It is through schoolboy Neville's eyes that we first see
Percival, and the circumstances are not at all solemn as Neville
thinks, "Now I will lean sideways as if to scratch my thigh. So I
shall see Percival" (25). Neville falls in love with Percival, and yet
qualifies his admiration of Percival's straight nose and pagan indifference by later speculating that the rather stupid Percival—in
Neville's eyes—"will coarsen and snore. He will marry and there
will be scenes of tenderness at breakfast" (34-35). Perhaps the
same quality that Neville found stupid Bernard finds merely "conventional." Observing the admired Percival during the farewell
dinner, Bernard muses about his hero, "He is conventional; he is a
hero. The little boys trooped after him across the playing-fields.
They blew their noses as he blew his nose, but unsuccessfully, for
he is Percival" (88). Instead of glamorizing the notion of convention
by linking it to myth or even to pagan indifference, Bernard here in
effect defines it mockingly, by recalling the viewpoint of Percival's
very young admirers, as a certain inimitable manner of blowing
one's nose.

Perhaps it is because of Bernard's respect and love that he understands more completely Percival's significance than the others
seem to. Visiting Jinny after Percival's death, Bernard recalls (in
his summing up) that he was suddenly aware of the danger of senti-
mentalizing and trivializing their memories of Percival. "Let us
commit any blasphemy of laughter and criticism rather than exude
this lily-sweet glue; and cover him with phrases, I cried" (188).
Whenever, in the course of their friendship with Percival, Bernard
or Neville utters a "blasphemy of laughter" against their "god," it
is a laughter of respect, and it means that they have understood
Percival's own laughter at Bernard's effort to pin down a life by
means of a story, a sequence.

There are, however, many images that escape the blasphemy
of laughter. Unlike Percival's life story, these are usually static
images, not stories or sequences, but they, like Percival, represent
intimations of insight and meaning. These include the rather nega-

tive image, behind the shape and story of Neville's life, the threatening and blocking image of the apple tree. In the mind of Louis the recurring image of the women carrying jars along the ancient Nile (48, 69, 91) secures a shape for his life story and implies for him a continuity with the human story over the centuries. After Percival's death, Bernard, still seeking with a phrasebook, as he says, "the true story, the one story," leans over a parapet in Rome and sees "far out a waste of water. A fin turns" (133-34). Moved and thoughtful, he makes an entry in his notebook. "I note under F., therefore, 'Fin in a waste of waters.' I, who am perpetually making notes in the margin of my mind for some final statement, make this mark, waiting for some winter's evening" (134-35). There is more than a hint of the ludicrous, not in the fin image, but in Bernard's precise note-taking, and especially in his practice of alphabetizing visionary moments. Eventually Bernard ceases to look for phrase and story, and ceases to alphabetize his life. In the final section of the novel, as he talks to his anonymous dinner companion, the notebook slips to the floor, and Bernard lets it lie; he gives up the attempt to find phrases for the moon, for love, for death (209).

There is another image, a prominent and frequently repeated one, which is absolutely preserved from any laughter. This is the image of the woman who sits writing in the garden. Bernard as a boy apparently discovers her by surprise when he develops his story about Elvedon. Although there may "really" have been a woman writing in the garden of the white house, Bernard immediately places her in the context of his imaginary adventure into Elvedon. Bernard has been describing Elvedon as a fairy-tale location where no human has ever been, a place of primeval firs and giant toads. Bernard speaks to Susan:

> "Put your foot on this brick. Look over the wall. That is Elvedon. The lady sits between the two long windows, writing. The gardeners sweep the lawn with giant brooms. We are the first to come here. We are the discoverers of an unknown land. Do not stir; if the gardeners saw us they would shoot us. We should be nailed like stoats to the stable door. Look! Do not move. Grasp the ferns tight on the top of the wall."
>
> "I see the lady writing. I see the gardeners sweeping," said Susan. "If we died here, nobody would bury us."

"Run!" said Bernard. "Run! The gardener with the black
beard has seen us! We shall be shot! We shall be shot like jays
and pinned to the wall! We are in a hostile country." (12)

Why the fierce imagery of this episode? Why has the quiet lady, so
absorbed in her writing, given orders (apparently) that her gardeners are to shoot any children who might see her, and nail them to the
wall? This violent imagery seems at first inconsistent with the
usual interpretation of the woman's significance—that is, that she
represents the presiding and creating consciousness of the author.
Of course there is a certain logic to the idea that characters who discover their author risk destruction; they supposedly would recognize their complete fictionality, their nonexistence. ("If we died
here, nobody would bury us." True; a mere fiction can simply be
discontinued by the imagination.)

If this figure of the woman writing is indeed an image of the
authorial consciousness (and I think it is), the brutality of the imagery affirms that this writer is certainly no Angel in the House. She
is an Angel in the Garden, and she is a killer—potentially, at least. It
is significant that such an image appears in Virginia Woolf's most
complex book, the one that most thoroughly and luminously develops her style, the book generally recognized as her finest work. The
figure of the author in her garden implies contemplation *and* control, vatic vision accompanied by a knowledgeable and complete
control of form, character, style. This symbol of the writer suggests
that she is not at all afraid of the "aggressive act of creation" which
Anais Nin saw as being the province of male writers only, not of
women writers.[21]

The woman writing in the garden is a complex mythic and
symbolic figure. Although she is mostly offstage, appearing and
reappearing chiefly in Bernard's mind, she is always "numinous";
she always halts, attracts, even frightens, Bernard's attention. For
him she is a fateful presence. Her numinous qualities suggest that
she is indeed a kind of angel in the sense of a messenger from God or
the unconscious.[22] For Bernard, the woman writing remains one of
"these presences" (171), "those fabulous presences, men with
brooms, women writing," presences which are yet mutable "shadows" (202). In his summing up Bernard examines such persistent
psychological images and sees them as a kind of fate: "The lady sat

writing. Transfixed, stopped dead, I thought, 'I cannot interfere with a single stroke of those brooms. They sweep and they sweep. Nor with the fixity of that woman writing.' It is strange that one cannot stop gardeners sweeping nor dislodge a woman. There they have remained all my life. It is as if one had woken in Stonehenge surrounded by a circle of great stones, these enemies, these presences" (171). Seeing, in his mind's eye, the woman writing and the threatening gardeners, Bernard is "stopped dead" as though by the psychological walls of his world, the givens of his mortal existence. These mental images, like the ritual stones of Stonehenge, suggest both limits and mysterious illuminations.

The woman who sits and writes is as much a god as Percival is. Percival, dying young, and with a name taken from a secular Christian grail legend, brings with him mythic shadows of a Christ figure, and of older figures as well, particularly Attis, as Harvena Richter has observed; Attis is the dying tree-and-sun god whose mother (or beloved) is the rather fearsome Earth Mother, Cybele. Richter suggests that Susan, whom Percival loves, is a kind of Cybele, for Susan chooses the country, "nature," and family.[23] In this connection, it is significant that Susan is the only one of the women to see the lady writing in the garden; Susan, like Bernard, later recalls the awesome and terrifying moment. If Bernard feels both trapped and enlightened by the "presence" of the woman writer, so does Susan. Later, feeling somewhat "sick of natural happiness," she recalls how she "saw the lady writing and the gardeners with their great brooms. We ran back panting lest we should be shot and nailed like stoats to the wall. Now I measure, I preserve" (136-37). The combination of terror and motherhood (or, metaphorically, any kind of creativity) suggests Cybele.

More important, however, than the imagery of Cybele as a god figure in yet another novelistic restatement of a cultural myth is her significance as the psychic core of a work in which the point of view is that of a woman, a female seer. *The Waves*, like *Orlando*, apparently took its impetus from Woolf's perception of a book that would be the "semi-mystical, very profound life of a woman." If we turn for a moment from anthropology to psychology and consider the symbols of Percival-Attis and Cybele as archetypes within the psyche, within the contemplating consciousness of the woman who "thinks" the novel,[24] a very strong psychological landscape, a female one, emerges. Of course, if we put aside the idea of a woman's consciousness encompassing the whole, and if we consider Bernard to be the questor, the "ego" (and Percival a double image of this questing ego), then the lady in the garden becomes a fierce, creative-destructive "anima" of Bernard; she is his "soul," envisioned by him in his fantasy of Elvedon, and an enduring presence both threatening and sustaining. But if we assume that the total consciousness of the novel is a woman's then Bernard and Percival must be read as two aspects of the animus image, which is the soul image of the female narrator. Then, Bernard's creative effort to control and express his world and his courage in confronting mystery and death become images of these capacities in a woman's psyche, capacities symbolized by the animus, the positive male fantasy-image. Now, however, the figure of the woman writing in the garden needs to be read as an archetype which is deeper, more profoundly numinous than the animus. She is the archetype of the Self, in effect the deity image in a woman's psyche, an image usually manifesting some of the characteristics of Demeter or other mother images including Cybele.[25] The woman in the garden is indeed a symbol of the artist, of the artist who writes the book. She is at the same time, as suggested by her more numinous and even terrible aspects, an image for the Self archetype *of* the female consciousness whose contemplation, whose mystic vision, the book itself is. It is very appropriate, and a little uncanny, that in Virginia Woolf's most mature and profound novel, the figure of the woman writing in the garden gives us a kind of archetypal signature of the mature and potent, cunning and creative, Demetrian mother-Self who "thinks" the book.

This image remains completely solemn. Percival and Bernard, on the other hand, are sometimes mocked. To the extent that Percival is a "god," he is a mock-god, a mock-Christ. Harvey Cox, tracing the tradition of Christ as comedian and as victim-clown, asks whether one could have a comic perspective on one's own, believed religion. Cox thinks such a perspective is possible, but he summarizes the opposition (Kierkegaard and Heidegger). "For Kierkegaard one always has to be 'inside' *some* order of existence. Though a person can have a sense of comic distance about someone else's ultimate symbols he cannot have such a perspective about his own. Otherwise he would not be existing at all."[26] Virginia Woolf, at least when she was writing *The Waves*, would probably have agreed with Kierkegaard. As we have seen, she offered the opinion that women writers will want "to alter the established values — to make serious what appears insignificant to a man, and trivial what is to him important." As her work indicates, by established values she sometimes means the policy of domestic relationship, but sometimes she means myth, the cultural "story" or "sequence," truly the "established" values and images of religious tradition. While she does not reduce Percival to triviality, she does not make him the god figure of the novel: only the six speaking characters, mistakenly, perceive him as such.

Her Percival does not at all reflect her first impression of the *Parsifal* of Wagner which she had seen twenty years earlier at Bayreuth. She wrote in a letter of 1909 that the emotions in the opera "are all abstract — I mean not between men and women." She notices that the opera had "no love in it; it is more religious than anything."[27] In connection with *Parsifal* she uses the word "abstract" and the word "religion." She also here phrases a preliminary intimation of her later remarks about fiction, a fiction that would be free of "love interest" and have no comedy in the "accepted style." Ultimately, in *The Waves*, the "abstract" work which shows, of all her books, the least conformity to a novelistic and "accepted style," she writes her response to the abstract, religious emotions of *Parsifal*. But she changes the Parsifal figure; he becomes lightly comic, though he lives with a dedicated and casual courage. The most solemn and awesome of the "abstract" and "religous" emotions in *The Waves* are given, not to the Parsifal figure, but to the female figure, to the Stonehenge "presence," the woman writing in the threatening garden. Woolf seems to be writing — especially when we consider just the figures of Percival and the woman — from the point of view of a woman's "civilization," a woman's anthropology and psychology, one which is, as she held, different from a man's.

The book, however, is called *The Waves*, not *Percival* and not *The Lady in the Garden*. Anthropomorphic — or gynomorphic — images finally succumb to the prevailing imagery of waves. The human-shaped "presences," like the human-shaped egos of the six characters, are but manifestations of the wave-filled sea of psychic and phenomenal reality. In the end Bernard confronts and fights death; in imagination he rides, like Percival in India, to oppose the final enemy. Bernard says, "And in me too the wave rises." He exclaims, "Against you I will fling myself, unvanquished and unyielding, O Death!" Then there is the single italicized line which indicates a return to the nonhuman world of the interludes, a world now dim in the predawn: *"The waves broke on the shore"* (211). Bernard rises on the wave of life, but then breaks and dies as that wave breaks. Although Virginia Woolf evidently had not read Bergson, the ambiguous Bergsonian imagery of the waves coincides, as Hafley notes, with the twofold gesture of Bernard, who fights, yet is the thing he fights (the ascending and descending waves of the sea of reality).[28] The library of the Woolfs did contain Jane Harrison's *Epilegomena*, and Harrison speaks there of a modern "new religion" in which evolution is the assertive principle and reality. She paraphrases Bergson: "This new religion, this bettering of life, involves conflict. It is the setting of the will towards what Bergson calls the 'ascending wave' of the *élan vital* against the descending wave which he calls matter. We belong in part to that descending wave, hence the conflict, its pull is always upon us even to the rending of flesh and spirit."[29] Harrison's statement gives the image of the wave the same ambiguous implication that it holds in the final lines of Woolf's novel; human life is *both* an ascending wave and a descending one. On the other hand, Woolf's use of the wave image does not reflect the duality of matter and spirit which is indicated in Harrison's image of the "new religion." The material world of the interlude landscapes fairly glows; the nonhuman world is as luminous as a jewel. Sunlight renders this world simultaneously more luminous and more substantial, more heavy; in the absence of sunlight the landscapes, in this sort of "death," are not more gross or material, but less so, less substantial. Whether falling or rising, the living and dying world, and the human beings inhabiting that world, are spirit and matter in one fluid, one reality, one sea of waves.

The presence of the sun girl, however, does introduce a qualification into my assertion of unity, of nonduality. The interlude image of the jewelled girl, the image of the sun rising and making the waves visible, perhaps implies a transcendent realm; the sun woman herself is not a "wave" evidently, but an element that reveals the waves. Something, some light from the "outside," must first of all illuminate the "waves" of phenomena, of human personality, of human image-making, even of the psychological "presences" or archetypes. The image of the sun woman, if she exists in a realm other than that of the waves which she illuminates, suggests that the "seer" *sees something*, and sees something (light, a woman, a transcendence) that is not as vulnerable, as temporal, as Bernard and Percival, or even as vulnerable as the woman writing in the garden, who is the archetypal image of the author-seer, of her "Self." But the transcendent shape of light is itself imaged as a woman, and the presence in the garden is also a woman. The sun woman creates the world; the woman in the garden creates a book. The similarity of image suggests a unity after all, the sun woman becoming a further image for the creative Self.[30] The images speak of the same reality perhaps, though one is light and one belongs to the imagination of earth, to Bernard's imagination. *And* to the imagination of Virginia Woolf. To whom also belongs the sun woman. The paradox and circularity of the fictional imagery itself parallels the traditional paradoxes of mysticism: where does the human soul end and God begin? Neither saint nor novelist has ever indicated the precise boundary.

In *The Waves*, we have not so much the liminality of a particular counterculture as the liminality of a counterconsciousness; this holiday of meditation is a *via negativa* that points to, and discards (or dissolves with a wave), every image, every "story," every "phrase," that God or truth is *not*. As Bernard realizes, leaving his phrasebook behind, the truth is nonimageable, ineffable.

The Years and *Between the Acts*

Late in 1931, Woolf writes that she is "full of ideas for further books, but they all develop from *The Waves*"; she cannot, she says, return to the style and form of *Mrs. Dalloway* or *To the Lighthouse*.[31] Her subsequent novels, *The Years* and *Between the Acts*, both have an unfinished quality, as though neither quite represents the promise of development that Woolf could see as she completed *The Waves*. *Between the Acts* of course had not received the author's final revision before her death, but Woolf's long struggle with the form and emphasis of *The Years* is perhaps an indication that this novel resisted completion. Both novels develop from *The Waves* in that they continue Bernard's quest for an adequate "phrase" — an adequate means of expressing a hidden reality. In her last two novels this reality is not so much mystical or psychological as it is political, and its hiding place is the future. The major characters in *The Years* often attempt to state their perceptions, but their sentences are unfinished or interrupted. Since, in earlier drafts, many of these statements were completed, Woolf apparently decided that the ravelling remarks would be symbolic of the difficulty of shaping an idea in a shapeless, deteriorating culture.[32] And in *Between the Acts* Isabel Oliver, composing phrases, scraps of poetry, seeks a radically new, still undefined "plot" for her life. In both novels the new "plot" — new structures for institutions and for human relationships — is explored by means of festive and seasonal imagery. Or rather, the potential for human renewal is tested by such liminal images, and these will be the focus of my brief look at the two novels.

In *The Years*, Woolf or a persona very much like Bernard's phrase-persona if he had ever used his phrases in a novel seems to be going through an alphabet of sketchy patterns, and crossing them out one by one or placing each in parentheses, all equal and none prominent or underlined. Woolf's refusal to subordinate characters or to subordinate imagery contributes to the uncertain status of any brief glimpses of meaning or truth. In this novel Woolf supplies no Mrs. Ramsay or Bernard or a lighthouse. Over the span of decades, pigeons coo, characters repeat words and actions, a hammer taps in imagination or in reality, the moon is like a coin and the aging Eleanor clutches coins in the final section as she thinks of a center or a knot which could be called a self, a life.[33] But no single image is allowed prominence; there is no symbol as a major focus of meaning for all the characters.

Even the two most comprehensive structures employed in *The Years*, that of the family novel and the suggestion of cyclic, seasonal renewal, are underplayed. The Pargiter family and the patriarchal institutions of power and possession go downhill in the course of the years, but don't quite emerge as anything other than what they were. Further, the turning years of the introductory sections sometimes reflect the personal or the institutional, and sometimes do not. The broken human adventure, with its decaying former institutions and its uncertainly defined new ones, is no longer securely linked to the ritual harvest and seed time of the natural world.

Neither order nor liminal and satiric disorder has strong definition. In *The Years* order lacks the power to affirm and secure, and disorder lacks the power to renew.

Much of the satiric disorder expresses itself from a feminist perspective, and recent scholarship has done much to illuminate these elements. Quoting from *Three Guineas* the hypothetical letter-writer's assertion that laughter is "an antidote to dominance," Joanna Lipking points to the laughter which Sara directs at her cousin Martin, "Almighty Mr. Martin," whom the old servant Crosby nearly worships, enshrining a photograph of him in military uniform.[34] Establishment institutions — the church, the family, the military — receive considerable miscellaneous satiric jabbing. In Woolf's previous novels patriarchal habits and institutions were mocked (heroism, an infatuated lover), but the female institutions were spared, or at least spared the roughest attacks. Mrs. Ramsay may have channelled her creative abilities too rigidly into the institutional molds of possessive motherhood and matchmaking, but her creative energies are still very constructive for others and even for herself. In *The Years*, however, the older sister, the spinster-mother of the rest of the family, Eleanor, is almost a caricature of Mrs. Ramsay, as Victoria Middleton observes; Eleanor does not create large unifying experiences for those around her.[35] Nor does anyone else. Although Delia organizes the large dinner party that comprises the final section of the novel, her consciousness does not dominate it, as Mrs. Ramsay's would have, or Clarissa's; there is no rich, complex female consciousness, hostess to others and to itself, receiving, collecting, and focussing experience into vision and meaning. Instead, there are several scattered and poorly articulated intimations of meaning. As Schaefer has observed, the final events of the novel are "almost a parody" of the moments of vision which arose from the dinners and parties of earlier novels.[36]

The imagery and the rituals of liminality have changed; women are no longer, in *The Years*, the guardians of a kind of counter-culture, a celebration and release in contrast to the masculine arena of dominance in politics and in love. Instead there is a miscellaneous group of outsiders — Sara, the mocker; the feminist Rose, who throws a rock and is arrested; Nicholas, the homosexual; the sensitive Renny, who has a capacity for weeping and for laughing loudly; and Eleanor, free and single, a world traveller in her seventies.

As Jane Marcus notes, the outsiders have their own nonpatriarchal "rituals," the lovemaking of Nicholas and Sara, for instance, being their mutual affection and mockery.[37] Yet these rituals are not given the heavy luminescence that Woolf gave to Mrs. Ramsay presiding at her dinner table.

Nor does a glowing natural world supply an orderly and sustained reflection of human "passages" as it did in *The Waves*. The introductory descriptive passages which initiate each chapter of *The Years* imply a relationship between the vitality of nature and the human need for renewal. The connections between the two are haphazard, however. An "uncertain spring" begins the novel, and no one knows whether to expect rain or not. Describing the moon, the narrator offers a series of interpretive nouns, but commits herself to none of them. "At length the moon rose and its polished coin, though obscured now and then by wisps of clouds, shone out with serenity, with severity, or perhaps with complete indifference" (2). In this uncertain spring evening the children of Abel Pargiter wait for the kettle to boil, for their father to come home, and for their mother to die. Eventually all these things happen, and they happen with serenity, with severity, or with complete indifference. Eleanor remains serene now and in later years; Delia expresses a severe hatred of oppressive family life and a desire to find beauty and freedom somewhere else (11); the children and their father are indifferent at the burial of Rose Pargiter, except for Delia, whose barely controlled fury silently accuses the others of pretending sorrow and reverence. The narrator refuses to exploit the fact that the first long chapter takes place in spring. This spring was so "uncertain," it might just as well have been any other season. And that may be the only connection that Virginia Woolf wanted to suggest.

The chapter dealing with the year 1891 is another matter. Now it is autumn. London nervously tries to settle down to work after the summer holidays. "It was difficult to work after the holidays" (94), the narrator notes in the first paragraph, and shortly thereafter, observes that "it was October, the birth of the year" (96). The birth of the year, in October? Yes, it is the birth of London's business year, and Eleanor, who has spent the summer in the country with her sister Milly and her husband, is glad to be back in London. Once again she is overseeing the Pargiter rental properties. She likes the stir of "everything beginning again in October" (100). In

1891 we are also given a more mythic and ancient symbol of begin-
nings and of birth. Kitty, married and living in the north, observes
smoke drifting across the lawn, and remarks, "Burning weeds"
(95). In London, Eleanor explains to her father, "They're burning
weeds" (98). At the home of Digby Pargiter, it is Maggie's birthday,
and she and Sara, dancing with excitement, toss armloads of leaves
onto a bonfire. Their mother explains to their visiting uncle, Abel
Pargiter, that the bonfire is "for Maggie's birthday" (129). Bon-
fires, to celebrate an autumnal birth of the year were, according to
Frazer, an ancient custom among the Celts.[38] The spiritual concom-
mitments of such a festival are expressed in an exchange between
Sara and her father, Sir Digby. Surveying the soot-covered dresses
of his daughters, he says that birthdays should provide a reason "to-
er-to-er reform one's habits" (135). Sara mimics his words exactly,
but without her father's meaning; her uncle laughs at this early instance of what becomes Sara's very typical mocking attitude. But
her father does not laugh. A birthday, and especially a New Year,
may indeed be an occasion of reform, or renewal in the sense of reaf-
firming the values of the community; such a celebration also supplies traditionally an opportunity to flout and mock those values.
Sir Digby, the older generation, speaks for order and cleanliness;
the ash-covered jester, the child Sara, speaks for the liminal elements of such events, for the festive mockery of order, and as she
grows up she continues to speak for these elements.

Twenty years later it is again "the holiday season," though the
August of 1911 is hot and dry (206). Eleanor's father has died and
she feels that her life is starting all over. In an episode that presages
Between the Acts, Eleanor visits her brother Morris in the country,
arriving just after a fête which was graced by the presence of the
bishop. An outdoor drama, held in order to raise funds for repairing
the church steeple, was produced by the symbolically named "Miss
Green" (211). During dinner, and again on the terrace, Eleanor and
Morris's family watch the cows slowly munching and moving
across the meadow — as the guests at Pointz Hall will do in *Between
the Acts*. The idea of holiday and renewal is reflected in Eleanor's
feeling that her life is just beginning. Perhaps it is reflected also in
the lines of Dante which attract her attention as she reads at night:
"For by so many more there are who say 'ours' / So much the more
of good doth each possess" (228). The notion that possessions and

goodness are "ours," rather than "mine," links Eleanor's musings here to the communal solidarity of traditional seasonal festivities.

There is no real solidarity, however, among the questioners, the rebels, in this novel. Images of community remain images, though prophetic perhaps of a world of radically changed institutions. The spring day that introduces the 1914 chapter, for instance, emphasizes the discord even among the outsiders. In 1914 the clocks on the churches are "irregular, as if the saints themselves were divided" (241). Similarly the episodes in this chapter are affirmative yet scattered; the outsiders are divided. The chapter moves from Sara's intoxicated mockery of prayer-book phrases as she eats in the chophouse with Martin, to their afternoon pastorale in the park as they join Maggie and her baby, and then to Kitty's party from which she herself eagerly escapes, taking the night train north to her home. The next day she climbs a hill, where she lies down and hears "the land itself, singing to itself, a chorus, alone" (300). In this novel there are a handful of vigorous characters who recognize themselves as social misfits, mockers, or protestors, but they are not a society. About a year after portraying this miscellaneous collection of outsiders, Woolf published *Three Guineas* (1938), a book that developed from what were originally the "essay" sections of the novel; in *Three Guineas* she urges women, as outsiders, to form a "society."[39] The characters of the novel, however, lack a communal and uniting ritual; they lack a society, and they do not seem to understand each other. Maggie would "hate" going to the political meeting that so attracts Rose (187). Eleanor does not go to Kitty's parties, and Kitty is hurt by this (283). Each of these disaffected people is like the land that Kitty hears, "singing to itself, a chorus, alone."

Nevertheless, the Pargiters persist in their efforts to enunciate their vision. Eleanor, riding in a cab with her niece Peggy during the light-filled evening of "Present Day," speaks for absolutely new, radical combinations; in her future travels she wants to see "another kind of civilisation. Tibet, for instance" (360-61). And Eleanor can hear and respect another kind of music. She is the only one who can venture the word "beautiful" for the strange, fierce, meaningless song which the two caretaker's children render just as dawn culminates the all-night party. The incomprehensible song is a kind of audible silence; it is like those ellipses and pauses which have, throughout the novel, characterized the sporadic efforts to formulate verbally a concept of new lives and new institutions. Joanna Lipking's interpretation of this singing emphasizes the radical nature of the necessary changes; the strange song is "a suggestion of something beyond, outside history, some unknown and more authentically divine spirit borne in through a speaking in tongues."[40]

In *The Years*, the words of the characters falter before the enormous attempt to define "another kind of civilisation." Similarly, in *Between the Acts* the more sensitive characters are searching for a "new plot"—for a new vision of how society and personal relationships might be ordered. The imagery of seasonal liminality, however, is more focussed than in the earlier novel, and the experience of the characters, especially as they respond to the pageant and to the rural landscape, is less disparate than was the experience of the characters in *The Years*. The Oliver family and the guests are united at least in their decision to participate in this festival day, though many of them are mildly skeptical of the traditional machinery of rural festivity—amateur actors, a mediocre pageant, a priest who pronounces upon the play's meaning.

As I have suggested elsewhere, the novel is in many respects a "festive comedy," to use C. L. Barber's term for those comedies of Shakespeare in which a community is renewed after experiencing the "green world."[41] The festive occasion observed in *Between the Acts*, however, is without the gaiety and confidence of Shakespeare's festive comedies; the society portrayed in the novel is threatened and seems to be on the edge of collapse. In *A Midsummer Night's Dream* the jealousies and thwarted passions are resolved after the overnight in the woods on the eve of May Day; a new governmental harmony, in *As You Like It*, coincides at the end with happy marriages for everybody. *Between the Acts* does not have such a neat resolution, and though several readers have briefly noted the presence of comedy in the novel, they also point out the severe frustration and fury which stir uncomfortably beneath the surface.[42] The liminality is unresolved. Passion and protest do not return at last to an affirmation of order. In this decaying culture there is no perceivable order to affirm. Instead, Isa Oliver demands a "new plot," for civilization apparently, and certainly for human relationships.

The ritual patterns of seasonal liminality are themselves often mocked in *Between the Acts*. Miss La Trobe's pageant is to some extent a burlesque of all such pageants.[43] Mrs. Manresa, who can say and do what civilized restraint forbids to others, who expresses the "license" of the seasonal festival, is an ambiguous figure; sometimes she is seen as a breath of fresh air, and at other times she is recognizable as a sham. The meal, the semisacramental tea, which is served in a barn reminiscent of a Greek temple, has fly-blown cakes, and tea that tastes like rust boiled in water.[44] (By contrast, Mrs. Ramsay's Boeuf en Daube, served in the green world of the Hebrides, was perfect.) The green world of the Pointz Hall grounds is not always expansive or fertile. Sometimes it is the comforting and absorbing view, which the audience has during the pageant, of contented nature continuing its own pageant of trees and cows; at other times it is restricted to a symbolic greenhouse which the passionate and jealous Isa visits with the homosexual William Dodge during an intermission. The clergyman, Mr. Streatfield, is an important symbolic figure in any communal celebration having its roots in seasonal religious rites. Priests have attended since the time of the Greek Dionysia, the annual community dramas.[45] Both the narrator and La Trobe's audience, however, find it hard to take Streatfield seriously. He seems to be something of an heirloom.

The presence of ritual elements traditionally associated with liminal observances would seem to suggest a mood of joy and spontaneity. Yet such a ritual is inadequate to supply this frustrated and war-threatened society with regeneration. The community represented by those gathered on the lawn at Pointz Hall is too much infected by values that contradict those of festivity. Virginia Woolf describes—or at least sketches—both sets of values in *Three Guineas*. She was still responding to reviews of this book while working on *Between the Acts*,[46] and some of the ideas expressed in her feminist-pacifist work became dramatized in the novel. In *Three Guineas* Woolf advocates new patterns for society, patterns that would eliminate the pomp and power of male-dominated institutions. She also provides some hints of society as it might become once the debilitating egotism of judges, soldiers, and other patriarchs has been mitigated. She gives us a glimpse of what the "new plot" might be. If the state, for instance, paid women a living wage for rearing the children, the men would no longer need to be such struggling heroes of the business world. Their financial burden would be eased, and "culture would thus be stimulated." The men could see their children and see the spring bloom; "the half-men might become whole." The caricature-man might cease, and human beings might then be able to celebrate. The Society of Outsiders—women who refuse to participate in society as it is now structured—would eliminate medals, gowns, and the symbolic public ceremonies of the war-culture, but the society would not want to do away with beauty. "On the contrary, it will be one of their aims to increase private beauty; the beauty of spring, summer, autumn; the beauty of flowers, silks, clothes" (199-207).

In the novel, the persistent images of garlanding, maying, and bringing the green into the lives of a frustrated and threatened society make the book glow with a kind of bitter hope, as though the vision of a radically changed society, a Utopia, is briefly perceived and then lost. The pastoral imagery is reminiscent of the hay-making festival described by William Morris in *News from Nowhere*: a socialist time-traveller, in a dream, tours a magnificent empty house (as William Dodge and Mrs. Swithin do), observes a handsome old Roman town (cf. the Roman road, site of the Oliver's cesspool), and joins the celebrating community in a large old church, its arches hung with flowers.[47] The new world in Morris's story is only a dream, and the sporadic and thwarted intimations of a renewed world in *Between the Acts* are similarly insubstantial. The temple-like barn is garlanded, but with paper roses. The members of the chorus at one point during the pageant "seem intoxicated by the music," and they sing "a-maying, a-maying" (112-13), but on many occasions their words are blown away. Sir Spaniel Lilyliver in the play thinks the aging Lady Harpy Harraden overdoes her dress and amorosity; he says, *"She's rigged like a barber's pole of a May Day"* (153). Mrs. Manresa evidently does not see this grotesque parody of herself any more than she uses the mirrors, during the last part of the pageant, for self-scrutiny and moral evaluation. Instead she adds a little powder to her nose (217).

With Isa the imagery of maying becomes especially poignant, and symbolic of the classic struggle of Winter with Spring, Death with Life. During tea in the barn she murmurs poetry to herself. She feels desolate among the "china faces, glazed and hard," as they seem to her. She thinks of going away "under the nut tree and the may tree, away, till I come to the wishing well." The imagery of water seems to release something in her, but she is not sure what wish she should make at the imaginary well—perhaps to drown in the water. She asks, "Should I mind not again to see may tree or nut tree?" (124-25). Isa here incorporates into her thoughts fragments from a Mother Goose rhyme, "Nuts an' May" which is a game of tug-of-war, as Nancy Bazin has pointed out; the verses imply that Isa hopes to be taken away by death or by the man she is in love with, Rupert Haines.[48] In a larger context, Isa is torn between "Death" and "Life." She is torn between a threatened society, a limited domestic life, on the one hand, and a longing for a new structuring of human emotions and imagination on the other. The tug-of-war was sometimes a part of seasonal festivals, and Jane Harrison describes an Eskimo tug-of-war which was symbolic of the struggle between summer and winter.[49] Isa's tug-of-war is in a sense the tug-of-war of the novel itself, the conflict between a restricted society and the restless exuberance of human passion and its creative energy.

Isa later formulates this conflict in more distinctly sociological images. At the end of the day, she is sitting with Giles in the library and notices his uniform for the evening:

> Both had changed. Giles now wore the black coat and white tie of the professional classes, which needed—Isa looked down at his feet—patent leather pumps. "Our representative, our spokesman," she sneered. Yet he was extraordinarily handsome. "The father of my children, whom I love and hate." Love and hate—how they tore her asunder! Surely it was time someone invented a new plot, or that the author came out from the bushes . . . . (251-52; the ellipsis is Woolf's)

Priests and stockbrokers, in their special garb, are the spokesmen for society, the priest speaking for the flock, the husband speaking for the wife and family; those who have power speak for those who do not have it. La Trobe, hiding in the bushes, refused to appear and to receive the condescending thanks of Streatfield. Isa's sneer associates her with La Trobe's resistance to the official "spokesman."

Isa's desire for a new plot, coming after her contempt and frustration as she regards her husband's dress, widens the meaning of the word "plot"; she wants a new structuring of domestic and social institutions.

On a day whose roots are in fertility rituals, Giles as stockbroker represents a society whose values are opposite to fertility. And yet Giles is, in conscience, an outsider. He has been bothered for ten years about Mrs. Swithin's criticism of his marketing stocks to the beautiful and naked "savages"; at lunch, he tries to apologize to himself: "Given his choice, he would have chosen to farm. But he was not given his choice. So one thing led to another; and the conglomeration of things pressed you flat; held you fast, like a fish in water. So he came for the week-end and changed" (59). Giles has caught himself. His former self, which would have chosen a different life, catches the frustrated businessman he has become. He is now very much like the businessmen in *Three Guineas* who have no time to watch their children or see the spring. Nevertheless, the festival day gives to Giles some clarification and insight. He suspects that the competitive world of stockbroking conflicts directly with his own happiness.

If Giles is the most tormented by what he dimly sees, it is Isa's imagination which most often provides images of flexibility, hope, and renewal. During the Elizabethan section of the pageant she is momentarily confused by the bawling of the actors and the complicated plot. She thinks: "Did the plot matter? She shifted and looked over her right shoulder. The plot was only there to beget emotion. There were only two emotions: love; and hate. There was no need to puzzle out the plot" (109). Isa looks over her shoulder because Rupert Haines, the object of her present emotion, is seated in that direction. Later she adds one more emotion, peace (111). Her insight—that the plot is there only to beget emotion—is an idea common among Woolf's friends, and is nearly a quotation of Roger Fry. It is also an idea developed by Jane Harrison, who observed that art, since it has its roots in fertility rites, still retains as its main impetus the creation of emotion; the believers in the rite hope by their own dancing and shouting to reproduce magically in nature something of their own vitality.[50] Seen in terms of the novel's main conflict, Isa's thoughts here suggest that the emotion, which gives rise to the pageant's plot and which also results from it, is the most important thing; if so, then the plot, in literature and in social structures too, may change, the surviving human vitality being always present. Liminality remains, ready to rejuvenate an inadequate institution.

Between the Acts celebrates this capacity of nature, and of human nature, for regeneration. Yet the novel also implies that such regeneration is thwarted by the "plot" which political and domestic institutions have imposed on the heart, on the imagination, and even on festivity itself. Some of the elements by which festivity is expressed are themselves too closely linked to false or oppressive institutions—the straight-collared priest who carries greenery, the simultaneously trivial and sinister Mrs. Manresa, who tries to be a "wild child" of nature. Both of these figures are too tainted by the culture which they, on this festive occasion, are traditionally supposed to criticize and to renew.

In *Between the Acts*, and also in *Three Guineas*, Virginia Woolf is saying in effect that springtime must become political; that is, the regenerative energies of human beings must discover or devise not only new institutions but new rituals for renewing these institutions. Festivity, traditionally a renewing ritual, must itself be renewed; in the process, some very ancient and rooted symbols may need to be discarded if they are too closely linked to an oppressive and patriarchal past. Although Woolf draws upon Frazer and Harrison, she perhaps at the same time implies a critique of the symbolic liminal observances which they describe. The ending of the novel, with its imagery of evolutionary renewal, suggests that the new plot, which Isa longs for, is so radically new that human beings will have to start all over in order to find new images, new symbols of festivity.

As we have seen in Woolf's novels, these new symbols are for the most part identified with the subculture or counterculture of "female" activities—activities and attitudes traditionally given to women. The glimpses of an idyllic society in *Three Guineas*, one in which both sexes are chiefly occupied with increasing the "private beauty" of silks, flowers, season-watching, and child-raising, affirm the values of immediacy, perception, sensuousness, relationship—values and activities traditionally allowed, or relegated, to women. These values, like Clarissa's flowers and parties, are opposites of those "masculine" activities of developing one's own ego and career, of pursuing Mr. Ramsay's "R" or Giles's stock-market success, or the war by which Septimus seeks to define a tough masculinity. When springtime becomes embodied in political institutions, these will be institutions with a precedent in the female "civilization," in the Society of Outsiders, in the women's counterculture. The politics of holiday will become the politics of politics.

On the other hand the more ascetic vision of *The Waves* suggests that any "plot," any culture's quest paradigm or festive pattern, is a mere "sequence," a "phrase." Percival's story, Mr. Ramsay's scholarly quest, Lily's painting, Clarissa's party, and Jacob's climb up to the Acropolis are all mere human hedges against what Betty Flanders called the "oppression of eternity." There is a sometimes poignant, sometimes comic fragility to any cultural "plot," any metaphysical quest, any myth, whether its imagery is masculine or feminine.

4

Muriel Spark:
The Irrational Norm

In Muriel Spark's novels springtime does become political: anti-structure figures — the artists, bachelors, radical teachers, pilgrims, servants, and other "outsiders" — invade tradition, overturn the mind or the heart or the institution, and leave the formerly trustworthy realities lurching as alarmingly as jarred stage scenery. Spark's comic novels are traditional in that they employ the liminal patterns of inversion, life crisis, or festivity, but these patterns are used in massively concentrated doses, and the novels do not finally circle back to an affirmation of the old order — the old order scrutinized and renewed but still the old order. The characters, who have often adventurously and deliberately set out on some daring psychological pilgrimage, tend to remain in awkward exile from themselves: a cloistered nun gripping the bars that separate her from the world, a comic and anguished ghost searching for death, or a one-time seminary student still chafing at his surprise vocation, that of a "first-rate epileptic." In the fictional worlds created by Spark, there is always something like the Fall; something is disastrously overturned.

Spark's first eight novels deal primarily with the overturning of a psyche; but in the last seven novels, the landscape is larger, more social (even "global," to quote the glib investment shyster of *The Takeover*), and the action elaborates the overturning of economic institutions and social conventions. Virginia Woolf's Isa Oliver had hoped vaguely for a radical "new plot," and Miss La Trobe's play held broken mirrors up to the old. In the fiction of Spark the diffident artists Lily and La Trobe are replaced by artist-outlaws corrupted by a sinister confidence or sheer faith; the outsiders come inside, infiltrate, and lay new plots everywhere like traps and mines. The festivity — aristocratic, meditative, and nostalgic in Woolf — is in Spark loud, even impudent. Muriel Spark, whose early novels often look back at the same war Virginia Woolf anticipated with discouragement in *Between the Acts*, illuminates her characters' wars, loves, and crimes obliquely with a severe, even menacing, hope.

Both writers claim for themselves the status of outsider, and they examine the outsider character in their novels; for Spark, the condition of exile — which she does not link to feminism — has become a "calling," leading her to sojourn in London, New York, and Rome, since her native city of Edinburgh did not provide an environment congenial to her work.[1] Feminism is an active undercurrent in the work of both novelists, although for Spark the issue is most often latent, matter-of-fact, assumed rather than analyzed or professed. Both writers could perceive Hitler as a comic creature, and Spark, as did Woolf, advocates the weapon of laughter against such violence.[2] Although she began writing in the fifties, a time uncongenial to the experimentalism so prominent in the fiction of Woolf and the other "moderns," Muriel Spark has consistently manifested in her novels the playful and significant eccentricity of a writer conscious of style and form. But while Virginia Woolf violates realism in order to sound, depth by depth, the sensuous ocean of consciousness, and gives us repeated and richly illuminated epiphanies of fins and lighthouses, Muriel Spark's experimentalism can be said to move in the opposite direction, into thinner and thinner air, so that we perceive her characters at a distance. She is stingy about epiphanies (though they do flash occasionally); she teases and denies the reader and manipulates the characters through moral mazes into really frightening corners.

Most of Woolf's major characters seek and find glowing, if obscure, intimations of eternity. Spark's fictional seekers, on the other hand, are likely to be wary about visions or any sudden "transfiguration of the commonplace"; some will even turn numbly away and avoid if at all possible any insight into themselves or into moral or metaphysical realities. Like Betty Flanders, in *Jacob's Room*, they seem to prefer a protective if narrow blindness, and like her "would fain ward off a little longer — oh, a little longer! — the oppression of eternity." Yet the weight of eternity oppresses them and catches up with them because a brooding, nonimageable moral luminescence is at the center of all of Spark's fiction. Many have said, often but accurately, that she writes *sub specie aeternitatis*; she looks at the world — as Cardinal Newman urged everyone to do — the way God looks at it.[3]

Spark insists on "the full irrational norm" as the sounding board for her comedy; this norm is never more than slightly visible in the world, as Spark, a Catholic convert, understands the world and divine reality behind it and within it. Only paradox and a diffident and crafty imagery can point toward an ultimate reality, compared to which anything else, even the commonsense norms of everyday run-of-the-mill collusion with one's bad conscience, even the venerable attachments and relationships of primary socialization, are potentially ridiculous, being (spiritually considered) provincial, incomplete as bases for decision and action. In her "Foreword" to a selection of Newman's sermons, Spark notes that when most people speak of "the moral standards of Christianity," they mean "those codes of decency which have evolved in the chivalrous West from the Christian faith."[4] In her novels, morality-as-chivalry withers into the ridiculous under the humbling and mocking light of her severe vision. Chivalry is too often a pose, a false crossing of the threshold into spiritual adventure, a parody of initiation or conversion. The last of Spark's many convert characters, Barbara Vaughan, in *The Mandelbaum Gate*, expresses the contradictory quality of any psychological adventure. On a personal and religious pilgrimage in Israel, she has ventured into the Jordanian side of Jerusalem, even though she is partly Jewish. Barbara finds it humorous that a mother-oppressed diplomatic clerk, Freddy Hamilton, has so far found himself as to "rescue" her from a convent where she is spending her first night in the Arab section of the city. She feels both amusement and admiration concerning Freddy and his "madness," which she too seems to have caught; he is "flowering in the full irrational norm of the stock she also derived from: unself-questioning hierarchists, anarchistic imperialists, bloodsporting zoophiles, sceptical believers."[5] Freddy's burst of chivalry turns out to be highly dangerous for him psychologically, and fatal to his mother; his parodic quest parallels Barbara's to some extent, but veers crazily away from it also. The irrational norm can only express itself in paradox, in the doubling, twisting, and contrasting of myth patterns, or in the briefest hints of wholeness, or in the mocking and fugitive landscape epiphanies that more often imply judgment, not fulfillment.

The persistent theme in Spark's work is the necessity of the liminal action — of growth, initiation (often in the early novels imaged by conversion), or social change (usually implied by the liminal mockeries of inversion and outrageous festivity). The counterbalancing and equally persistent theme is the danger of false liminality: of presumptuous, misguided reformism or spiritual quest. Spark is fascinated by liminal figures, by those for whom the ordinary rules or norms (social hierarchy, sex identity, and sexual expression) do not apply: bachelors, converts moving toward a new self, the reformist spinster teacher, the epileptic, nuns, the very old, or even the dead. She treats harshly any straying or presuming pilgrims, and mocks the Nazi in the teacher, the Nixon in the nun, the professional outsider, and the "professional victim," to use a phrase from *The Mandelbaum Gate.* Even those characters who undertake spiritual or social heroism with humility have an acute wariness — as does the narrator always — regarding the manifestations of truth in a fluctuating material world. The norm can be found, can be imaged, only with the greatest difficulty in this world, and there is consequently no rest for the wicked, and hardly any for the good either.

All of Muriel Spark's novels have been written since her conversion in 1954, and she has said that Catholicism provided the norm for her work as a satirist: "The Catholic belief is a norm from which one can depart. It's not a fluctuating thing. I'm not advocating the Catholic Faith as this for everyone, but for me, it's provided my norm. The Catholic Church for me is just a formal declaration of what I believe in any case. It's something to measure from."[6] Just how this norm expresses itself in her fiction has been the subject of much critical attention. Although a few critics have suggested a connection between a conservative religious view, in Spark's work, and what they perceive as the narrator's arrogant and judgmental omniscience, others point out that her work has neither a distinctly Catholic ethos nor ethic, Spark very often portraying her Catholic characters as ridiculous or sinister.[7] Spark's extremely deliberate control and her use of the omniscient point of view have been consistently defended by Frank Kermode, who argues that this aspect of her method suggests a playful and illuminating connection between God's world and the novelist's.[8] The other-worldly norm in her novels manifests itself as some kind of "frame," or implies a coherent vision, a unity that derives from the strong sense of an obscure Providence.[9] Her fictional norm is perhaps best described by Anthony Paul as a concept of God's grace portrayed as "a sort of dazzling blank," and her method by Bernard Harrison as one which demands over and over again that readers revise, as the novel proceeds, their previous interpretation of character and events.[10] Certainly Muriel Spark distrusts the emotion-laden iconography, the rich Catholic costuming, which might have given the dazzling blank norm some character; her work is free of the jewelled imagery which manifests itself in the occasional highly wrought passage of a novel by Graham Greene, for instance, or in Waugh's *Brideshead Revisited.* Her biographer Derek Stanford has suggested that Spark, at the time of her conversion at least, was somewhat disenchanted with the material world, and a reviewer has seen in Spark's stringent style and her nonluxurious imagery an indication of "a kind of impatience with the material."[11] Spark herself, in an introduction to an edition of Newman's letters, often refers to his mistrust of material reality; she writes that "this motif of external mistrust and an intense personal relationship to God, is a constant factor among the many apparent inconsistencies which Newman's life presents."[12] What Spark says about Newman's life could very well be said about her own work; the "constant factor" is the personal relationship with conscience, destiny, or God, but this is linked to a singular mistrust of the traditional "external" stereotypical myths and actions, patterns that might tempt a character to express a calling or a psychological rebirth in a narrow, destructive, and indeed ridiculous fashion.

To imply an essentially imageless norm, then, Spark approaches it like Perseus approaching Medusa, backwards and with mirrors. She uses the conventions of liminal comedy which were discussed in the first chapter, but especially those paradoxical motifs which have parallels in the more radical moments of the New Testament and in Christian literature. She uses inversion as flamboyantly as the medieval broadside designers; as Derek Stanford has aptly observed "her world-picture is ours inverted."[13] But the Christian world-picture is itself an inverted one, as Newman emphasizes many times, especially in the sermons for which Spark wrote an introduction. He notes the paradoxes of the Beatitudes, and recalls Christ's washing the feet of the disciples; he quotes and paraphrases such stringencies as "many that are first shall be last, and the last shall be first." Newman gravely warns that "under the dispensation of the Spirit all things were to become new and to be reversed"; strength, knowledge of human nature, experience of life, are merely local values, for "in that kingdom which Christ has set up, all is contrariwise."[14] The principle of inversion, of turning the world, as in revolution or judgment, "contrariwise," produces a fiercely playful mocking of norms in Spark's fiction.

A positive, transcendent norm is implied, but it is always implied by a kind of finessed absence, a procedure to which Spark gives a clue in her poem "Elementary." In the first two stanzas a woman questions whether she really did see a vision of herself in the dark night over a dark street; she realizes that *something* must have been there, because that same something has left behind it such a palpable sense of absence, and she uses the analogy of a cat to describe this peculiarity:

> The void exists as bulk defined it,
> The cat subsiding down a basement
> Leaves a catlessness behind it.[15]

With some exceptions, the hidden province of values behind Spark's comic novels is expressed by a catlessness, a strong sense of what has just left or just been lost or may any moment assert itself again to a guilty conscience or a nonchalant community. The positive implications travel usually on a network of negatives. John Updike sees in Spark's work a "comic mysticism,"[16] and the linkage of comedy and mysticism is not such a peculiar tandem as it might at first appear to be. If "catlessness" is a peculiar phenomenon—as well as a peculiar word—to a person used to perceiving cats, and if a "cloud of unknowing" is an awkward phrase and concept to someone used to clouds and used to the assumption of "knowing," then to the one dwelling close, psychologically, to some extreme or ultimate perspective, the ordinary world of cats, clouds, and material reality, basic assumptions of social and psychological identity, may seem odd, unusual, and comic. Spark has said that she thinks children are capable of mystical experience and that to her, as a child, life itself seemed odd, unusual.[17] Viewed from a certain perspective, a quite sensible and upright world will be seen as inverted, grotesque, flawed, and comic, even its basic moral arrangements all awry. A perspective something like this, and one that combines comedy and Christianity, the latter interpreted according to its most liminal, radical values, is found in Kierkegaard, in his *Journals*, for instance, which a character in one of Spark's short stories was reading with great interest.[18] In the *Journals* Kierkegaard affirms that Christianity's ideal is "so great that all others disappear alongside it (the romantic and humorous aspect of Christianity)."[19] The "comic mysticism" in Spark's fiction results from a similarly extreme ideal, grace as a dazzling blank, the norm as catlessness.

Spark typically refuses in her fiction to engage the reader's emotions by building up sensuous physical details or to move by means of rich epiphanic revelation; she uses action and image as parables, as allegories representing an unrepresentable moral and metaphysical reality. She has asserted that her fiction is "a kind of parable," that "it's not true." For Spark, the physical world provides the artist merely with an "economy" of material imagery, with hints and symbols, just as it provides, in Newman's understanding of "economy," the sacramental manifestations of a hidden truth.[20]

Chief among the material images, the hints and symbols drawn from the world of the senses and from cultural patterns, are the liminal patterns of initiation and inversion, as I have suggested. Spark shows a lot of caution even here, however, and she will use mythic quest-patterns, for instance, only if she also teases and tests them. Spark claims that she doesn't use myth except as plot, though she hopes the plot has "something universal in it."[21] Even the nearly universal plot of initiation has a particular meaning for Spark; initiation-conversion meant, for her personally, "finding one's own individual personal point of view."[22] Similarly, her major questing converts accept no pat values or stereotyped modes of action. Those among her characters who do fall into a well-trodden primrose path, who arrogantly conceive of themselves as spiritual heroes, are subjected to ridicule and to unnerving intimations of where they are heading.

Most of Spark's convert-searchers are women, and the mythic patterns that appear assume a distinctly female imagery. One could as accurately say that the imagery is androgynous, for the women heroes do not fall into the stereotypical patterns of "feminine" passivity, or of all-nourishing and sympathetic mother to males or children. The female hero is intellectually and physically qualified for the arduous self-confrontation, and for assertion in relation to others, that a spiritual quest requires. These qualities are essentially taken for granted by the woman hero herself and by the narrator and are not apologized for, argued for, or advanced as polemic. Perhaps the close attachment between Muriel Spark and her mother contributed to this matter-of-fact portrayal of strong women. Spark's maternal grandmother, an active feminist who knew Mrs. Pankhurst, may also have contributed to Spark's strong female characters. In a semiautobiographical short story, "The Gentile Jewesses," the narrator tells how her capable and imaginative grandmother would elaborate upon Old Testament imagery, substituting a woman for a man as liberator of the oppressed; according to the grandmother's version, "Miriam, the sister of Moses, banged her timbrel and led all the women across the Red Sea, singing a song to the Almighty." The grandchild-narrator herself carries the fanciful imagery further: "I see her [the grandmother] in the vanguard, leading the women in their dance of triumph, clanging the tambourine for joy and crying Alleluia with Mrs. Pankhurst and Miriam the sister of Moses. The hands of the Almighty hold back the walls of the sea."[23] Such lavish instances of jubilant female heroism do not appear in the novels. Instead, a more subtly strong woman claims, as a matter of course, her right to self-knowledge, adulthood, or adventure, or to crime, sin, or self-destruction. When feminism occasionally emerges in Spark's novels, it is enmeshed in a larger context of personal or social liberation. Mrs. Pankhurst, Miriam, and an entire society need to walk together into a God-promised freedom. For Spark herself, "feminism" means legally assured equality of pay and employment, and she notes that she is "an independent woman."[24] Women in her fiction are as likely as the men to demonstrate strength and independence. They venture hardily into liminality, into the "betwixt and between" threshold world of inverted and mocked norms, where comedy tests the subtlety and humanity of their spiritual courage.

Spark's adventurer in the early fiction usually is a Catholic convert, and usually a woman. Yet the novels are not really about conversion, or about Catholicism. They concern instead the alarming and creative questions that occur to a sensitive and, it seems, rather mischievous heart and intellect in transit to self-knowledge. Muriel Spark exploits fully the comic potential of this world of liminality, this phase of "initiation," in which values and identities have been overturned; the central character proceeds to conquer the false answer and the false self by means of wit, betrayal, or physical force. Usually the central character is a chosen "daughter" in some sense, a student or co-worker or servant who is favored by an older woman, a mentor-mother figure with a penchant for overwhelming the younger person with oppressive nurturance and guidance. In every case the younger woman, often a writer, gets rid of this tyrannous "angel in the house." Caroline Rose, in Spark's first novel, drowns Mrs. Hogg, the caricature Mother Church of plentiful bosom and herdlike instincts, and in *The Mandelbaum Gate*, the prying and domineering Miss Rickward is effectively dismissed by ridicule. After this novel, Spark's eighth, the conflict of nuturing mentor and rebelling daughter disappears, apparently resolved, and the comic liminality is no longer that of personal crisis but social and economic crisis, inversion, intrigue, and festivity.

The Comforters

Muriel Spark's first novel, *The Comforters* (1957), was written shortly after she become a Catholic, and after she recovered from a nervous illness which she perceived as being somehow connected with the conversion.[25] The hero of the novel, Caroline Rose, shares these characteristics: she, too, is a recent convert and seems to be emotionally ill. She has begun to hear a typewriter, followed by words which mimic her own thoughts. A writer who has just left a retreat at a self-consciously Catholic community, St. Philumena's, Caroline is not yet sure about the next decision she must make — whether to marry her lover, Laurence Manders, who works with the BBC. When she starts hearing voices, she tries to determine the identity of the "Typing Ghost," and once she suspects that the typing noises and words are those of an author who is typing Caroline's own story, character-Caroline begins protesting, holding back, trying to waylay the plot, which she perceives as "phoney." She is the only one among the characters to protest; the others are perfectly satisfied to act as if they are straight out of a silly story of blackmail-ers, smugglers, occult aficianados, and stereotyped group-centered Catholics bemoaning their status as victims in English society.

Caroline's most important relationship is with the author of the book, and this constitutes the central comic inversion of the novel: the character rises up against the author. The author-Caroline ad-mits, breaking into the narrative, that the character-Caroline is ex-erting an unexpected influence on the action,[26] even though the author has tried to silence the character awhile by putting her through a car wreck and into a hospital. Caroline "hears" the words typed by the author, but the author evidently "hears" Caroline's thoughts (and then types them out). There is an exchange of cre-ative energy between character and author, and when the two merge into one, the implication is that someone named Caroline has "found herself"; she has recognized and accepted her vocation as a novelist. She has survived both her nervous breakdown and the misguided sympathy of her acquaintances, who are false "com-forters" like Job's friends.[27] The other characters in the novel are really parodic spin-offs from Caroline's process of self-discovery. They are figures who caricature responsible and real creativity, with their frenetic intrigues and doubtful "miracles": Mrs. Hogg, fleshy, warmly prying caricature of concern, thinks she has heard the Virgin speaking; crippled Andrew Hogarth may have been healed at the European shrine. They possess readily contrived new identities; Willie Stock, who suspects satanists have smashed the religious statues, is nicknamed the "Baron," and Mervyn Hogarth, a bigamist with a new name, used to be husband to Mrs. Hogg. The preoccupations of the other characters ultimately lead to nothing, except to Caroline's book. Her reality is the one that survives, and her story, as the character becomes the author, is the "real" one.

Caroline moves toward herself, toward a balanced and appro-priate identity, through a classic symbolic terrain. When we first meet her, the character-Caroline has already descended, like the archetypal hero, into her unconscious; she *is* her unconscious. Her most horrific opponent throughout most of the novel is the egre-gious Mrs. Hogg. A same-sex parody of Caroline's Catholicism, Mrs. Hogg is a destructive, interfering, tricky "shadow." According to Jung—and Spark was acquainted with Jung's ideas by means of theory and therapy—the "shadow" is usually confronted and dealt with first; then the opposite-sex image, the soul or "animus," may lend its allegorical aid or challenge.[28] Spark briefly describes the process of the masculine archetypal entity rising from the earlier feminine one during a time of psychological probing in her poem "Evelyn Cavallo," which employs as its title a pseudonym of Spark's. The poet irritably refers to Evelyn as a "momentary name" that gives "a slight stir in a fictitious grave," and she scolds the troublesome Evelyn:

> Therefore, therefore, Evelyn,
> Why do you assert your so non-evident history
> While all your feminine motives make a mystery
> Which, to resolve, arise your masculine?[29]

Both the masculine and feminine of the poem can be understood as "Evelyn," a name applicable to both sexes. Some of the "Evelyn" characteristics, however, suggest the feminine Mrs. Hogg particularly. Like Mrs. Hogg, who can disappear, the mysterious Evelyn has a "non-evident history," and a few lines later she is called "Evelyn of guile." These are "shadow" characteristics, the shadow being a subtle trickster, a sabotaging element within the unconscious personality. After the shadow is recognized, however, the animus archetype may appear, just as Evelyn's "masculine" arises to resolve and complete the androgynous unconscious.

So in *The Comforters*, after Caroline drowns the Mrs. Hogg nuisance, the author-Caroline takes a fresh look at Laurence. Although character-Caroline had previously dismissed his advice, his ideas, his proffered comfort, author-Caroline apparently admits to the criticism he offers in a letter to character-Caroline. He says she sees herself as a "martyr-figure," and he is amazed, we are told, to discover that his letter winds up in the book that author-Caroline is writing, since he decided not to send the letter (223-24). (Laurence, of course, does not understand that the author-Caroline can overhear his thoughts.) The biblical imagery used in the description of Laurence's tearing up the letter implies its beneficial effect on author-Caroline: "He saw the bits of paper come to rest, some on the scrubby ground, some among the deep marsh weeds, and one piece on a thorn-bush; and he did not then foresee his later wonder, with a curious rejoicing, how the letter had got into the book" (224). Compare the parable of the sower, especially the description of where the seeds fell: "Some seeds fell by the way side . . . , some fell upon stony places . . . . and some fell among thorns" (Matt. 13:3-7). No wonder Laurence is surprised that his letter bore fruit, since its pieces, like the seeds in the parable, fell upon unpromising ground, even among thorns. Caroline's mature heart, like the good ground (the fourth to be described in the parable), is receptive, however; the fact that she receives his criticism of her victim complex under-lines her new self-knowledge. Caroline has matured from the ner-vous insecurity of a new convert and untried writer who was self-consciously comfortless, and who sought the image of herself in grotesque or merely misguided, and misguiding, "comforters." By accepting the accurate criticism of her internal guide-lover, the ani-mus-Laurence — a criticism which is in part a critique of the book she is writing as well — Caroline shows herself to be a convert to her better professional and personal self, to have found her own "indi-vidual personal point of view."

Robinson

In many ways, *Robinson* (1958) is the counterpart of *The Com-forters.* Spark's second novel modifies and complements the earlier emphasis on finding and trusting one's personal response to a large public ideology and to the people who embody it. Although *Robin-son* is Spark's least typical work, and is generally considered to be a lapse among her achievements,[30] its imagery and even its allegori-cal plot provide important counterweights to *The Comforters.* Further, the book as a whole sketches in an elaborate, if rigidly stated, female myth which Spark more subtly employs in her later novels. Whereas Caroline forcefully drowned the oppressively nur-turing Mrs. Hogg, the oddly androgynous island Robinson, which is "a landscape of the mind," [31] sinks into an ocean of obscure and beneficent memory which the female hero, January, never force-fully denies, rejects, or represses. On another level, just as the im-agery of the first novel ruthlessly caricatured certain aspects of Catholicism that are typically assigned a female imagery (Mother Church as Hogg and herd), the second novel with equal vigor carica-tures the male-imaged aspects of Catholicism — arrogant masculine authority that withdraws from the pollution of the flesh and of women.

The action and characterization are conspicuously stylized and invite these allegorical interpretations. January Marlow and two men survive a plane crash and are nursed by Miles Mary Robinson, a recluse who lives on an island named after himself (and shaped like a human figure). The only other person on the island is Miguel, an orphan whom Robinson takes care of and possibly the child of one of the boatmen who arrive annually to harvest the island's pomegranates. All of these men are evidently aspects of January's personality, which is in need of integration after the "crash," symbolizing mental illness or at least an emotional crisis. Robinson, a Catholic who had studied for the priesthood, decided not to be ordained because he perceived the increasing veneration of the Virgin Mary as a dangerous, unhealthy, inauthentic movement. Soon after the arrival of the castaways, he fakes his own flamboyantly bloody demise by killing a goat, scattering its blood, and throwing the remains into a volcano, and so withdraws from the survivors into the solitude he prefers. His departure leads to increasingly dangerous threats and suspicions among the three adults, who accuse each other of Robinson's "murder."

The Freudian interpretation sees Robinson as January's superego; when he leaves, the other elements become active and destructive. One of the more sinister survivors, Tom Wells, the editor of an occult journal and a peddler of Celtic statuettes, may be an id of passion, superstition, and creative energy.[32] The Freudian interpretation works well as far as it goes, but there are other important implications. Peter Kemp has observed that Spark seems to be sketching the difference between a female and a male attitude, the former being associated with matter and instinct, and the latter with rationality.[33] There is in fact in *Robinson* one of the few paradigms in modern literature of a positive female myth. The pattern of the hero's quest, described by Campbell, Frye, and Jung, might yield insights into the female experience, as Annis Pratt has observed, if the male myth were "turned upside down."[34] This is just what Spark does in *Robinson*. The female hero is the only "real" character in the novel; she is distinctly the subject, and the males are "other."

Like Caroline, January is a Catholic convert, still in the liminal state of initiation into her new identity. She is "new" in several ways, having been born on the first of January, and then named after that new month. The rebirth crisis is for January a descent episode typical of the classic motif. Trying to protect her journal (which she thinks could provide evidence against Tom Wells if he decides to falsify the story of the apparent murder), January hides it deep in one of the tunnels on the island—the Pomegranate Bay Tunnel, in fact. The typical male hero usually descends into a geographic context reminiscent of a woman's body; January, a female hero, descends into an island shaped like a human being, supposedly a male human being, but one also with female associations. Significantly, whereas the male hero usually meets and conquers a female threat in the far reaches of his descent (or travel, or dream), January violently confronts the sinister Tom Wells, who threatens her with a knife. He is a sinister animus (in archetypal terms comparable to Circe's threat to Ulysses), a kind of Hades, who would have killed January-Persephone, leaving her in the hellish sulphurous underworld of the pomegranate island. Karl Malkoff has pointed to the significance of the fact that January shines her light in Wells's face, an action suggesting the sudden illumination of one's darker self.[35] It is also significant that she strikes him with the flashlight and escapes; her new psychological illumination would have meant little if she had not successfully thwarted the attack and climbed out of the tunnel.

January as subject is taken seriously by the author; the men, however, and the stereotypically "male" attitudes which they represent, are often treated satirically. January's own dependence on male chivalry and her own tendency to admire and emulate romantic, aloof authority are mocked only in the persons of Jimmie Waterford, Robinson, and to some extent Wells. While still at the airport January had singled out Jimmie Waterford as her traveling companion and protector; she explains that if a lone woman picks out one man, it keeps away other men, the "numerous chance pesterers all along the line" (23). Jimmie's protective attitude toward January is adequate for defending her from the condescending flirtations of Tom Wells, who calls her "honey" and "sweetie." In his derivative and comic dialect, Jimmie confronts Wells: "And any indignities vented upon this lady, I black your eye full sore" (63).

When his lady is really in a serious plight, however, Jimmie's knightly efforts in her defense are a hazard to everyone. He had persuaded January to give him the gun she had been carrying (al-

ways with the safety catch on): "Many ladies do not understand
what is a gun. In the event that words should occur, pouff—the
lady will shoot and the gentleman is killed" (158). He himself tries to
shoot Wells after hearing of his attempt on January's life in the tunnel, but the pistol seems not to work. During the ferocious fistfight
that follows between the two men, January picks up the gun and
sees that the safety catch is still on (168-69). The noble-intentioned
Jimmie Waterford is a caricature of the valiant hero defending his
threatened "lady"—in this case a lady who has vigorously been her
own hero in the tunnel and needs no bookish, sentimental defender
such as Jimmie.

The fistfight ceases because Robinson, returning from his own
contrived death, chooses that moment to reappear. His return
marks a change in January's estimate of him. Although she dis-
agrees emphatically with his position on Marian doctrine, and even
though she has been teaching the rosary to Miguel (against Robinson's wishes), she had begun to perceive him, during his absence, as
"an austere sea-bound hero, a noble heretic," and "a pagan pre-
Christian victim of expiation" (137). When he returns from his
faked death, however, she mocks him and her own romanticizing
by adjusting her attitudes; she thinks with chagrin, "a noble heretic indeed" (171). With this rejection of her former idealizing about
Robinson, January rejects the authoritarian in herself, the authoritarian who had, in Robinson's absence, imitated his iron rule and
kept the keys to the arsenal.

In rejecting the anti-Marian heretic, she perhaps also rejects
her tendency to be severe on some of her own "pagan" impulses.
True, she carefully argues, against Tom Wells, for a distinction between a pagan goddess and the Virgin Mary, but January has sometimes felt a desire to worship the moon (her grandmother did so,
repeating a good-luck charm). The island, paganism, a moon god presumably female, are elements of her experience which January
apparently carries away with her, although the island itself sinks
into the sea some years after she and the other survivors are rescued. It becomes for her "an apocryphal island" (185), symbolizing
the noncanonized elements beneath the surface of her official self,
her beliefs, her Catholicism.[36] In the last words of the book, the island becomes a reminder that "all things are possible" (186); the
island of mingled religious impulses, the island belonging to a de-

spiser of Marian enthusiasm whose middle name is Mary, the peculiarly androgynous island, leads to January's legitimate, even scrip-
tural thought that with God all is possible.

The most hidden yet pervasive and implied presence on the island is a female ambience linked to January's impulse to use the
moon charm of her grandmother. This ambience is implied also by
the pomegranate orchard. Although Robinson tells January that
the legendary King Arthur planted the pomegranate orchards
(138), the pomegranates have a feminine and religious heritage as
well. In the Song of Songs pomegranate orchards are images of the
sponsa, the bride; Jung in his *Answer to Job* (a book which Spark
read) quotes one of these passages and offers it as an image for the
feminine "Wisdom," or "Sophia," who is elsewhere described in
Scripture in terms very similar to those applied to the Holy Spirit.
Jung points out the biblical parallels in characterization and diction
between this same complex of imagery and the Virgin Mary.[37] The
pomegranate island in Spark's novel is female as often as it is male.
On this island January is visiting her female heritage, and when she
leaves, she does not entirely deny it, for a strictly male-imaged faith.

Female imagery is not identified so thoroughly with matter as
it is in *The Comforters*. After reading his book on Marian doctrine,
January rejects Robinson's "sterile notion" that Mariology, Earth
mythology, superstition, and evil are linked in meaning (82-83).
Later, January confronts Robinson when she suspects that he has
taken her rosary, and during their altercation she realizes that he
fears "any material manifestations of Grace" (102-3). Perhaps Robinson saw in Marian doctrine a threat to what he conceived of as the
orthodoxy of the masculine image for any heavenly figure. He may
have sensed some of the implications that Carl Jung perceived.
Again, in his *Answer to Job*, Jung discusses the newly promulgat-
ed doctrine (1950) of the Assumption. In some of his other work, he
had ambiguously, and somewhat like January, linked female imagery to the concept of matter; he went further sometimes, and like
Robinson, implied that the feminine, evil, matter, flesh, darkness — all belonged to the same complex of imagery and meaning.[38]
Especially in *Answer to Job*, however, Jung emphasizes that biblical imagery links Mary to the feminine "Wisdom," or "Sophia,"
God's companion before Creation; interpreting the new doctrine of
the Assumption, Jung writes, "Mary as the bride is united with the

son in the heavenly bridal-chamber, and, as Sophia, with the God-head."[39] Whether or not Spark was recalling in *Robinson* Jung's wide interpretation of Marian imagery, the female images in the novel, and especially those implied by January's own heroic actions on the pomegranate island, are strong, positive ones. They illuminate and conquer the benighted, male-imaged superstition of Tom Wells.

January's own experience on the island does not identify her with matter, flesh, and evil; she herself, considered as an image of female qualities, is strongly intellectual, meeting the anti-Marian arguments of Robinson with thoughtful good sense. Her story and the female atmosphere of the island itself give a feminist significance to the Virgin Mary as a symbol; to January's Catholic consciousness in the mid-twentieth century, the Virgin is a very much hidden female element closely associated with the Godhead and taking on a mysterious prominence very threatening to men. In reaction, Robinson seems to be regressing. In order to maintain his distance from the intruders, among them an advocate of Marian devotions, he carries out a crude, mocking sacrifice; with the blood of a goat, he covers his retreat into isolation and into his own unmolested masculine heresy. His gory departure is an inverted, parodic sacrifice; it does not give, it takes. A self-centered would-be priest performs it, relishing the purity of a private doctrine that clings to a male deity. Robinson's simulated death and resurrection mock the death and resurrection of the male God he so severely defends.

Robinson lacks the excitement of Spark's other novels because it lacks the contrast between a world of assumed normality and the intrusion of some violently peculiar, abnormal world. When a recognizable novelistic context of social relationships is violently interrupted by a nonrealistic intruder, by a Typing Ghost or by "Death" making nuisance calls, this juxtaposition of two kinds of literature reinforces the clash of two kinds of reality. One reality has the recognizable structures of human relationships in society; it is the "home" world, described by Berger and Luckmann, that was examined in the first chapter. The other reality, the one often implied by an allegorical figure or by hallucination in Spark's novels, is the area of liminality, the area of transition, psychologically, socially, and biologically. This reality is uncomfortable and often threatening but concomitant with mortality, with an existence occurring in time that necessarily involves birth, growth, change, leaving former structures behind at "initiation" perhaps, or marriage, or death.

Memento Mori

The liminal areas are vulnerable ones for people, and hence surrounded by taboo, but these human weak spots are Muriel Spark's favorite domain for perpetrating her guerilla-warfare comedy. In *Memento Mori* (1959) she chooses the most liminal of all events, death, as the allegorical intrusion, as a personified jester on a macabre holiday inverting all of the ordinarily cherishable comforts, even malices, of mortal life. By definition and fact, death is not — for the dying individual — resolvable into the ordinary structures of life and society; it is a great negative to the socializing and ordering forces of life, as anthropologists and sociologists have observed. For these reasons, it should theoretically hold vast comic potential, potential for inversion and for liminal attacks on norms.

Spark deftly elaborates that potential. A mixed group of couples who have known each other for sixty years in varying relationships, — as spouses, lovers, in-laws, servants — begins to receive phone calls reminding them that they must die. Their reactions to the voice on the phone indicate the strength of their attachment to the world-as-usual, to their own tense social arena of jealousies (often lingering from infidelities of fifty years ago). They spend their time making competitive attempts on the last will and testament of a recently deceased friend, or vengefully altering wills, or congratulating themselves for being slightly less feeble than someone else. Most are attached to a self-image that is decades younger than the reality. They live in a world that has slowly turned upside down, right on top of them, but they haven't noticed; their actions are in a way reminiscent of the medieval broadsides, where a young child feeds a bearded adult in a cradle and both figures maintain an air of complete normality. In *Memento Mori*, the aging characters are nourished by the passions and jealousies of their youth.

Not all are grotesque. Mortimer, the retired policeman whom Dame Lettie Colston calls in to work on the nuisance phone calls, is a happy stoic and humanist who delights in his wife and in their grandchild. When he receives his phone call, the grim message is

given by a soft-voiced woman, and Mortimer has a healthy acceptance of the admonition. There are two Catholic converts, Charmian Colston (once a well-respected novelist) and her servant Jean
Taylor, who has retired into a nursing home because of arthritis.
Much of the time, Charmian refers to her new servant, Mrs. Anthony, as "Taylor," and the former novelist's husband, Godfrey,
uses this lapse, and any other vulnerability, as a means of torment-
ing his wife; he urges her to move into a retirement home. She sees
that he is taking revenge for the many years of being subordinate to
her fame and income. Everywhere there are reversals which provide the opportunity for self-discovery, but which—like the phone
calls—usually only lead to a more rigid self-deception. There is a
revival of interest in Charmian's novels, and her physical health im-
proves as a result; as another result, Godfrey sinks into discouragement and into a blackmailing plot with yet another servant, Mrs.
Pettigrew, who easily gains control of the household.

The more fortunate reversals buoy the characters and provide
a counterpoint to the solemn phone calls. The phone calls, and the
response of each character to them, reveal the extent to which the
receiver of the message is morally corrupt.[40] The eighty-seven-
year-old Charmian, who accepts the telephone admonition, reply-
ing that she has indeed remembered her death for the last thirty
years,[41] is more sensitive and humane than her sister-in-law Lettie.
Lettie is frantically suspicious; she dismisses her servant, and at last
renders herself unprotected by all her efforts at protection. She is
beaten to death by burglars. Mrs. Pettigrew, only sixty-nine, is the
crafty servant of comedy; she works her way into the confidence of
a household and then blackmails her employer into altering a will in
her favor. She has such an agile subconscious that, immediately
after the phone call, she doesn't remember it happened.

There is, in addition to the phone calls, a contrasting and more
subtle indicator of corruption in the arrival of good news: it is as
though a character occasionally receives the message, "Perhaps
you will not die," and this leads to a sudden and amusing revival of
energy. Godfrey's corruption is revealed by the alacrity of his response to the news that Charmian was unfaithful to him decades
ago. Alec Warner, an amateur sociologist of aging, brings Godfrey
this message at Jean Taylor's request, for she has decided, from
mingled motives of jealousy and of supplying Godfrey with a wea-

pon against Charmian, to betray her former mistress. As things turn out, Charmian takes Godfrey's accusations with equanimity and lets him know that she has known these many years about his infidelities to her. Even so, Godfrey refuses to be deflated, and he drives home feeling assured that his new knowledge has evened the scale between him and Charmian. Usually a dangerously reckless driver, "Godfrey drove more carefully than usual. Having satisfied himself that Warner's information was accurate he felt that life was worth taking care of" (208). Now that he has an equal chance in his long-term marital battle, he relishes a sense of triumph. The solemn telephone warning of inevitable death has been countered; for Godfrey, a little corruption goes a long way toward restoring good cheer and love of life.

If one can neither accept the telephone admonition nor fight it with the life-restoring malice of old jealousies, one can try to explain it, as Alex Warner does. To label death anything but "death" is Alex's way of exorcising it. When he himself receives one of the phone calls already famous among his friends, he calmly asks the voice to repeat its warning; then he makes a card on the event, and puts it into his elaborate file of data on the physiological responses of his elderly acquaintances. In his diary he writes: "Query: Mass-hysteria" (140). For Alex, as for several of Caroline's "comforters," an attempt at a scientific explanation brings the intrusive event — the voices or phone calls that turn the world upside down — back under an umbrella of normality. Alex's cards serve the same purpose as Godfrey's regenerative revenge on Charmian. The ritual of scientific study and the ritual of marital arm-wrestling restore the identity of "scientist," of "husband" and "wife," and so postpone the fear of losing these identities in the liminal event, the final negative comedy, the jest of death as prank caller. To give in to such a fear would mean the ultimate inversion of the customs and values that had made mortal life credible and moderately comfortable.

Muriel Spark treats satirically the sociological insight that was quoted in Chapter 1: "All social reality is precarious. All societies are constructions in the face of chaos." As Berger and Luckmann observe, "All plans end in extinction. All houses eventually become empty."[42] And the people become empty along with them. When Alex Warner's house burns and all his records in it, he tells Jean of his sense of unreality: "He felt, sometimes, he said once, that he was really dead, since his records had ceased to exist" (222). Ironically, some of his records still do exist in his head, and even after his stroke he recites the terminal diseases of his friends: "Godfrey Colston, hypostatic pneumonia; Charmian Colston, uraemia; Jean Taylor, myocardial degeneration. . . ." (224). The macabre proof — according to his own stated equation — that he himself still exists is the card index he still carries in his head. By the end of the novel, the fact that had once seemed to be the alarming unreality, the fact and approach of death, has emerged as the simple reality of Jean Taylor's meditations; in contrast, her former lover, Alex, meditates not on death but on his scientific life-metaphors for it, the scientifically precise names of diseases. A sort of caricature of Alex's lifework fills his head ironically, grotesquely. "Life," as a file of mocking data, is now the jesting intruder.

The Ballad of Peckham Rye

In Spark's next book, *The Ballad of Peckham Rye* (1960), the voice of the telephone prankster, the jester who overturns the customary if shabby comforts of ordinary life, is visibly and more fully characterized. Dougal Douglas, hired ostensibly to overhaul the morale of factory workers, holds a position in this novel's structure similar to that held by the telephone voice that warned of death. As symbols, the two jesters have almost opposite meanings, however. Both characters try to give people a new "vision" — Dougal's word — and both cause considerable distress among people reluctant to accept this vision. But Dougal, more than the disembodied voice of conscience or allegorical figure of death, belongs to a comic tradition of pranksters and pretenders, usually somewhat likeable liars and boasters who, from their status as outsiders, mock the values of the respectable citizens around them; the pretender character is always a great talker and a great actor.[43] Dougal shares many of these typical qualities with Falstaff, for instance, who is also a pretender, who mocks and mimics respectable things like "honor," and who is sometimes, like Dougal, described with devil imagery. Falstaff, like Dougal, is associated with the liminal world of festivity, play-acting, and mocking the rules; but the rules mock back, though much more severely for the banished and dying Falstaff than for Dougal. In Spark's novel, the disruptive comic figure is not finally dismissed, nor is the disruption subsumed by an affirmation of order, as it is in Shakespeare. While the community of Peckham Rye settled back uneasily into its torpor, Dougal travelled, prospered, write "a lot of cockeyed books, and went far in the world."[44]

He went far in Peckham also. He managed to get himself hired to do "research" and improve morale at two competing textile factories in a small London suburb south of the Thames. Dougal's presence in Peckham injures morale, however, and his "human research" consists largely in convincing people that they are tragic victims of life and are therefore entitled to take a cheap revenge on others or on themselves. He easily undercuts their fragile self-confidence, their never-questioned, and therefore never consciously affirmed, values and patterns of behavior. He frequently assumes the manner of a concerned counselor, a priest, or a psychiatrist and encourages people to confess some unhappiness; if they are too numbly bourgeois to have any doubts or grudges, he sees to it that they invent some reason to demoralize themselves.

And he succeeds. Mr. Druce, head of one of the textile firms, learns, from Dougal's solicitous psychological nudgings in a very comic scene, to see himself as a sensitive man whose career has been ruined by a nonsupportive wife (72-76); later he kills his mistress as passionlessly as he had made love to her. The personnel manager, Mr. Weedin, has a nervous breakdown. The absenteeism which Dougal's research was supposed to eliminate increases alarmingly because he tells employees, who are only too willing to see themselves as overworked victims, to take days off. He tells the workhorse Dixie, who is saving money for married life, to take Monday off. "Take Tuesday off as well. Have a holiday" (39). But Dougal is not really advocating holiday, not really urging rest and restoration of the soul.

Dougal's admonitions and counsels are dishonest, unlike the one solemn admonition uttered by the voice on the phone in *Memento Mori*. The voice on the phone was a true and terrible "holiday" voice, a voice that warned of the approaching, quite natural absenteeism from all the responsibilities, jealousies, and the attachments of life. What Dougal offers is a false holiday, a false initiation. A central portion of the action does in fact take place on a holiday — on Midsummer Eve, as Peter Kemp points out.[45] On that evening, Mr. Druce and his mistress Merle Coverdale routinely make love,

Dixie rebukes Humphrey's efforts to do the same, and Dougal play-acts in the ballroom, rowing, fishing, dancing, all with a trashcan lid as his only prop. Almost no insight, no "clarification," arises from this false festivity, however, though such illumination is a part of festive occasions and of festive comedy.[46] Only in the last sentence of the novel is there a brief illumination, and only for Humphrey; driving away with Dixie after their wedding, he observes the Rye "for an instant looking like a cloud of green and gold, the people seeming to ride upon it, as you might say there was another world than this" (160). The clarification of Shakespeare's festive comedy illuminates the orders of this world, political and domestic and psychological, as a part of the surrounding order of a divine creation; further, the community as a whole rejoices in the common vision of unity and harmonious order. Humphrey's brief vision has no such unifying effect. There is no indication of how Humphrey feels when he sees the bright green Rye, or that he even sees what he sees. The citizens of Peckham Rye are hardly visionaries, and Dougal's parodic posing as an awakener of souls results only in disorder, not in the harmonious illuminations which accompany traditional, nonironic festive comedy.

Dougal mocks everyone he approaches in Peckham because its residents are comically and pathetically incapable of the glamorous melodrama which he juxtaposes on their industrialized and trivialized hearts. Most critics see Dougal as essentially a neutral or even a creative figure, a moral catalyst, whose tremendous energy merely goes to waste on people who might have sprung to the occasion of enlightenment.[47] Yet Dougal offers only the clichés of insight and of advice. He is made of phrases, of the kind of phrases he is collecting for use in his ghost-written autobiography of Miss Cheeseman, an actress. When the electrician Trevor Lomas steals Dougal's notebook, he finds phrases like "I thrilled to his touch," "I revelled in my first tragic part," and "We were living a lie" (102-3). Dougal has picked up some of these lines from his acquaintances in Peckham, but he himself does not have a significantly contrasting idiom. He offers such phrases to everyone. He is trying to rewrite a glamorized story of every person's life — not just Miss Cheeseman's life — and then sell the person that story. Dougal seems to have either read or intuited (he claims to be psychic) a book like the one Mr. Druce keeps in his desk, *Marital Relational Psychology*. Even before Mr. Druce shows Dougal the book, Dougal has spoken, imitating a marriage counselor, "There is some question of incompatibility, I should say" (73). And he continues with a soothing, ego-inflating jargon: "You have a nature at once deep and sensitive, Mr. Druce" (74). He does not uncover deep truths about people and then encourage them to make responsible decisions in their future behavior.

If, as Kemp suggests, the excavations of the old convent in Peckham parallel Dougal's psychological excavations,[48] the parallel does not imply the uncovering of truth, but rather, a voyeuristic teasing of denuded lives. Dougal, walking through the tunnel on his way out of town, juggles six shinbones from the excavations. He is as cynically playful with the psychological relics of Peckham's demoralized citizens as he is with the bones of the long-dead nuns. Most of the people to whom he affects to offer "vision" are about as inert as the excavated skeletons and do not resist him. There are a few exceptions, however: Dixie knows that she doesn't like him; the eccentric prophet of the streets old Nelly Mahone eventually refuses to work with him or send him messages mingled with her public prophecies; Trevor, who was always suspicious of Dougal, fights him in the tunnel as Dougal is leaving town. They fight with bones, Dougal beginning by throwing a hipbone at Trevor's head, and Trevor finally using a bone to stab Dougal in the eye. Dougal's resurrection of Peckham is as full of casual contempt as his interest in the excavations; the only wound to his proffered "vision" is delivered by means of a bone.

The vision that Dougal tried to give to people is that life can be "cured" — that reality can be made into literature, into melodramatic autobiography or into a book on marriage — but by his own admission, Dougal's "fatal flaw" is a fear of the proximity of illness. Even a hint of mortality, of the memento mori theme, is an antidote to Dougal's power. He avoids friends when they get a cold, or have a stroke, because Dougal's message is opposite that of the voice on the phone. Instead of waking people up, he tries to lull them into an even murkier complacency then they suffer from already. He peddles a cure for life by encouraging people to turn their lives into fiction, into shoddy melodrama. He is a personification of evil, not of death; the latter can be seen as a human good, and it is presented this way in *Memento Mori*. Although Muriel Spark is not famous for compassion toward her characters, there is a subtle compassion implied in *The Ballad of Peckham Rye*. Inert and petty though the concerns of the community of Peckham are, and helpless as the people are in Dougal's manipulation, their simple, mortal fragility threatens him as much as Trevor's suspicions do. Evil is driven away by the honest presence of disease and frailty, and Dougal's deceiving vision, his eye, is battered with a bone after he so contemptuously juggled the bones of Peckham.

The Bachelors

The people of Peckham belong to each other in a dependable way, and without much passion or interest. No one of them is a Faustus; if this renders them mute and inglorious, it also trivializes Dougal's efforts to seduce them into a belief in their own importance, and reduces him to a ridiculous sort of tempter. In *The Bachelors* (1961), on the other hand, each character is a singularity, a bachelor, an outsider, either by pose or by vocation. They are an eccentric group, and their eccentricities have some of the characteristics common to liminal groups generally. Their lives do not correspond to the usual patterns, especially the basic domestic ones: they are all unmarried. Some are celibate, some homosexual, and some maintain relationships outside the usual social and religious blessings. Like most outsiders, they are critical of established structures; the medium and crook Patrick Seton is scornful of nondreamers and nonvisionaries, and the homosexual Father Socket prides himself on the fact that he was ordained, not by human hands, but by fire and the Holy Spirit. The daily routines of bachelors are counter to the routines that fit into the normal social roles and sex-linked duties; buying groceries, "these bachelors would set out early, before a quarter past ten, in order to avoid being jostled by the women, the legitimate shoppers."[49]

Most of the bachelors have some characteristic that puts them on the outside of easily identifiable and "legitimate" categories. The epileptic Ronald Bridges, a handwriting expert who gives evidence against Patrick Seton in a fraud case, makes the point for all bachelors, though his situation is a particularly poignant one. When he refuses an offer of casual lovemaking, the woman accuses him:

> "You think I'm not good enough for you," she said. "Not your class."
>
> "I'm an epileptic," he said. "It rather puts one out of the reach of class." (186)

All of the bachelors are outside the reach of "class" in several senses of the word. Elsie is not "good enough" for Ronald; she has only reluctantly returned the stolen letter to him, a letter that he was analyzing and which is important evidence against Seton. Elsie had hoped to get a little sex from Ronald in exchange for the letter. The other bachelors are, like Ronald, far from the mean of any given definition of character or behavior. They are not "good enough" for society; they are beyond "class," because they have a class of their own.

Some of them are extremely far beyond. Patrick Seton, a medium of real ability, goes from one crime to the next, each one an exercise of his idealistic greed, or his dreamy, destructively sentimental ego. Now that his diabetic girlfriend, Alice Dawes, is pregnant and urging marriage, Patrick pursues his inspired plan to give her an overdose of insulin, and so release her ethereal spirit from the body that Patrick perceives as dragging her earthward. Alice, completely oblivious of his sinister qualities, is saved, much against her will, when Seton is convicted on fraudulent conversion charges; she marries another bachelor, the journalist Matthew Finch, who is alone among the singles in really wanting to lose his bachelor identity. The other sinister bachelors are Father Socket and his lover, Mike Garland, who run a pornographic cinema, with real girls as follow-up entertainment.

The bachelorhood of Spark's characters in the novel has been seen as "a territory of damnation."[50] The isolation among these people, notes Alan Kennedy, is an expression of a false, heretical dualism of body and spirit, an idea most clearly enunciated by Seton, the spiritualist, who prefers his dreamy egotism to the encumbering flesh; the subject of the book is "bachelorism of the spirit, or dualism."[51] Since Ronald's conduct is honest and generous, it is not the *state* of bachelorhood that is heretical or blameworthy or damaging to one's humanity. While working on the book, Spark said, "I wrote a book about bachelors and it seemed to me that everyone was a bachelor."[52] If everyone is a bachelor, even those who are not, then the word is being used metaphorically to indicate some basic condition, or perhaps opportunity, arising from the fact of being human.

Bachelorhood for Ronald Bridges is linked ironically but sturdily to a calling — to what he thought was his calling to the priesthood. When his attacks begin, he learns that epileptics are barred from becoming priests, and he considers also that many other professions are now no longer open to him. He and an old priest have an uncomfortably humorous exchange about this:

> "You were never meant to be a first-rate careerist."
> "Only a first-rate epileptic?"
> "Indeed, yes. Quite seriously, yes," the old priest said. (7)

Restated in the light of the basic metaphor of the book, everyone in it is "meant to be" a "first-rate" bachelor. Bachelorhood is the condition of being special and separate and alone, and this condition is rooted in the imperfections of human existence; theologically perceived, all the bachelors (i.e., all human beings) have a "Falling Sickness," which God is the "vigilant manipulator of," as Ronald perceives (121-22). The idea of a fallen world, a world which then gives people both individuality and aloneness, is implied ironically by the many pseudo-idyllic garden images in the names of the characters: Elsie Forrest, Mike Garland, Freda Flower, and perhaps Matthew Finch and Alice Dawes — a couple of birds who eventually become lovebirds, since they marry. The vicious weed in the garden is of course Seton (maybe "Satan"), whom Elsie calls "that little weed" (179). Bachelorhood means, as it must to everyone in a mortal and imperfect world, a "calling" to become a "first-rate" individual capable of forming honest and affectionate "bridges" to other people — as Ronald Bridges manages to do.[53] He is indeed a priest, a "pontiff" (literally "bridge-maker").

Everyone in *The Bachelors* is a soul cast out of Eden and into history. Ronald, after the trial, muses upon the "fruitless souls" of his acquaintances who, like himself, sometimes seem to belong merely to "demonology." Their criminal or helpless or merely frenetic separateness provides him with meditative material, producing "indifference or amusement or wonder." His meditations describe the condition of a fallen world. "It is all demonology and to do with creatures of the air, and there are others besides ourselves, he thought, who lie in their beds like happy countries that have no history" (240). Suffering from the falling sickness of a fallen world, Ronald and each of his bachelor acquaintances do indeed have a "history." They have entered history, and life itself is being defined as ordeal, as trial, as an extended liminal process, a transition rite, a passage or bridge between Eden and death, between God and God again. History, bachelorhood, an anguished singleness that must seek out others and bear fruit, is the ordeal and test for everyone in the novel — not just for Seton, who is in fact brought to trial and convicted.

Ronald in all his actions is fruitful, giving, generous; he reserves his mockery of his friends for his own private thoughts, and even there he counters his "demonology" by enumerating the good qualities as well. For instance, at a party given by Isobel, the mistress of Martin Bowles, Ronald tries to take the frivolous event in stride, but its triviality becomes worse than boring when the guests begin to look like "automatic animals": "Isobel's party stormed upon him like a play in which the actors had begun to jump off the stage, so that he was no longer simply the witness of a comfortable satire, but was suddenly surrounded by a company of ridiculous demons" (116). Nevertheless, Ronald can quiet the grimmest visions of his friends by repeating Scripture. The fact that he bothers to counteract his impression is important; he troubles to enumerate to himself the more positive qualities of his friends (121). He rejects, as dehumanizing, their demonic bachelorness and thereby keeps open the possibility of communication with their eccentric, lonely selves. Ronald, mocking himself and others, is still a first-rate epileptic, a first-rate fallen person, and he is amused as well as saddened by this knowledge.

Others are not so fruitful because they are not willing to meet another person; instead, they seek to impose their own singleness, their own image of themselves, on others. Ronald's girlfriend Hildegarde, for instance, wanted to be a mother to him, to protect him, rather than ever fully see him and love him. Ewart Thornton, grammar school teacher, enjoys gossiping by phone to Freda Flower, but doesn't want their relationship to become any more closely connected than a phone call. Freda herself, although Seton has defrauded her by forgery, is excited by him and remembers when he recited to her, "Season of mists and mellow fruitfulness." She tells

Ewart that "it was a deepening experience" (197). Freda's single-ness, her bachelorhood, is a self-reflecting mirror; it is not fruitful because it never shares or gives.

Nor does Seton's egocentric liminality. Of all the bachelors, he most strongly caricatures the revolutionary idealism of a reformist cult that sets itself up in opposition to a stodgy and oppressive con-vention. The "dreamy child" of over-indulgent parents (171), he is still merely a child-bachelor. He is amoral and casually destructive. All his politics and religion are confined to his fuzzy brain as though he were continually in a trance, continually unconscious. His ex-pressed views, however, are parodies of some famous ones; he is amazed, for instance, when an American woman accused him of taking money from her purse because he had been thinking of her, "in his poetic innocence, as a kindred soul to whom money does not matter" (171-72). The prose continues, in a parodic distortion of New Testament ideas and of Christ's assurances to the disciples that separation would endure for only "a little while" (John 16:16-20): "A little while, and he learns from a man that the early Christians shared all their worldly possessions one with the other, and Patrick memorises this lesson and repeats it to all. Another little while, and he has sex relations with a woman, and is upset by all the disgusting details and is eventually carried away into transports" (172). The narrator's mocking recollections of Seton's career incor-porate some of those antihierarchal, reformist ideas that Newman quoted in his sermons; Seton's understanding of a revolutionary ethic, however, is limited to the benefits that might accrue to him if he can get enough followers to enter his dream. Seton is the most separate of all the bachelors, the one most confined to his own head; that is why he is the most destructive.

Ronald Bridges, whose similarity to Seton is there mainly to draw attention to all the contrasts between the two, is the least con-fined and least confining personality among the bachelors. Al-though his epileptic seizures very much resemble Seton's medium-istic trances, Ronald's epilepsy is an illness and symbolic of the general human condition. Ronald certainly does not pursue his ill-ness, whereas Seton actively works to heighten the theatrical ele-ments in his trances, even taking a drug to increase the impressive physiological effects. Ronald's life is a calling; Seton's, like Dou-gal's, is a cliché, a theatrical parody of a creative soul with a vision.

The Prime of Miss Jean Brodie

Miss Jean Brodie is a radically creative soul, but she pursues her vision in a more practical context than Seton does. Unlike Seton, who gathers a lunatic coterie and remains on the fringes of respected institutions, the reformist educator of *The Prime of Miss Jean Brodie* (1962), attempts the real thing: revolutionary action in a limited but potentially powerful arena. By teaching in a traditional school for girls, she differs — as the narrator is careful to observe — from other Edinburgh spinsters. Although the others direct their "war-bereaved" energies into new political ideas or into reform measures in the fields of education and social welfare, they do not attempt such things within the staid conventions that surround Jean Brodie's revolutionary efforts. Endowed with private means, reasonably wealthy fathers, and the spirit of reform, the Edinburgh spinsters are in some ways the Scottish equivalent of the English "daughters of educated men" whom Virginia Woolf admonishes to become "outsiders" as a means of social protest. Jean Brodie, however, is an outsider who steps *inside* and attempts a revolution there. Whether she does so because the conventional institution gives her a challenge, or because it provides a self-protective context, is a question that she herself never faces.

For the ten-year-old girls who become the chosen set of Jean Brodie in 1930, the world of adolescence is turned upside down. The socially recognized ritual of education is always potentially a liminal one, being an extended period between childhood and adulthood and socially an initiation into the roles and values of adult life. For the Brodie set, initiation becomes a much more dangerous and daring ordeal than it normally would be in Edinburgh. Instead of the rules that come with the school, these six girls learn that "safety" is not first, but goodness, truth and beauty.[54] Instead of the usual curriculum that is to prepare them for their exams, they learn history and art from life — from the life, both real and imaginary, of their teacher. Instead of words and dates and sums, their education is to be flesh and fantasy.

Their teacher tells them to eschew "the team spirit," particularly because they are women. In this admonition Jean Brodie's feminism shows its individualistic, noncollective character; she asks the girls to admire the loners Florence Nightingale, Cleopatra, and Helen of Troy (115). The condescending, perhaps contemptuous phrase that Jean Brodie offers to Mr. Lowther by way of explaining Mr. Lloyd's large family, "Roman Catholics, of course" (135), dismisses peremptorily the teams of love, family, and religion. (Jean Brodie is her own religion; she has "elected herself to grace" [160], and she rotates her Sunday attendance among the Protestant churches of Edinburgh.) As usual, she overstates to the point of fanatacism the "insight" and "instinct" which her "prime" has brought to her and which she shares, in her emphatic benevolence, with her girls. Ironically, her ferocious individualism demands a team for its support, as the aspiring peak of a pyramid relies on a base. Miss Brodie denies the team spirit to anyone except the members—the six students—who belong to her team and who define love, truth, and beauty as she defines them.

"Love" is her relationship with Hugh, who died in the war and who receives her tributes of fantasy year after year perpetuating and redesigning his memory according to her recent interests, especially her developing love for the married art master, Teddy Lloyd, and her compensatory sexual attachment to the unmarried singing master, Gordon Lowther. "Truth" is her fantasy, her way of "making patterns with facts" (106), a characteristic which Sandy Stranger much admires. And "beauty" is Giotto. "He is my favourite," she tells her students (18). Her students are impressed by Jean Brodie's cool rebellions and are excited by the discovery that those in authority over them can disagree. When they first learn that the headmistress believes in "Safety First," and Jean Brodie does not, the knowledge is a revelation. "Indeed, to some of them, it was the first time they had realised it was possible for people glued together in grown-up authority to differ at all" (17). By demonstrating this revelation and by living it out before their eyes, Jean Brodie supplies her students with the essential awakening, with the knowledge that social and educational structures and attitudes are merely human constructions, and vulnerable to question and change. Their teacher gives them the invaluable perception that creation is possible, the perception and faith which January Marlow carries away with her from the sinking island: "All things are possible."

The motif—persistent in the earlier novels—of a younger woman both receiving and resisting the powerful influence of an older one appears again in *The Prime of Miss Jean Brodie*. Caroline Rose drowned the large-bosomed Mrs. Hogg and her oppressive "team spirit." In *Robinson*, an ambiguously human-shaped island of moon and pomegranates, of pagan prayers recited by a remembered grandmother, is also "drowned." Yet January retains the faith that all things are possible, just as the narrator of the short story "The Gentile Jewesses" retains the triumphant vision of her grandmother and Miriam crossing the parted Red Sea along with Mrs. Pankhurst. Jean Taylor, sufficiently influenced by Charmian Colston to emulate her in becoming a Catholic, decides, apparently out of both love and jealousy, to betray her confidences. In *The Prime of Miss Jean Brodie* this tension between a mother-mentor and a daughter-student finds its most painful and complex manifestation.

The leader of her special "set," Jean Brodie is sometimes seen as a "Roman matron" (163); she is a kind of godmother to her initiates and even, ironically and fantastically, a "female god," as Nina Auerbach suggests.[55] Miss Brodie sees herself as beyond the important norms, not only in her teaching methods, but in her modes of sexual expression. To her girls, she seems "outside the context of right and wrong" (126). She is outside the context of the usual; the mere earthly mothers "don't have primes," as Sandy and Jenny realize with awe and mirth. "They have sexual intercourse" (25-26). Jean Brodie's famous prime, mocked and ironic as it is, still is creative in a most basic way. The greatest gift from the wealth of her prime that Jean Brodie gives to her favored girls is this notion that the rules can be countered with antirules, that the authorities are plural, that the world is still creatable.

Miss Brodie's manipulative efforts to create the lives of her girls fail, however; her carefully chosen "community" is full of tension and is a parodic image of the mystical body of the Church, Brodie being a caricature of Christ heading a group of spiritual radicals.[56] Her plans fail most drastically where Sandy is concerned. Between them there exists the passionate mentor relationship, described by Daniel Levinson, in which the older person is exemplar and guide. Muriel Spark herself seems to have benefited from such a relationship with a strong teacher; according to Stanford's biography, Spark kept up a correspondence with an influential teacher long after her school days.[57] In the best of these relationships the teacher fosters the dream of the student, the dedication to a lifework, and Jean Brodie does try to cultivate a "vocation" for each of her girls. The calling must be the student's own, however, and this qualification is difficult for the older party in the relationship to accept. According to Levinson, mentoring is much like a love relationship and "is difficult to terminate in a reasonable, civil manner"; it usually ends bitterly.[58] The relationship between Jean Brodie and Sandy Stranger shows the mentoring features of dream-fostering, intense emotion, and rancorous termination.

The relationship is further complicated by insecurities in both women. Both are afraid. Sandy perceives that Miss Brodie thinks of herself as Providence, as the God of Calvin (176), and the student is frightened when she sees Miss Brodie assigning roles to the girls, but Sandy is also afraid of losing her role in the group. She is afraid of psychological tyranny and confinement, but she is equally afraid of losing her place in the privileged set. During a tour of Edinburgh, Sandy, to regain her position, teases the group's official scapegoat, Mary MacGregor, but Sandy is still unable to quell her anxiety:

> Sandy was unable to cope and decided to stride on and be a married lady having an argument with her husband:
> "Well, Colin, it's rather hard on a woman when the lights have fused and there isn't a man in the house."
> "Dearest Sandy, *how* was I to know. . . ." (46)

Why this particular fantasy at this time? Does the daydream about a protective husband who can keep the house well lit quiet Sandy's fear of winding up as a lonely outsider? Her fantasy places her solidly in the conventional world of a marital quarrel, where she can both protest and receive protection.

Later, on the same tour, when the group observes the shabby men lined up to receive the dole, Sandy is again afraid; the line looks like a "dragon's body which had no right to be in the city and yet would not go away and was unslayable" (60). As a relief from her fear, Sandy wants to cry for starving children, or for a street singer or beggar. She shivers, pleads a cold, and goes home. "She wanted at that moment to be warmly at home, outside which even the corporate Brodie set lived in a colder sort of way" (60). On the brink of adolescence, Sandy flees to the security of childhood again. At home she writes another chapter to "the true love story of Miss Jean Brodie" (61).

Sandy's has been a very protected childhood in which her

mother did not allow her to go out alone, as the other girls could, until Sandy was well into her teens. As a consequence, she is uninformed, unsophisticated, and fearful as she learns the astonishing realities: sex, love, desperate outsiders such as people who must accept charity from the government. Her later rebellion against Miss Brodie's intrusive personality perhaps reenacts Sandy's restless relationship with a mother who protected and controlled her too rigidly. The mother and the teacher are alike in some ways. Mrs. Stranger does not conform in manner and dress to the mothers of Sandy's friends. Mrs. Stranger is English; she calls her child "darling" (to Sandy's chagrin) and wears a flashy fur-trimmed coat (27-28). She is an outsider, a stranger, like her daughter and like Miss Brodie.

The outsider Jean Brodie is also afraid, and Sandy probably notices it as early as the Edinburgh tour. Maybe Sandy projects her own feelings when she perceives an inconsistency in her teacher's scornful rejection of the Girl Guides. "Perhaps the Guides were too much a rival fascisti, and Miss Brodie could not bear it," Sandy thinks; she briefly considers joining the Brownies, then rejects the idea, afraid of losing her place in the privileged fascisti, the Brodie group (48). During the tour Miss Brodie has been talking on and on about an upcoming meeting with the disapproving headmistress. Although Miss Brodie appears to be offering reasons for her confidence that she will keep her position, she is overprotesting, arguing at length, while Sandy drifts in and out of daydreams. Jean Brodie admits her vulnerabilities, noting that the education she received at the university was not as good as that of the more recently qualified, and younger, headmistress; Miss Brodie defensively asserts, "But her reasoning power is deficient, and so I have no fears for Monday" (58). No fears? Then why talk about one's lack of fear at such length, and to a specially chosen group of very young people, chosen because they are to be reflectors of herself? Sandy was to have reflected Jean Brodie's power by assuming the role of reporter concerning Rose Stanley's affair with Teddy Lloyd, Miss Brodie's vicarious love affair. Instead, Sandy thwarts Miss Brodie's plan by entering into a brief relationship with Teddy, and then telling the headmistress that the eccentric teacher is an admirer of fascism. The teacher's fears concerning dismissal are made real by her most frightened student, the student who can no longer admire or trust her idol.

Having tea with Miss Brodie after her forced retirement, Sandy looks at the distant hills and sees in them an image of the power the teacher has lost. The hills are "so austere from everlasting that they had never been capable of losing anything by the war" (82). Later in the conversation Sandy again regards the hills, as Miss Brodie's voice whines on about her renunciation of Lloyd, her affair with Lowther, the mysterious betrayal by one of her students. Sandy "was looking at the hills as if to see there the first and unbetrayable Miss Brodie, indifferent to criticism as a crag" (89). Sandy is apparently discouraged to see that her own plans and actions have had such thoroughgoing success.

The frightened Sandy, like the frightened Miss Brodie, wanted to put her faith in something that was unbetrayable; Miss Brodie chose Mussolini, and Sandy chose Miss Brodie. Both chose revolutionary figures, figures of radical disorder, people who were going to remake the world, who were "outside the context of right and wrong." Both the older woman and the younger one, her godchild, had themselves been first nourished, and then "betrayed," by traditional institutions — Jean Brodie by a romantic attachment and the war that destroyed it, Sandy by a restrictive, overprotective mother. Both wanted to control relationships, to have "love" free from the pain of being in love, for neither Jean Brodie nor Sandy share a bed with anyone they love. Jean Brodie is not only a reformist in educational and political matters, but she seems to be trying to revolutionize her heart — to make it run on schedule, with the efficiency of Mussolini's Italy. Her renunciation of Teddy Lloyd is a self-protective excuse rather than an action in response to one of her principles, since she does everything to encourage Rose to participate in the adultery which the instructor "renounces." Miss Brodie chooses "safety first" after all, not the safety of her position in the school primarily (though she does not want to lose this), but the safety of not risking her heart again.

Jean Brodie and Sandy Stranger, hiding behind fantasy, scripted for each other a fictitious, idealized role. They tried, in effect, to see each other — and politics, education, the world — in a "transfigured" light. They attempted a "transfiguration of the commonplace" on each other, and both failed, because — as the narrator and the novel's action suggest — real transfiguration does not intrude, does not tyrannize or impose. Although Miss Brodie professed to *educate* (to "lead out," as she explains, calling her students' attention to the root), she does in practice *intrude*, just as she accuses the headmistress of doing (54-55). By contrast, a sudden epiphanic sunset illuminates and perhaps admonishes, but without "intruding." Walking with Miss Brodie on the beach near Lowther's house, Sandy and her companion Jenny are describing Lloyd's family portrait, his many children "graded downwards to the baby on the floor" in a diagonal line; the sunset provides a sudden illumination for the discussion of the painting:

> "They are all facing square and they all look serious," Sandy said. "You are supposed to laugh at it."
> Miss Brodie laughed a little at this. There was a wonderful sunset across the distant sky, reflected in the sea, streaked with blood and puffed with avenging purple and gold as if the end of the world had come without intruding on every-day life. (140-41)

The context of this epiphany is important; the painful and avenging sunset, and the metaphorical analogy ("as if"), carefully hedge and frame a statement of ultimate judgment on even the most ordinary and comfortable institutions of everyday life, even on marrying and giving in marriage. But the laughter of Miss Brodie and her students is judged also. An ultimate perspective silently gazes into the action of the novel, an ultimate revolution, a "new plot" more radical than the one Woolf's Isa was hoping for, and yet the sunset with all its frightening splendor does not violate the everyday life that it transforms.

Human efforts at transfiguration, however, tend to impose the will of the person who attempts the transfiguring. The attacker and reformer of institutions confuses the fictional world of possibility with the factual one that exists, confuses a mere "economy," or parable, for the truth it represents. Although Sandy, as Sister Helena, writes a treatise on ethics called "The Transfiguration of the Commonplace" and may have argued in that book that such a visionary view of things is good (we aren't given any selections from her book), she herself suffered, at the hands of Miss Brodie, from too much transfiguration. She became for several years a nervous but obedient fiction contrived by her teacher. Although some critics perceive Sandy as having sorted out fact and fiction while Miss Brodie confuses the two, others argue — more convincingly I believe — that Sandy remains almost as deluded by fiction as Jean Brodie is.[59] Protected, frightened, Sandy clings to Jean Brodie and the team as a vision of secure daring, an image of defiance and change which would "lead" Sandy away from her fear and the ambiguously comfortable security of her childhood. When Jean Brodie becomes as suffocating as Sandy's mother, Sandy destroys the teacher's own illusory, fear-concealing defiance, and in so doing assumes the mantle. Sandy takes a daring if defensive woman's vision and puts it back in the closet. The narrator quietly steps in to assert that Sandy has "tiny eyes, which it was astonishing that anyone could trust" (147); this untrustworthy Sandy becomes a nun and writes a book. She is again confined, unable to go out, as she was confined as a child. Behind the grill of the cloister, she has the safe fame of admirers, of impressed pilgrims who come to see her, curious about her and her past. We do not hear them asking questions about the book's content, but about Sandy (Sister Helena) and about the important influences during her school days. Her response is, "There was a Miss Jean Brodie in her prime" (187).

Sandy acts on the principle of "economy" in betraying Miss Brodie (149). This concept is essentially a positive one when understood as a description of Muriel Spark's own fictive method, her use of parable. But Sandy's understanding of "economy" is much less subtle and much more crass, more thrifty and restricted. She admires the economy of Teddy Lloyd's method of painting (149, 183), a method which changes his subject, by "a magical transfiguration," into Miss Brodie; members of the Brodie set become another portrait of Jean Brodie (162). Such a transfiguration is an obsessive mockery of the transfiguring presence of red and gold light filling sky and water while Miss Brodie and the two girls walked on the beach.

We are never assured that Sandy's vocation is a real transfiguration for her; it may be a parodic one. Sandy did not want her mother to play Providence; she did not want Jean Brodie to do so; she strains in her cloistered interviews, as if she chafes while the Catholic Church plays Providence or — a more cruel possibility — while her own misapprehended vocation plays her a false Providence. On the other hand, Sandy's religious vocation may be her real one, and the tension in her manner may be the remnant of the guilt and anguish that accompanied her rejection of her mentor, a painful but utterly necessary act. No mentor, no mother, no political leader, has a right to play Providence; in the novels of Spark, only Providence plays Providence. All other players are mocked.

The Girls of Slender Means

The mockery in *The Girls of Slender Means* (1963) recalls that of *The Ballad of Peckham Rye* in some respects, for there is almost no interiorization of character in either work. The later book also looks forward to Spark's last eight novels—those beginning with *The Public Image*—in which characterization is extremely light, mere watercolor and ink. There is in *The Girls of Slender Means* the convert character typical of the earlier novels, but he is kept at a distance, while the working girls of slender means and slender souls, the girls of the residential May of Teck Club, are the dominating presences. Nicholas Farringdon, the convert and later a "martyr," begins as an anarchist who is trying to publish his miscellaneous political treatise called *The Sabbath Notebooks*. There he affirms that the modern anarchist must use ridicule instead of bombs.[60] Nicholas does not take his own advice, however; he is very serious and idealistic. In the mingled chronology of the novel, he falls in love with Selina during the 1945 sections and tries to convert her to his politics by sleeping with her; these sections are juxtaposed on those dealing with Jane's later efforts to put together a story about Nicholas's martyrdom in Haiti. In the context of Jane's research, the narrator, and Jane herself, provide the events between V-E Day and V-J Day, events which include the explosion of a bomb buried in the garden of the May of Teck. As the building burns, the trapped girls who are slender enough to do so escape through the bathroom window, and the heavier ones are rescued, except for Joanna Childe; the last one to grasp the escape ladder, she goes down with the collapsing house.

The cruel story is an expanded joke, a pun on the meanings of *slender*. The foolish idealizer of women and politics Nicholas Farringdon turns to Catholicism and the priesthood when he sees the slender quality of his girlfriend's humanity. Her slender hips allow Selina to slip through a narrow window and go back into the flaming house, past the sweating, as yet unrescued heavier girls; she plucks the Schiaparelli dress from the burning, and Nicholas takes her action as a symbol of the fragility of human goodness generally; he crosses himself as he observes this act of savagery.

Nicholas had been in love with all the girls collectively, as an ideal society of communal sharing and poverty (76), but he fastened his own fuzzy Utopian dreams especially on the poised and slender Selina (who recited twice a day two sentences about maintaining poise). An anarchist whom the anarchists would not accept, a pacifist who decided after all to fight in the war, he hovered socially among writers, potential publishers, and the girls of the May of Teck. When he and Selina became lovers, his own revolutionary conceptions were so slender that he perceived in the thrifty gracefulness of her body a symbol of his Utopian vision. There is subtle comedy in the scene in which he attempts, through passionate lovemaking, to infuse his politics into her body and mind: "It was not the first instance of a man taking a girl to bed with the aim of converting her soul, but he, in great exasperation, felt it was, and poignantly, in bed, willed and willed the awakening of her social conscience. After which, he sighed softly into his pillow with a limp sense of achievement" (112-13). When he looks at her, however, he realizes that "her austere and economically furnished" body (113) is as poised as ever, and her heart is as untouched by his love as her mind is by his vision. If Joanna, in Nicholas's view, substitutes for sex the recitation of poetry, Nicholas as surely substitutes passionate and greedy sex for significant political action. His ambition to turn Selina into his own daydream is equivalent to that of the vaguely political and reformist Jean Brodie, who hoped to perform such a transformation on her chosen girls.

Although Nicholas is intellectually sensitive to moral and political issues, he is completely egotistical—in 1945, at least. He is a man so proud of his own sensitive heart and intellect that he will not condescend to discuss new poets with women; he and a companion can sit and talk of anarchism, while two May of Teck girls must just admire. The men "were bored with educating the girls for this evening" (19-20). When he is invited to the May of Teck for the second time, another guest rises in courtesy whenever the girls get up to serve and remove food from the table; however, "Nicholas lolled like an Englishman possessed of droits du seigneur while the two girls served him" (84). He refuses to indulge in mere social amenity or in the humanity of conversing with stupid people. He makes an exception of Selina because he is inspired to use his more romantic methods of communication with her. He seeks discussion by means of passion, conversion by means of orgasm.

Though his means are different, morally Nicholas is like the girls; he too is a child of slender means. We have some evidence that he uses the same visionary egotism as a priest in Haiti that he had used in trying to convert Selina's soul. As a convert, he seems to have transferred his greedy love to God and to have spared little of it for misguided human beings. One of Jane's contacts says: "From what I can gather, the man was making a complete nuisance of himself, preaching against the local superstitions. He had several warnings and apparently he got what he asked for" (143). This report—and it is only circumstantial evidence—would not mean that the "martyr" Nicholas was a fraud; it would indicate merely that he carried with him into his new faith a characteristic failure to perceive that other people have interests, no matter how paltry or misguided, of their own. He dies a priest, but a priest of slender means.

The very slenderest soul, however, belongs to the chubby Jane Wright. It is the unattractive Jane whose image Nicholas retains as emblematic "of all the May of Teck establishment in its meek, unselfconscious attitudes of poverty, long ago in 1945" (176). It is Jane Wright ("maker" and "worker," "writer," and perhaps "right"—all in an ironic sense) whose information-gathering about Nicholas provides one-half of the book's structure; the counter-pointing half is the chronology of events between May and August 1945. Jane sees people as stories for a newspaper, as data, and in this she is a little like Alex Warner in *Memento Mori;* like Godfrey Colston in the same novel, she gains renewed vitality from corruption. When Nicholas asks her to prepare a fake letter that will praise his book as "a work of genius," Jane, who had been feeling gloomy and tearful, experiences a regeneration. "Jane's life began to sprout once more, green with possibility. She recalled that she was only twenty-three, and smiled" (119-20). Although Selina's poise is more famous among her friends, Jane possesses an unforced, unthinking animalistic poise. Selina returns for the Schiaparelli dress, but Jane, after the explosion, runs into her room and with animal instinct gulps a chocolate bar (145). Her "means," her moral capacities, are even more slender than Selina's, if lack of reflection is a criterion. Selina has established a ritual for maintaining poise, as though she felt the necessity for seeming calm in situations that would threaten her equanimity. She tries for poise, loses it finally, and screams (when Nicholas visits her after the fire). Jane thrives on gossip and chocolate, weeps readily, and selfishly, revives easily, and does not need to practice anything so fancy as poise.

The novel ends with a picture of Jane. Nicholas and she have gone to Buckingham Palace, along with the huge pressing crowds, to celebrate V-J Day. Here Nicholas, alone of all the crowd, sees a sailor idly stab a woman, no one else in the congestion being aware of the murder. This act is the second vision of savagery which Nicholas observes (the first being Selina's rescue of the expensive dress); it is the final trigger to his conversion, for he takes Jane's fake letter from his pocket and thrusts it into the murderer's shirt, a gesture that rejects lies and perhaps the slenderness of his own past illusions. As Nicholas and Jane move away from the crowd, she stops to replace a hairpin, and he marvels at her calm self-possession. She stands, "sturdy and barelegged on the dark grass, occupied with her hair" (176). Jane, heavy and unreflective, associated with vegetable and animal imagery, possesses a sensitivity too slight, too slender even for the screaming that shakes Selina's carefully cultivated poise.

The Girls of Slender Means is a comic fugue on the theme of moral and political slenderness. The massive celebrations of victory which occur in the first and last chapters of the book are ironic affirmations of order. The crowds applaud the waving royal family, but the huge masses of people seem to be celebrating disorder instead of order, even indulging in casual murder. Both celebrations are sinister, disorderly festivities, liminal occasions during which the rules are abandoned. An older resident of the May of Teck comments on the festival nature of the first celebration; she says the V-E Day event "was something between a wedding and a funeral on a world scale" (16). It is the end of a war and of a world. The two celebrations envelope, embrace, the end of the smaller world of the May of Teck Club, the world of Nicholas Farringdon's facile Utopianism, and the world of Joanna's passionate recitations. As world and house and ideals collapse, there is a counterpointing of ironies. On the one hand, it is ironic that Nicholas Farringdon's slender, poetic, political ideal is betrayed by its own slenderness (and by Selina's trim figure, which allows her to rescue the dress and so shock him into Catholicism). Considered in this light, the exploding bomb and succeeding fire are psychologically shattering, apocalyptic. On the other hand, a deeper irony lies in the fact that such an apocalypse—like the fiercely vivid sunset in *The Prime of Miss Jean Brodie*—can pass "without intruding on every-day life." Certainly the fire scarcely intrudes on the life of Jane Wright as she replaces a hairpin during a casually savage festivity.

The Mandelbaum Gate

Unlike *The Girls of Slender Means*, which foreshadows the more thinly textured satire of Spark's later novels and their more withdrawn narrators, *The Mandelbaum Gate* (1965) gives a fuller treatment of the convert character than any of the earlier novels supplied. The liminality in this eighth novel is again that of a life-crisis transition, and the imagery of quest appears, but this imagery is teased and mocked at every step, especially the elements of its pattern that are linked to the stereotypes of sex roles. Barbara Vaughan is a complex character who is much preoccupied with her identity; her preoccupation suggests a movement away from identity as a mere habit, to identity that questions psychological and social habits.

Barbara's life is in some ways fairly conventional: she is a teacher in a girl's school, she becomes a Catholic, she marries in her thirties, and she has a daughter. Into this unadventurous thread, however, is woven a spectacular braid of shining mockery. The book is a departure from Spark's typically more stringent style, and has been seen by some as a failure. One critic can even see in the Catholicism of the hero a reminiscence of Waugh's *Brideshead Revisited*.[61] The heavy and sentimentalized Catholic iconography of Waugh's novel, however, has no counterpart in *The Mandelbaum Gate*, and there is no attempt to clutch at the reader's heart with gilded Catholic imagery. Barbara's religious musings are more intellectual than emotional, and her dangerous and hilarious quest mocks everything in its path: the chivalry of the Western male, a spinster's sexual awakening, political earnestness, the "professional victim." *The Mandelbaum Gate* is not Muriel Spark's *Brideshead*

Revisited; it is her *Orlando* — a fiction of "everything mocked," as Virginia Woolf said of her book.

The historical context, Jerusalem during the Eichmann trial in 1961, provides a clash of cultures and countercultures of several kinds, and Spark turns this ambience of political, personal, and sexual insecurities into comedy. All the important characters are outsiders, strangers, and they treat the various insider social and political structures to mockery, lies, disguise, and subterfuge. Spark exploits the comedy latent in an area of the world where one culture — an English culture, or an Israeli culture, or an Arab culture — is continually under attack, verbally and militarily, by an opposing counter culture. All of the prominent characters in *The Mandelbaum Gate* seem to have read *The Sabbath Notebooks* of the anarchist Nicholas Farringdon, and the chief mode of attack is ridicule, not bombs. This ridicule, and the other elements of festive liminality, are most apparent in the communal flyting that occurs at the makeshift coffeehouse and tavern located in the cellar of a laundry in Acre. Here college students and teenagers of many races, though they are mostly Jews and Arabs, meet to sing, dance, and partake of varied narcotics.There is a strong communal feeling, blurred ethnic identity, and no social hierarchy; it is a festivity of equals. Among these is Abdul Ramdez, an Arab who is dedicated to making an interesting and profitable life for himself instead of supporting a political cause. He and his emancipated sister Suzi have "a pact of personal anarchism" (111), and Abdul is "deeply bored" by the duty held out to every Palestinian Arab — that of "becoming a professional victim" (115). At the party-cellar in Acre, he and his Israeli friend, Mendel Ephraim, launch into their popular chant called the "Song of Freedom." They chant phrase after phrase of mockery at the heroic slaughters carried out by their two peoples throughout the centuries; all these things are past and merely "dead history," they say. One of them praises both Allah and the God of Israel: "It's all a long time ago. Great is the God of Israel! Mighty is Allah! We dance and sing and make love with each other, it is better than all that religion and hatred all the day long" (129-30). The scene itself, and the thrust of the mock chanting, are analogous, in the structure of the novel, to the scenes in the East-cheap tavern in the King Henry IV plays, where nothing but fun is

made of the political matters taken with life-and-death seriousness
by the leaders of the contending factions. Both the plays and the
novel indulge, in these scenes, a license that mocks the norm. Stead-
ier values of order and honor are again reasserted at the end of each
history play; but Middle Eastern politics, unresolved in the novel
and in history as yet, provide a context of sustained disorder, sustained transition, through which the major characters — the "passionate pilgrims," as a chapter title calls them — pursue their own
difficult, hilarious, and uncertain quests.

On her own pilgrim's progress, Barbara Vaughn questions herself about love and identity, her past and her future, while she takes
sight-seeing excursions through symbolic landscapes, through
"holy land" psychologically and politically. A Catholic convert whose
mother was Jewish, a spinster schoolteacher whose lover, Harry
Clegg, is an archeologist digging in the area of the Dead Sea scrolls,
Barbara hovers in disunity and contradictions while she and Harry
await the Church's decision on the annulment of Harry's previous
marriage. The prognosis is not hopeful, and Barbara decides she will
marry him whether or not he gets the annulment, her decision thus
leaving her future identity open to continuing painful irresolution,
since she would be unable to practice the faith that she believes.

The contradictions of psychological transition express themselves in the classic comic devices which have their counterparts in
liminal rituals. Barbara leaves the safety of Israeli Jerusalem and
crosses into the "darker" side of politics and of self by entering the
Jordanian side. Motifs of disguise, inversion, and confused or
blurred sex identity accompany her journey. Her casual acquaintance Freddy Hamilton, with the British diplomatic service, decides
that she is in danger and so "rescues" her by night from the convent where she is staying. The next day she becomes a servant of
her servant, in a sense, because she wears an all-covering voluminous Moslem garb and pretends to be the mute servant of Suzi
Ramdez, Barbara's guide and chauffeur among the shrines of the
Jordanian sector. Barbara's comically mistaken identity reflects
ironically on more painful circumstances when her former teaching
colleague Miss Rickward accosts the Arab Barbara at the Holy Sep-
ulchre and asks her to decipher an Arabic address. The jealous
"Ricky" is in hot pursuit of Barbara in order to prevent her marriage. Disguise, intrigue, lies, and flight surround Barabra's so-

journ, along with surprising sexual alliances, and revelations about old friends. The more farcical quests of Freddy and Ricky cross and recross Barbara's pilgrimage, especially in a combination brothel-spy station in Jericho where Barbara recovers from scarlet fever. Everyone in the establishment is led to believe that she is a prostitute. Here the repressed Freddy sleeps with Suzi (probably because she looks like her brother, Abdul), and Ricky recites Islamic poetry as Ramdez senior seduces her.

The comic chaos of roles and disguises symbolically suggests the multifaceted possibilities for renewal, for shattering the habit of former identities and former political structures and moving toward new ones. It prepares too for the benign conclusion which arises, not from finding one's true identity, but from finding a perfectly adequate false one. Disorder triumphs in the Barbara Vaughan plot; order is not restored, but disorder is falsely perceived as order. Ricky forges a birth certificate for Harry which asserts that he was baptized a Catholic. (In the real certificate, which she found, he was baptized a Methodist.) She assumes that her forgery will prevent Harry and Barbara from marrying, but in fact it smoothes the way. Harry's previous marriage—a Protestant one—is not one that the Catholic Church can recognize if Harry was a Catholic at the time (whether he knew it or not). The misguided Ricky thus ironically fosters the marriage that she so vehemently opposed.

Likewise, Freddy Hamilton's quest ends on a pleasantly false note. It also begins on one, as his burst of chivalry toward Barbara is lightly mocked, and his behavior generally while he is in Jordanian territory is taunted by the narrator's benignly judging diction. He and his friend Alexandros, an Arab merchant, plot the great rescue of Barbara: "Freddy's had been the idea of getting her up in Arab disguise, while Alexandros, his hand clapped suddenly to his brow to hold intact the brimming tide of inspiration, had contributed the Ramdez daughter as her best possible escort" (173). The narrator is amused at the solemn concentration of the two heros, as they seek to intervene on behalf of a threatened woman. Freddy's departure from the convent, with Barbara's baggage, is also comic: "He lifted the case, whispered, 'We're off!' and opened the door. He whispered again, 'Not a whisper,' and stopped to listen lest anyone in the house had been aroused" (177). Again, the diction is amused, emphasizing the excited Freddy's whispers prohibiting whispering. Nevertheless, it is a big night for Freddy. His heroic impulse to rescue Barbara has been fortified by his decision to dispose of his letters to his mother, her servant, and a doctor. He turns his back on his dominating mother's problems and even the threat to her life; he flushes the letters away at the merchant's house. He later learns, however, that the servant attacked and killed his mother; he recovers from what might be some qualms of shrugged responsibility, and in later years remembers his Middle Eastern adventure as having made "a free man of him" (166).

Freddy takes leave of his identity for a few days, as he suffers amnesia after travelling, spying, and lovemaking on the Jordanian side. Gradually the incidents return "like a cloud of unknowing"; the experience "seemed to transfigure his life, without any disastrous change in the appearance of things" (165). The metaphor from the title of the anonymous medieval mystical work *The Cloud of Unknowing* implies that Freddy has moved safely close to some ultimate understanding of himself, without clearly seeing it. His transfiguration has occurred benignly; the end of his former world has arrived, like the ominously unobtrusive sunset in *The Prime of Miss Jean Brodie*, without shattering him entirely as a human being. The narrator suggests that Freddy may have gained his self-confidence by falsely interpreting — to his own best advantage — his Middle Eastern crisis; nevertheless, he feels like a new person. "And whether this feeling of Freddy's subsequent years was justified or not, it did him good to harbour it" (166). Freddy is a comic character whom Spark, for once, decides not to prosecute. She lets him bumble his way to redemption instead of to damnation.

As Barbara says, on learning that Harry has obtained the annulment, "With God, everything is possible" (296). Even lies, even a "mistaken" identity, can work toward one's regeneration. The comic ironies of this novel imply that order and truth — the world's order and truth — are sometimes mocked and even overtaken by beneficent falsehood. There need not be a general unmasking at the end of the action. Occasionally the liminal world itself continues into the common one; holiday continues into the everyday to constitute "the full irrational norm."

The Mandelbaum Gate is often taken too seriously by critics who then criticize it for not being serious enough. Its more or less realistic, fully detailed, descriptions and characterizations mislead reviewers into expecting a general realism, and they must then express disappointment at the quite fantastic and coincidental turns in the plot and in the characters' decisions as well.[62] Or, Barbara's offhand attitude toward love and sex offends a critic who assumes the book is a love story.[63] Indeed, Barbara's attitudes about sex and love violate the serious romantic norm of literature and life. Her religious faith, she tells Suzi, "penetrates everything in life," including sex, which "is child's play in the argument" (344). Barbara does not perceive herself as a lover any more than she accepted the image of spinster earlier. In her words, "Every spinster should be assumed guilty before she is proved innocent, it is only common civility" (179). Barbara separates sex from the usual Western context of the grand passion, from the Laurentian mysticism of the flesh, from the sentimentality of high seriousness. Her friend Suzi Ramdez agrees: "I see what you say of the child's play is true. I hate the man in bed who plays at it like he conducts the military band for King Hussein to review the soldiers" (344). In contrast to Suzi and Barbara, Miss Rickward takes sex with a high solemnity which is mocked whenever the narrator, and Suzi, have a chance. On her mission to locate Barbara and prevent her marriage, Ricky unknowingly winds up in the same Jericho house where Barbara is recovering from scarlet fever. Informed by the aging Joe Ramdez, her "travel agent" (who is also a spy), that he and she will sleep in the same bed, Ricky recites Islamic poetry, and Joe exclaims, "My rose of Islam!" and, "Well of sweet waters!" (299). His daughter Suzi hears a sound like cats that night and tells Freddy the next day, in her unidiomatic English, that Ramdez "unflowered and nearly killed" Ricky; Suzi is convulsed with laughter at Ricky's request for a cushion as they begin a sight-seeing drive (314-16). In some ways Ricky is another version of Mrs. Hogg, Robinson, and Jean Brodie, but Ricky is thoroughly overthrown by ridicule, whereas Jean Brodie retains a shred of sad dignity. Barbara, the younger woman whom the older tried to control, carries no anxious vestige of the dominating woman in her heart, unlike the troubled nun Sister Helena.

Ricky's painful and comic transition into nonvirginity, like her subsequent transition into marriage (with Joe Ramdez) and into the Islamic religion, echoes the comedy and anguish in a novel of transitions, some political, some personal. Individuals, nations, and cultures of the Middle East are all passing through gates, as Barbara passed through the Mandelbaum Gate into Arab Jerusalem. The motifs of comedy and the motifs of social protest or political sabotage are both rooted in the creative disorder of liminality, of transition rituals. For this reason, both comedy and social revolution are close to danger. In *The Mandelbaum Gate* Spark overbalances the danger with a more generous portion of benign comedy than is her custom.

5

Muriel Spark: Takeovers

Not until *The Takeover* do we find anything like the good cheer of *The Mandelbaum Gate*, and never, in Sparks's last eight novels, is a character again interiorized as fully as Barbara Vaughan is. Instead of the motifs of initiation, so often present in Spark's use of the convert character, the social motifs of liminality appear. The inverted values of festivity, or of social and economic sabotage, become the moving forces behind the comedy. Often both festivity and social attack occur at once; a countercultural group will fiddle while Rome burns. For instance, the media artists, the mod servants, celebrate the aristocratic family's inevitable demise in *Not To Disturb*. Instead of the quest, the major narrative metaphor becomes the party, the holiday, the celebration of an overthrow. Parties are scattered throughout the later novels; there is much dancing and dining, while the burglary, murder, suicide, or "takeover" is completed. In the earlier novels an individual, or several people as foils or parallels, searched for identity. In the last seven novels, society is searching for identity, and the mockery is as radical politically as it is ethically and psychologically.

Spark has said that those who, like herself, grew up in the primitive landscape of Edinburgh's castle and crag, generally viewed the Whitehall government "as just a bit ridiculous"; she imbibed from Edinburgh "its haughty and remote anarchism." She draws the following conclusion; "I can never now suffer from a shattered faith in politics and politicians, because I never had any."[1] Never had any? This is going a large step further than merely arguing that Hitler's oppressive politics should be ridiculed. A tone of haughty and remote anarchism could well describe Spark's narrative voice in its distant and somberly satiric moments. In her fiction, and especially in her later novels, all comedy aspires to the condition of satire. That is, she strives in her work for the "desegregation of art," for the strictly unsympathetic mocking of "tyrannies" and of the "ridiculous oppressions of our time." In a speech delivered in 1970, she argued that if art solicits sympathy for the victim, it then segregates us from reality, cheats and lulls us into catharsis instead of spurring us to real knowledge and action. Well-aimed ridicule, she insists, is likely to leave "a salutary scar."[2] That assertion has the true satirist's boast and bite. Such an aim requires remoteness, an elimination of any positive concern for a character, and indeed Spark sometimes withdraws from her characters; she abandons them, like the Old Testament God giving creation over to the Flood.

Characterization in the last eight novels usually gives us only stick-figure representations, but very effective ones for the author's satiric purposes. Like parodic pegs, the characters move about on a map as indicators of the latest protest, the latest economic intrigue, or the latest ideological excitement. In the later novels Dougal Douglas becomes legion, and not always devilish, as the outsiders move inside, the servants, nuns, or religious crazies—all backed by the media—surge over the weakened traditional values. The antic inversions of "normal" order spill beyond season and taboo, and begin to threaten, or merge into, the deteriorating fabric of the political and economic structures.

The Public Image

The Public Image (1968) suggests in its title the thin-textured mask that passes for identity among the characters of the later novels. In the worlds of social and political manipulation inhabited by such characters, the public image becomes extremely important. And yet a projected image, a mere role, need not be destructive to oneself or to others; it can serve to explore new and possibly better ways of behaving.[3] The danger lies in accepting one's public image as the only one. Particularly in *The Public Image* and in *The Driver's Seat* (1970), the main characters accept too thoroughly, and without question, the socially available stereotypes of themselves. Unlike Barbara Vaughan, who knows that her straight-laced appearance does not conform to her real and changing self,

Spark's most desperate and defeated characters have taken to heart some public image, some cultural stereotype of themselves. As a result, they undertake completely parodic, cardboard quests. The various clichés projected by the media, and by a culture's expectations about people, become the people; it is as though the several vocations which Miss Jean Brodie tries to impose on her girls actually become the girls. A facile and brittle public image becomes dangerous — and desperately comic — only when it becomes private as well.

The public image becomes private (sociologists would say it becomes "internalized," believed) for Frederick Christopher; a producer and film-script writer, he begins to take himself seriously as a person of "seriousness," as a good-looking cultured man whose talents are not being encouraged by his wife and by ready opportunities. He is rankled by his wife Annabel's sudden success as a film star, a success due largely to her well-maintained public image. To her audiences, she is an erotic "Tiger Lady," though she is a fairly simple Englishwoman whose attractive body and minimal acting skills have given her a respected place among Rome's actors, journalists, and film-makers. Frederick, unlike Annabel, is much more addicted to his part in their combined public facade: "Frederick found himself rooted deeply and with serious interest in a living part such as many multitudes believe exists: a cultured man without a temperament, studious, sportsmanlike, aristocratic, and a fatherly son of Mother Earth, Annabel's husband."[4] Frederick is taking to heart clichés that are centuries old in the popular culture of Western civilization. "Fatherly son of Mother Earth" is the imagery of "home" for the male psyche, and Frederick has blanketed himself warmly in the media's exploitation of primary socialization. He accepts this norm of immaturity, this "living part such as many multitudes believe exists." Spark's diction is very careful and scary here: Frederick is *living* a part that does not *exist.* He is thus in a horrific condition, for he is "dead" even before he commits his stagey suicide.

Frederick puts together a melodramatic plot — his own manipulative suicide — which will glamorize his despair and take revenge on his wife for having failed, toward him, in her "Mother Earth" role. After inviting a loud, drunken crew to his flat, where they surprise and embarrass his wife with their boisterous partying, Frederick jumps from the scaffolding erected over some excavating work that is being done in caves beneath a church. He plants behind him some carefully written, sentimental, accusatory suicide letters. His purpose is to destroy his wife's public image, and he very nearly succeeds; the story spreads of an "orgy" in progress at the Tiger Lady's house while her loving and sensitive husband leaped to his death.

Annabel should have taken more responsibility for her husband's happiness,[5] as he indeed should have taken more responsibility for hers, but the novel's subject is not the spectacular gossip-column suicide of a man and a marriage. Annabel's Italian public wants very much to perceive the events in this sensational light, but the action of the novel concerns her growing competence in parrying such false images. It is her almost unconscious psychological iconoclasm that eventually liberates her from false images, some public, some domestic. She herself is surprised, for instance, at her own competence in obtaining a flat, and getting it decorated and furnished. This is the first indication of an unspectacular but very important change in Annabel's character. "Maybe I am strong, she had thought, when she arranged, all on her own, to buy a flat" (40). Her stupidity, which her husband has always been ready to reinforce, begins to disappear, or at least to become less significant, once her film career becomes successful:

> In those early days when she was working in small parts her stupidity started to melt; she had not in the least attempted to overcome her stupidity, but she now saw, with the confidence of practice in her film roles, that she had somehow circumvented it. She did not need to be clever, she only had to exist; she did not need to perform, she only had to be there in front of the cameras. (10)

Annabel begins to recognize the power of her effect on others; she becomes aware, if not clever. Even her husband notices a change as her successes accumulate; he "listened more carefully to what she said, and seemed not to think of her as being quite so stupid as before" (13). Reciprocating slightly, Annabel finds him to be "an interesting man compared with the rest" (13).

Annabel's lack of attachment to her image, or images (stupidity, Tiger Lady, Mother Earth), may contribute to her ability to per-

ceive how earnestly other people, especially men, are attached to
their projections of themselves. In this ability, Annabel manifests a
nonchalant, very nonpolitical feminism, and a sense of the comic as
well. In an environment of deliberate image-making, she can perceive—in her instinctive, "stupid" way—the false, manipulative
posturing of the men who surround her. She laughs at a "solemn
American student of drama" (11) when he shouts at the telephone
operator about his "priority call": "He looked at [Annabel] in hurt
confusion, with the shiny round face of a schoolboy, someone's kid-
brother who (as it might have been) now realised for the first time
that his mother hated animals. Annabel did not know why she was
laughing, but that was the reason" (12). She laughs again when the
same student, her lover at the time, gets sick after a party and expects her to make a solicitous motherly fuss over the fact:

> "But I'm sick!" he shouted at her. "I'm sick!"—so that she
> opened her eyes and saw him standing there on the rug, like a
> toy doll-man, his arms straight and sticking out from his sides
> as if they were made of cotton, filled with doll-stuffing and
> sewn-up. His eyes and mouth seemed completely circular as he
> stared in the face of her English callousness. She laughed at
> him the second and last time. (12)

Annabel's laughter is unreflective, but the narrator describes the
impetus for the amusement and points out "that was the reason."
The schoolboy image of masculinity is the reason, the "doll-man"
who sees himself as the incontrovertible subject for the solicitude of
any woman sufficiently trained in femininity to behave the way his
mother would—or any mother who had the decency to like animals.
Annabel does not feel obligated to perform some designated role in
private, a role imposed by a male companion. She uses roles, her
images, to make money for herself and for her baby; she sees roles
as roles, and sees no reason to pretend, aside from her own quite
practical purposes. Unlike the "newly-emancipated" press secretary Francesca, who promotes the Christophers' public image, Annabel is not deferential to men. (Francesca "even gave a kind of instinctive precedence to a male cat over a female cat" [24]).

Knowing the falseness of her own image and of those projected
by others, Annabel is adept at adjusting appearances, or at adjusting and falsifying the truth, when necessary. She rapidly learns to

use others as they have used her. After her husband's suicide, she manages a show of grief, gives out the story that Frederick was pursued by women, chased by them, till he leaped from the scaffold to escape. She sidesteps a blackmail attempt, then abruptly leaves the inquest and the country, choosing a new life and abandoning her lightly held public image.

Her new life is symbolized by her love for her baby, Carl. Her new identity is not essentially that of mother, though this had been part of her official, public image. Her new identity is herself *as* a child, as a person of possibilities, as someone with new growth ahead of her. Early in the novel we learned that the baby was "the only reality in her life"; his existence "gave her a sense of being permanently secured to the world which she had not experienced since her own childhood had passed" (38). It is not a sense of maternity that satisfies and liberates her but a sense of herself as a child, as a new being. As she waits in the airport, she feels "pregnant with the baby, but not pregnant in fact. She was pale as a shell" (144). The shell imagery belonged initially to one of Frederick's cruel suicide letters in which he denounced her for being merely a beautiful and empty shell. But Frederick's effort to tarnish and betray her public image is transformed by the final sentence of the novel: "Nobody recognised her as she stood, having moved the baby to rest on her hip, conscious also of the baby in a sense weightlessly and perpetually within her, as an empty shell contains, by its very structure, the echo and harking image of former and former seas" (144). Her emptiness turns out to have been an advantage; the fact that, unlike Frederick, she never accepted as her own a mere public image has left her free to listen to the "former and former seas" of her earlier self, a self which her baby may help her to learn or to relearn. The "former seas" are lightly reminiscent of the sea at the end of *Robinson*, where the island of possibility lay submerged.

The Public Image is a transitional novel in Spark's work, for it has still the central character of the earlier novels who is capable of some moral growth; at the same time, the increasing presence of the artificial, dehumanized world created by the press, and by a reciprocating, lazy faith in public images, points toward the later novels. In these, nearly all the characters are like Frederick in that they take seriously some "public image," some stereotyped caricature of themselves; Spark's characters increasingly become symbolic of popular, vaguely reformist social motions, not really "movements," but sputtering burlesques of people who are keen on self-renewal or who "want their equality." Spark's later novels often seem to embody her political skepticism. Few of her reformers are rescued; few are left with anything resembling the egotistical dignity that Jean Brodie retains in defeat.

The Driver's Seat

Particularly in *The Driver's Seat* (1970), efforts at social and spiritual renewal are themselves turned upside down. Earlier I said that in Spark's novels the motifs of festivity and of countercultural activities enter right into the official work-world of politics and economics: springtime becomes political. This happens especially in *The Driver's Seat*, the harshest book that Spark has written, and one that put its author in the hospital.[6] It shows regenerative attitudes and actions being cruelly mocked. To the humanistic reader, it may seem that various theoretically harmless "cures" for modern life — a southern holiday for a desperate office worker, a macrobiotic diet, feminism, therapy for the sex-offender, civil disobedience that jams the metropolitan traffic — hardly deserve the severe beating they get in the novel.

The novel is about "self-destruction," the author says,[7] and that is an understatement. A barely identified office clerk named Lise, who speaks four languages and lives in a northern country, perhaps Denmark, buys some exceptionally garish clothes and boards a plane for an obviously much needed holiday in an unspecified southern country. As she boards the plane, she spots her "type" of man (who fearfully moves to another seat to avoid her), and when she arrives in the city of her destination, she spends the afternoon and evening searching for this man, whom she finally persuades to kill her. During her miscellaneous adventures — which include shopping with the prospective murderer's aunt, slipping into hotels to look for her chosen assailant, picking up two other men who are not, after all, her type — there are many flash-forwards which let us in on Lise's fate, so that it seems to *be* fate and unavoidable. We have brief flashes of the investigation that follows her murder; a police officer is questioned, as is Carlo, a garage mechanic whose car she stole for a short time.

Lise is insane, but that is clearly not the point of the story, which is told in the present tense and hangs suspended outside the normal chronology of cause and effect, the chronology of a psychologically difficult past on its way to an unhappy future. The characters are stick figures in a cartoon tragedy. They are allegorical ciphers, empty in themselves and pointing to an emptiness behind them. They describe the void, by means of catlessness — as Spark does in the poem "Elementary," quoted earlier. In *The Driver's Seat*, and again in *The Hothouse on the East River*, the entire novel is the epiphany or the transfiguration; it is the vision — like the green in *The Ballad of Peckham Rye* and the sunset in *The Prime of Miss Jean Brodie* — of "another world than this," but it is a backwards vision.

Explanations of the novel's meaning in terms of "this world" — that is, in terms of psychology and characterization, as if the figures in the novel had been realistically portrayed — are a beginning, but they do not do justice to the brutally severe comedy in the novel. It is true that Lise can be seen as having certain faults or failings which, by a kind of poetic justice, lead to her uncomfortable fate. Her egotism and her determination after many years of passivity to take the driver's seat naturally lead to her destruction; her mania is echoed by other manias in a novel about fanaticisms.[8] In a world that dehumanizes people and turns them into objects, such manic obsessions and self-destruction are inevitable, as several critics rightly argue.[9] And yet, the fact that the self-destruction is represented chiefly by a woman character has been attacked by feminist critics; Lise seems to act out the very nonfeminist stereotype of "massive neurosis due to shortage of sex."[10] The novel sketches in all of these issues, but each one of them is presented as both a problem and an ironic, incomplete answer. The social or psychological problem is stated ironically in terms of a regenerative effort.

Lise, in her quest for her killer, for instance, runs into a mob of student protesters; her own holiday quest appropriately collides with the political quest of the students, since the protesters are also "outside" the official and presumably oppressive structures of business offices and politics. But social or personal attempts at renewal are ridiculed or thwarted. Self-destruction is depicted horribly by motifs of regeneration. Bill, who sits beside Lise during the flight, is zealously pursuing a special diet and a ritual sexual requirement that is outside the norm; he must arrange somehow for one orgasm a day. Lise is on a purposeful holiday, a pilgrimage that is a bizarre parody of Barbara Vaughan's; Lise is in transition between her stuffy, desperate office self and a new (dead) self. She puts on new clothes; she deliberately rids herself of her former identity as she stuffs her passport into the seat cushion of a cab; she will die to the old self and gain a new one—in fact, she will actually die. The sex-offender who kills her is amazed that his resolution to have a new life, after years in a mental hospital, has been destroyed at Lise's dictation. He tells the police: "She spoke in many languages but she was telling me to kill her all the time. She told me precisely what to do. I was hoping to start a new life." [11] His hope of regeneration, however, took the same terrible pattern of his earlier crimes evidently, except that he had not killed his victims until now.

The most prominently inverted social movement in *The Driver's Seat* is feminism. The first indication of radical imbalance between the genders is in Bill's distorted interpretation of the forces of yang and yin. To Lise, Bill explains that his macrobiotic diet consists mostly of yang, that is of rice and other "cleansing" foods. Most of the food during the in-flight snack that Lise is eating is yin, Bill points out, asserting that coffee, olives, and salami are full of toxins—"far too yin" (33-34). In his philosophy yin represents space. "Its element is water. It is external" (34). Bill does not say so, but yin is also the "female" aspect, yang being the "male," of the oriental concept. By implication, he lives on a strictly male diet and lives in a strictly male cosmos. In his view, poison, space, externality, and femaleness are lumped together. When Lise runs into him later that day, she knows he is not her "type"; she wants death, not sex, not an infusion of yang and masculinity.

Another obvious, yet upside-down feminist theme is Mrs. Fiedke's harangue against the men who "are demanding equal rights with us." She delivers an excited speech, as she and Lise leave a department store and look for a taxi. Mrs. Fiedke bemoans the loss of male deference (opening doors for women), describes the equality-demanding males who wear jewelry and long hair: "They don't want to be all dressed alike anymore. Which is only a move against us. You couldn't run an army like that, let alone the male sex. With all due respects to Mr. Fiedke, may he rest in peace, the male sex is getting out of hand. Of course, Mr. Fiedke knew his place as a man, give him his due" (77). She worries that men will soon "be taking over the homes and the children" while women conduct war. Soon men will want more than equal rights; "they'll want the upper hand, mark my words" (78). If Mrs. Fiedke's speech concerned women instead of men, it would have a very familiar ring as a catalogue of reactionary arguments against women's rights.

The plot itself, along with Bill's characterization of yin as poison and Mrs. Fiedke's equal rights speech, would have the archetypal familiarity of a Western myth if the gender of the main characters were reversed and if a *Mr.* Fiedke spoke against women's rights while a fanatical woman rejected yang (and males). Then, when a repressed young man (a male Lise) sought his enchanted death at the hands of a mentally ill Circe, the parts of the story would fit nicely, because they would coincide with cultural patterns — i. e., gender behaviors — that are familiar to us from movies and television. We would recall, after finishing the novel, *Uncle* Fiedke's prophecies about the dangers, to men, of women getting the upper hand; and the fanatic woman's macrobiotic rejection of yang (and of men) would be a classically sinister image of warning against the female principle, perhaps recalling the *Oresteia* or D. H. Lawrence in his more misogynist moments. In *The Driver's Seat* feminism is present by means of elaborate reversals; it is treated ironically, but it is not disavowed.

Feminism and the other reformist or regenerative motifs whether social or psychological, are presented in the novel as mere cartoon distortions of what they should be. As parodies of themselves, they point to a world in which they could be genuine forces of renewal, and at the same time they point to a dehumanized world which infects and stultifies even its reforming movements. For most readers and critics, the fault will probably be assigned to the oppressive data-collecting mentality imaged by the police uniforms in the last sentence of the novel: Lise's killer "sees already the gleaming buttons of the policemen's uniforms, hears the cold and the confiding, the hot and the barking voices, sees already the holsters and epaulets and all those trappings devised to protect them from the indecent exposure of fear and pity, pity and fear" (117). In the uniformed society of Lise's office and of the forcefully patrolled vacation country as well, regeneration — whether of the individual or of society — is extremely difficult and perhaps impossible. Tragedy and the cathartic emotions of pity and fear are not allowed to happen. The legal phrase "indecent exposure" assigns cathartic emotions, and Greek tragedy, to a twisted grubbiness. The world is one controlled by the Dr. Bradshaws, who, as Woolf's narrator observed in *Mrs. Dalloway* "penalised despair." For the socialists Leonard and Virginia Woolf, significant social and personal change was theoretically possible; a more reasonable and sensitive "new plot" could reform society.

For Muriel Spark, whose religious faith combines with a lack of faith in politics, human efforts at regeneration are probably fruit-less; the problem defined by *The Driver's Seat* is not amenable to humanly devised cures. Lise's frustration during her search for the right type expresses the unsettling and radical difficulty of her problem and, by implication, her society's problem. Mrs. Fiedke asks Lise how she will know the man when she sees him: "Will you feel a presence?" Lise replies, "Not really a presence"; instead, it will be the "lack of an absence" (76). A lack of an absence — this sug-gests again the imagery of Spark's poem, in which a void is defined by the shape that has just passed into it, the "catlessness" left by the disappearing cat.

Lise's search for the "lack of an absence" implies a search that can scarcely be defined in ordinary language, and certainly is not defined adequately for her in any of the structures of her world or in any of the countercultural protests against that world. Hers is evi-dently a religious search, a mystical one — a search for the "lack of an absence." We recall that even the feminists in Spark's short story, the grandmother, Miriam, and Mrs. Pankhurst did not quite liberate themselves; the "Almighty" held back the walls of the sea. The cruelly ironic, backwards feminism in *The Driver's Seat* is quite consistent with Spark's political anarchism, in which God is the only thorough reformer, the only complete feminist. What Lise — and Bill and the protesters — are looking for cannot be found, not in the terms by which they are defining it. A social movement might assuage, but there is no simply human "cure," the novel says, any more than there was a cure or solution for the death an-nounced by the phone caller in *Memento Mori.*

Not to Disturb

All of Muriel Spark's comedies are in a sense stranded in mid-air, and this contributes much to their unsettling quality and to their power. Particularly in the novels written after *The Mandelbaum Gate*, novels which lack the convert character, there is little indication of the norm; the other shoe never falls. Only a phrase, often at the end of the novel, may imply a positive — "fear and pity, pity and fear" — to counter the crackling negative energy of the satire. In *Not to Disturb* (1971), the "lack of an absence" is an even vaster blank than usual. On a wealthy estate in Switzerland, enterprising servants adroitly encourage an aristocratic love-triangle to follow its natural course into murder and suicide. Lister, the butler, with a shrewd eye to the media, calculates the most sensational and lucrative aspects of the story with delighted enthusiasm and without a qualm of compunction; he is a mathematician dealing with angles rather than with people. Mixing his geometrical metaphors, he writes in his memoir of the evening's disaster, even before the deaths have occurred: "To put it squarely, as I say in my memoir, the eternal triangle has come full circle."[12] The doomed triangle consists of the Baron Klopstock, his wife, and Victor Passerat, lover to both. Early in the evening they gather in the study and leave word "not to disturb." Lister frequently moralizes the tale that he is scripting for them and quotes gothic judgments from Webster and Shirley. He continually turns the expected disaster into rhetoric fashioned for the well-staged plot that he is directing: " 'Supper, never again,' says Lister. 'For them, supper no more' " (6). The servants speculate on how long it will take for the anticipated quarrel to reach its fatal peak. Lister thinks it will be at 6:00 A.M.; Heloise, pregnant by she knows not whom and relying on the intuition of her special physiological status, thinks it will happen at 3:00 A.M. By morning Klopstock has killed his wife and Passerat, and then killed himself. The servants have proceeded with a wedding that insures a smooth transition of the baron's wealth to them: Heloise has married the baron's idiot younger brother, who spends his life confined, howling, in the attic room. Movie rights have been arranged, and the household staff, having rehearsed their stories, have been interviewed, photographed, and recorded on tape. There is an ominous indication, near the end of the novel, that similar servant takeovers could happen all over the world. Clovis, the cook, cannot reach the youngest brother, Count Klopstock in Brazil; the count, according to his butler, is locked in the study with friends, and they are "on no account to be disturbed" (118).

Spark herself has said that the book is "very proservant."[13] It seems to be pro everything that the social and economic hierarchies usually place at the bottom or on the outside. The comic inversions in the novel seem fantastically to imply that the world could be overturned by mere style and energy, that revolution is a matter of communication between butlers and media, between Switzerland and Brazil, until the worldwide takeover is accomplished. The sounding board of a norm is almost completely absent, and yet there is an ironic pointer toward it; the very slickness of the night's work provides a moral resonance. Life and death are both just a matter of "style" for Lister. Heloise asks why Victor's two women friends (one turns out to be male in drag) did not wait boldly in the main drive, but instead pulled their car round to the side of the house:

> "The answer," says Lister, "is that they know their place. They had the courage to accompany their kinsman on his errand, but at the last little moment lacked the style which alone was necessary to save him. The Baron will arrive, and not see them, not enquire. Likewise, the Baroness. No sense, for all their millions." (13)

No sense, and no style; the latter alone would have prevented the deaths in the library, Lister notes. According to him, people who do not "know their place," and who are bold to emulate their employers by wearing their clothes and quoting their poetry will survive.

The action seems to prove Lister right. Perhaps mastery is mere drama and good press coverage, but there are indications that even Lister and his style may become tripped up by such an enormous undertaking. Very early in the morning, after listening closely to the complete silence on the other side of the locked library door, Lister confidently remarks, "There remain a good many things to be accomplished and still more chaos effectively to organise" (55). He proceeds to organize the quite chaotic wedding, which is duly sanctified by the presence of clergy and a shortened ritual, after which the new baron (the dead baron's cretinous younger brother) gambols about the room, breaks vases and furniture while the photographer's camera flashes. Eventually the new husband tears the zip fastener from his clothes and falls on his bride. (He has been "full of style" all evening [20]—a violent style, and rather different from Lister's.) Soon nature itself parallels, in gothic fashion, the drastic human events, but in comically analogous imagery. While Victor's persistent but frustrated friends wander the grounds, there is a great bolt of lightning:

> Meanwhile the lightning, which strikes the clump of elms so that the two friends huddled there are killed instantly without pain, zig-zags across the lawns, illuminating the lily-pond and the sunken rose garden like a self-stricken flash-photographer, and like a zip-fastener ripped from its garment by a sexual maniac, it is flung slapdash across Lake Leman and back to skim the rooftops of the house, leaving intact, however, the well-insulated telephone wires which Lister, on the telephone to Geneva, has rather feared might break down. (109)

Lister needs the phone lines in order to summon doctors, ambulance, and journalists so that his melodramatic masterpiece can be effectively presented to the media; luckily, the "well-insulated" lines hold. Lister's plot depends on well-insulated communications and well-insulated feelings; it depends on his style and on his perceiving the world as a lucrative story.

The lightning appropriately slaughters the two friends; they lack style. Then, like "a self-stricken flash-photographer," and like the mentally retarded antics of the new baron, the lightning chaotically flings itself about. The metaphors are very pointed. Do well-organized cameramen sometimes self-destruct? Could manipulatory members of the media damage themselves? Perhaps passion and craziness cannot be quite insulated by strong zippers and locked library doors. Is it *possible* "not to disturb" such human and natural forces, or to keep them from disturbing and destroying, in spite of Lister's ability to organize chaos? The sudden apparition of striking natural imagery usually signals, in Muriel Spark's fiction, that "lack of an absence," that vision of eternity or "another world than this"; the vivid and bizarre lightning here performs a similar function.

The sudden raging light somewhat qualifies Lister's masterful abilities, which he has employed only in the dark. At the end of the novel—another favorite spot for the author's suddenly proffered new angle on events—the weary servants go to bed. The final sentence tells us : "By noon they will be covered in the profound sleep of those who have kept faithful vigil all night, while outside the house the sunlight is laughing on the walls" (121). Perhaps the laughter implies nature's delight at the return of peace. Perhaps it is a more careless laughter, implying a muted ridicule of the confidently sleeping household. After all, Lister himself has just said that "we want to go to sleep and we don't want to be disturbed" (119). Such an announcement carries ominous implications—or at least it did for the former baron. Lister, by means of his organizing abilities and his style, keeps himself well-insulated, like the telephone wires. But "him in the attic" is "full of style" also, as are passion and lightning; these parallel the pity and fear in *The Driver's Seat*, chaotic, disturbing emotions pushed away by the epaulets and holsters, by the insulating uniform that serves the same purpose as Lister's formidable, undisturbed, and very remunerative organizing of other people's lives. The new baron and baroness and their well-run house may not be as secure from disturbance as they presume themselves to be.

The Hothouse by the East River

Lister is an adroitly manipulative character, skilled in keeping terror, death, and sex safely behind a locked door; he is skilled in the art of belittling such things and can even reap a large profit from their action on the souls of those with less foresight and style than his. Paul Hazlett, in *The Hothouse by the East River* (1973), has attempted something very similar, but on a truly outlandish scale. The novel is a *Memento Mori* after the fact. Paul and apparently his wife Elsa to some extent have almost locked beyond consciousness the fact that they have been dead nearly thirty years. Except for Elsa's peculiarly slanted shadow, she and Paul seem to be an ordinary frivolous, quarrelsome, middle-aged urban couple who have taken the sensible modern step toward reducing their anxiety and unhappiness; both are in analysis. Living in New York, in a warm apartment overlooking the East River, they torment each other about their past. Both served in an intelligence compound outside

London during the war, and Paul entertains a festering jealousy about Elsa's affair with a German defector and counterspy who was also at the compound, Helmut Kiel. Tension between the Hazletts increases when Elsa claims that Kiel has reemerged as a shoe sale-man in New York and may be putting coded messages on the soles of her shoes. The nervous action alternates between a present of domestic dissension, analysis, and visits from eccentric friends, and a past in the intelligence compound. Although Paul and Elsa accuse each other several times of being dead, the novel is within twenty pages of its end before we are given the confirming scene in a flash-back to the war years; Elsa and Paul were killed, along with several friends (who also "exist" in the "present" New York scenes), when a bomb hit their train as it pulled out of a London station.

Just before and after this flashback, Paul and Elsa are having a night on the town. They are being followed from club to club by the same group of people who were with them when the train was de-stroyed. Elsa is less concerned about the implications of being fol-lowed than Paul is, and she wants to dance; as she says, "This deadly body of mine can dance, too."[14] The words "deadly body" are used several times by the author of the medieval *Cloud of Unknowing* to describe the mortal or corruptible body. The phrase occurs in con-nection with the author's admonition to beware of the images, con-ceptualizations, and fantasies that enter into human thinking and contemplation while one is in this "deadly," i. e. , mortal, body. In Ira Progoff's translation the author of *The Cloud of Unknowing* warns: "And as long as the soul dwells in this mortal body ('deadly body') the accuracy of our understanding in perceiving spiritual things, most particularly God, is mingled with some manner of fan-tasy that tends to make our work unclean."[15] Neither Paul nor Elsa is in a "deadly" physical body any more, both of them having been dead for thirty years, and yet both are using fantasy — images and memories of their former physical life — in a way that hinders the soul's movement toward God. They are in deadly and corruptible bodies still, bodies built by their own imaginations, their still-flick-ering passions, their thwarted hopes for a worldly future. Their fan-tasizing has even constructed two imaginary children, Pierre and Katerina.

During the long night of dancing, however, Paul and Elsa ap-parently gain a self-knowledge that will free them from their deadly, corrupt fantasies. They become more and more tender toward each other, as they move from one night spot to the next, dancing and dancing. It is an uncomfortable, grotesque, and yet benign dance of death. Finally, Poppy Xavier, an obese friend from the compound days who has been following them all evening, insists that they get into her car; she points out that her other passengers (who also died thirty years ago) are asleep. Evidently her car will take them all back to truth and death. Poppy, her name linking her with sleep, is a benign parody of an earth goddess. She tenderly cares for the silkworms that hatch out on her large breasts, and she wears a perfume named Diane du Bois. She is Diana, goddess of upper and nether worlds; associated with the more earthly aspects of death, with sleep and worms, Poppy has a solicitous concern for Paul and Elsa. At last Elsa moves, with her shadow, toward Poppy's car and its sinister but kindly destiny. "She turns to the car, he (Paul) following her, watching as she moves how she trails her faithful and lithe cloud of unknowing across the pavement" (146).

Again the phrase from the medieval treatise on mysticism underlines the nature of Elsa's growth, and of Paul's, just as the same phrase implied a transformation of Freddy Hamilton's life after his Middle Eastern spying and rescuing led to temporary amnesia. In *The Hothouse by the East River* Elsa's shadow-cloud is an image that goes a long way toward explaining the eccentric, even strident, quality of her frequent mocking laughter. Further, the ultimate perspective of mysticism provides the viewpoint, the touchstone, of the novel's comedy; in this book the elusive norm of Spark's fiction is presented more clearly than in any of her other novels. Here we have a thorough instance of the "comic mysticism" that John Updike identified in her earlier work. This postmortem comedy is full of instances in which a rent or a gap in their experience allows Paul and Elsa to glimpse the truth. Paul especially has to be nudged toward a clearer vision because he is more tied than Elsa is to the emotions of the past. His fearful suspicions about his ontological status keep him from seeing that status, and from enjoying Elsa's zany good cheer about their predicament. When three policemen demonstrate in the nude ("except for their caps—that's to show they're policemen," Elsa notes), it is bizarre enough, but Paul's nostalgic farewell to the world of clothed policemen and other verities heightens the peculiarity into comic nonsense: "When the police

start demonstrating without their clothes on it's the end of everything. Your dreams...everything. The forty-eighth Street Pre-
cinct" (113-114; the ellipsis is Spark's). Paul's dreams have already
been destroyed, and by a fact more disturbing than a nude protest.
Since his farewell to his dreams is late by thirty years and is prompt-
ed by such an outrageous event, his misplaced nostalgia is both
moving and funny. As a symbol, the image of a nude policeman is
not entirely irrelevant to Paul's oblique, hedging, self-protective
vision of loss. The clothes of the policeman, the holster and epaulets,
were insulation against "fear and pity" in *The Driver's Seat*, and by
implication, they were insulation against the acknowledgement of
death as well. Also, "Death" has in the literary past made appearances as an officer of the law.[16]

Paul finds it very difficult to forget his past dreams and his past
in general. And yet, he must forget the past if he is to draw near to
the "cloud of unknowing" which surrounds God and which Paul at
last sees imaged in Elsa's unearthly shadow. There are two "clouds"
described by the medieval mystic and anonymous author. He ad-
vises followers to put a "cloud of forgetting" between themselves
and their past lives, their interests, emotions, and sins. And between themselves and God, there will be the comforting presence of
a "cloud of unknowing."[17] Paul cannot put that cloud of forgetting
between himself and his suspicions about Elsa's affair with Kiel. As
a result, he has failed to die properly. His "terrible and jealous
dreams," as Elsa points out, have maintained their nonlife, have
"set the whole edifice soaring" (98). He has in effect kept himself
from moving into the cloud of unknowing and into the presence of
God.

Elsa, on the other hand, is shadowed by a cloud of unknowing,
and she spends much of her time gazing out the window at "nothing." She very evidently derives satisfaction, and much hilarity,
from this preoccupation. Many times, to Paul's consternation, she
will look out the window and begin laughing (21, 43); at the window,
she seems to be "communing with a sort of friend about the high
humour of what [Paul] has just said" (11). Once, the nothing that is
Elsa's good friend is pointedly capitalized: "Elsa starts to laugh as if
in company with the Nothing beyond the window, high above the
East River" (108). The medieval mystic urged the meditator to
"choose this nowhere and this nothing."[18] Elsa clearly has done so.

She has chosen the cloud of unknowing; she has chosen God. She suffers some anxiety still from the memory of her relationship with the spy, Kiel, but her pain is perhaps purgatorial, as several critics have suggested.[19] Likewise the anonymous mystic notes that the person who seeks the cloud of unknowing may still feel pain from past sins, but the pain becomes less and less. "He considers it, therefore, to be nothing else than purgatory."[20] Eventually both Elsa and Paul surrender the suspicions, fears, and jealousies left over from the past. With no tension at all, they cheerfully enough join the group in Poppy's car, a group which includes Kiel himself. Elsa's "faithful and lithe cloud of unknowing" still follows the ghost whose lithe sense of the comic has itself been so faithful to the ultimate perspective of Nothing.

The Abbess of Crewe

The Hothouse by the East River recalls in meaning, though not in style, the more interior themes of the earlier novels; Paul and Elsa, half dead and half alive, naturally have identity problems, as did Barbara Vaughan, who was half Jew and half Gentile. In contrast, *The Abbess of Crewe* (1974) is all artifice and play. It has some qualities of a masque, and the last paragraph begins with the line from *The Tempest* (4. 1. 148), "Our revels now are ended." Like the revels staged by the spirit Ariel to celebrate the courtly betrothal of Prince Ferdinand and Miranda, *The Abbess of Crewe* is a ceremonial piece that celebrates ironically a particular political event, and the "court" it reflects is that of "the imperial presidency." In the masques of the Elizabethan and Jacobean period, members of the court themselves sometimes took appropriate roles in the entertainments, and in Spark's novel, the real historical figures are recognizable behind the characters of the nuns.

The plot satirizes the Watergate scandal. Desiring to secure her election as abbess, Sister Alexandra, after the old Abbess Hildegarde dies, leaves Sisters Walburga and Mildred in charge of a crooked campaign; they are, the abbess says, "two of the finest nuns I have ever had the privilege to know."[21] Alexandra's chief rival, Sister Felicity, is filled with liberalism and love, especially love for a young Jesuit named Thomas. The convent and its grounds are thoroughly bugged, and Felicity and Thomas's meetings in the orchard have been photographed. To damage the sweetly attractive Felicity's image, two Jesuits, sent by Alexandra's campaign managers, steal Felicity's thimble—just to show that covert access is possible; the next night, when they return for the incriminating love letters, they are caught. Sister Alexandra, duly elected abbess, manages the cover-up with her right hand, and never lets her left hand know. She frequently consults by telephone with Sister Gertrude, who pursues diplomatic negotiations throughout the world. On Gertrude's advice, Alexandra makes a very successful television appearance to allay public suspicions about the abbey. Then she takes the slow route to Rome—by land and sea—when she is summoned by the pope for an explanation of the thimble "and thimble-related matters . . . ." (115; the ellipsis is Spark's).

To some critics the joke is too small to be funny, but others appreciate Spark's transformation of history.[22] She transforms, and mocks, not just a particular historical episode, but the interplay between conservative and rebelling forces. Her lack of political faith or illusion is again apparent in her satire on both the insiders and the outsiders, on culture and counterculture. Indeed, the outsider, Sister Felicity, whose historical counterpart was the Democratic candidate, is subjected to a more reductive comic scorn than is the imperial abbess. The book's motto, a quotation from Yeats's "Nineteen Hundred Nineteen," suggests that Spark will "mock at the great," and then "Mock mockers after that." From its position in the political structure, Sister Felicity's party should be the one to do the mocking of those in power; hers is the liminal, idealistic counterculture that advocates justice, freedom, and a return to "the teachings of St. Francis of Assisi, who understood total dispossession and love" (39). Felicity, as Alexandra observes scornfully, "claims a special enlightenment," and "will never see the point of faith unless it visibly benefits mankind" (34). Felicity tells her sentimental, superfeminine nuns in the sewing room that love "and lovemaking are very liberating experiences, very"; if she is elected, she will destroy Alexandra's electronics laboratory and "install a lovenest right in the heart of this Abbey, right in the heart of England" (40). Love, poverty ("dispossession"), liberal sex—Felicity's sensual idealism has the marks of a counterculture platform. Her rebellion is fuzzy-headed and self-indulgent, however. In defeat, excommunicated after her attempt to accuse the abbess of theft, Felicity lives with her Jesuit in a small flat in London. The author abandons her to her petty fate.

In contrast to Felicity's honest if simpering banalities, the abbess is dignified by the vigorous perversities of her passions and her platform. As she herself acknowledges, her "passion" is English poetry, and during prayers she often recites poetry instead of the liturgy. Before she leaves for Rome, she instructs her nuns to release to the public a selection of the abbey's transcribed tapes, but she asks that the words "Poetry deleted" be used instead of her passionate, nonliturgical recitations (115-116). During the election days, with an eye on the popularity charts, she reminds her coterie: "We are made a little lower than the angels. This weighs upon me, because I am a true believer" (34). She is a true believer in herself, in her abbey, and in her capacity to create mythology. To persistent reporters, wanting her opinion about Felicity's "defection," the abbess at last sends a generously condescending statement that includes Milton's "I cannot praise a fugitive and cloistered virtue" (92). She assures her nuns that the press will "make some sort of garble" out of her statement, and this will aid the cover-up. She continues, outlining the rationale for her actions and, by implication, all political subterfuge:

> Garble is what we need, now, Sisters. We are leaving the sphere of history and are about to enter that of mythology. Mythology is nothing more than history garbled; likewise history is mythology garbled and it is nothing more in all the history of man. Who are we to alter the nature of things? So far as we are concerned, my dear Sisters, to look for the truth of the matter will be like looking for the lost limbs, toes and fingernails of a body blown to pieces in an air crash. (92-93)

There is a cheerful, sunny despair here. In Alexandra's opinion, "truth" has crashed, and therefore is virtually nonrecoverable; no one should go in search of it. The plane image recalls January's crash—mental illness, perhaps, and the subsequent rebirth of a stronger self. The crash imagery in *The Abbess of Crewe* may be Alexandra's theology of the Fall, but she sees no redemption, no rebirth. Instead, truth is completely lost, and its substitute, the "scenario" (stories that will encourage garbling among reporters), is in the hands of myth-makers like the abbess. She demonstrates, in her views on mythology, a complete lack of context, indeed a "cloistered virtue" that does not even perceive evil.

Unlike Nicholas Farringdon, Alexandra has no vision of evil such as he gained when he saw Selina rescue the dress. Alexandra interprets the loss of truth as merely "the nature of things," and she calls it good, just as she once looked at the chanting nuns "as if upon a certain newly created world. She contemplates and sees it is good" (26). The convent setting for the Watergate satire is not just a cute joke, but an image of political power so protected, so cloistered, that it recognizes no moral context, no criteria for good and evil, no history. The abbess protects her "cloistered virtue," which could just as well be called a "cloistered evil." Her "wrongdoings"—which she delights in reciting—are sins that remain grossly pure, never having been corrupted with good. They are quite free of any non-mythological, nonscenario notion of what "good" or "evil" is.

The final image of the book expresses Alexandra's perverse innocence in a stunning allusion to Thomas Traherne's *Centuries*. Several of these seventeenth-century prose-poems describe the glowing aura which people and natural objects seemed to have when the poet was a child: "The corn was orient and immortal wheat, which never should be reaped, nor was ever sown."[23] Alexandra is likewise surrounded with such glowing imagery as she embarks for Rome: "She sails indeed on the fine day of her desire into waters exceptionally smooth, and stands on the upper deck, straight as a white ship's funnel, marvelling how the wide sea billows from shore to shore like that cornfield of sublimity which never should be reaped nor was ever sown, orient and immortal wheat" (116). Such imagery is moving and beautiful when it describes a poet's childhood in Traherne's *Centuries*, but it is shocking and ironic—though still beautiful—when it is applied to the magnificent corruption of the abbess. It suggests that she has preserved into adulthood a stupendous innocence whose "mythological" quality makes it all the more persistent and dangerous.

The Takeover

Most of the characters in *The Takeover* (1976) are, like the abbess, involved in thefts and cover-ups, but none of them has a heart as coyly ruthless as hers, and they are not trying to "take over" themselves. That is, they are not dedicated to becoming a myth. The one exception is Hubert Mallindaine, who has "encamped himself in his legend,"[24] a legend that he is a descendant of the goddess Diana of Nemi. Eventually, even he modifies his enthusiasm about his ancestry, however, and he and the other characters spend most of their time trying to take over each other's money, real estate, and valuables. Maggie Tullio-Friole, Hubert's landlady, for instance, is trying to evict him from his beautiful house near Frazer's famous Nemi, a house that she custom-built for him; she suspects he will try to sell its expensive furniture and paintings. Her suspicions are true but not subtle enough, for Hubert is surreptitiously having the furniture and paintings duplicated and is selling the originals. Fraud and robberies are committed with gamey high spirits and a relaxed conscience. No one in the novel has a serious vocation for either good or evil. There is no Dougal, no Jean Brodie, no Nicholas, no desperate Lise or hopeful Else, no aristocrats sealed in their passionate doom behind a locked door. The book is the most cheerful, light, playful comedy that Spark has written. It even seems to some reviewers to be all surface, or another of Spark's failed attempts at a long novel.[25] But the length gives greater scope to the satire, as one reviewer notes,[26] and the continuing elaboration of surprising subplots allows the title to become intricately ironic. No single "takeover" emerges as *the* takeover, and in fact the nature of a takeover seems to be that it is particularly vulnerable to a future countertakeover, just as the ancient priest at Nemi, having murdered his predecessor in order to attain his position, was himself subject to a takeover of the same kind.

The several takeovers in this novel ultimately cancel each other out. Hubert is finally persuaded to switch his religious enthusiasm from Diana to the Catholic church, especially to the charismatic movement within the church. His own new religion, which preached the combined female imagery of "the late Diana and the early Mary," flourished in numbers and revenue during the two years following the oil crisis of 1973 (139). He was especially concerned that the charismatics recognize themselves as "schismatics from the true and original pagan cult of Diana" (206). Hubert's faith, which has its headquarters in his house on Maggie's property (or rather, on property that she thinks is hers), has its sinister as well as its comic expressions; like Seton and Dougal, Hubert preaches vision rather than truth. "Truth," says Hubert during a sermon, "is not literally true." He advocates magic, allegory, and mysticism, and scorns materialism (138). His new religion has the hallmarks of an attitude that is usually attacked and punished in Spark's novels. In *The Takeover*, however, the laughter falls equally on the just and the unjust; whether the Catholic church has taken over the charismatics (along with Hubert's briefly prosperous Diana cult) or the charismatics have taken over the church is an issue left in delightful doubt.

Hubert's elaborately planned rally, well-staged outside his house at Nemi, ends in brawling and even bloodshed, in hilarious farce. His sermon is interrupted by his secretary-housekeeper Pauline (whose zealously New Testament name is significant). Dressed ludicrously like a "huntress" — that is like a woman on an African safari — she reads aloud from Acts 19 the account of Diana's corrupt silversmiths. Hubert manages to distort Pauline's testimony in his favor, and his motley congregation, which includes two Catholic priests, is soon clapping and singing to guitar music provided by Pauline's boyfriend. Then the priest of Nemi is again interrupted by a young Englishwoman who tutors in an Italian family. She begins tearing off Hubert's liturgical vestments, and soon all are fighting and tearing off their own or each other's clothes. (Even the Catholic priests, Cuthbert and Gerard, lose their clothes in the festive levelling and stripping.) Hubert, bloodied by his disastrous celebration with the Friends of Diana, feels all the more confirmed in his title as a priest of Nemi (233).

Between Hubert's zany religion and the Catholic church during the Holy Year of 1975, there is a curious cross-fertilization, or perhaps just a similarity in a few significant areas. The American priest, Father Gerard, Maggie's friend and Hubert's, would probably call the relationship between the two faiths an "ecology." He studies the local pagan legends of Italy and points out, in his American pop-science jargon, that the "Church continues to absorb many pagan nature-rituals because the Church is ecology-conscious" (105). Gerard's use of the word could pass for a modern translation of Newman's "economy," in one of the senses in which the latter uses the word: as a method of conversion which utilizes pagan allusion or readings in the process.[27] In the ideological ecology of the novel, there seems to be an exchange of spiritual energy between the

Christian charismatics and Hubert's ecstatics. Pauline attends a Catholic charismatic prayer meeting and reports back to the excited Hubert; the two priests show up at Hubert's Diana celebration. In the end, Father Cuthbert, friend of ecology-conscious Gerard, invites Hubert to lead the Catholic prayer meetings; according to Pauline, "Cuthbert said it wouldn't be in conflict with Diana as the preserver of nature, not at all" (261).

What has taken over what? Spark seems to enjoy asking the question and letting nonsense and truth speak for themselves. When the narrator attempts to speak for truth in a passage of unsuccessful lyricism, the result is not convincing. A rather solemn and digressive passage offers us a meditation on "eternal life," the ongoing reality behind the noisy clutter of gossip, lovemaking, buying and selling, and the excavating in Diana's sanctuary; apparently it is this reality, "invisible and implacable" (180-81), which the well-meaning imagery, the "ecology," of church and cult attempts to express. This extended epiphanic description, however, is not effective; as an economy of the truth it pales beside the tightly wound complex of human efforts to find security or ecstasy, to "take over," to monopolize the meaning or the material of life.

Territorial Rights

In her subsequent novel, *Territorial Rights* (1979), Spark again builds a complicated plot around takeovers. Indeed the complicated plot is often the focus of reviewers, who are divided as to whether it is an efficient vehicle for Spark's comedy in this instance or merely a "whirlwind of unnecessary invention."[28] The characters deserve their contorted, "unnecessary" plot. They work themselves into their own amazing jams, though only the American art-collector Curran seems to recognize this fact. Spark provides these characters with much less warmth, energy, and moral substance than she gave to those in *The Takeover*. We seem almost to have returned to the very commonplace world of Peckham Rye, although the setting is Venice. But this is Venice in the off-season, and the hearts of these frenetic visitors to the holiday city are off-season also. They are not seeking relaxation, or old gods or new ones; most of them are not "global" enterprisers. Except for the Countess Violet de Winter and Curran, these are people of modest ambition; they lack the means and style for the jet-set relationships and intrigues of Maggie and Hubert. *Territorial Rights* swarms with small people claiming to be on large missions. They pursue holidays and pilgrimages, yet most of them do not really want to risk leaving home psychologically; they continually claim "rights" as though they were signers to a cosy constitution which they carry around in their heads.

Ironically, Lina Pancev, a defector from Bulgaria, talks most frequently and vaguely about her rights. The thirty-five-year-old Lina, an artist and teacher, defected not from informed political commitment but because her well-travelled cousin's tales of Western life attracted her with the promise of easy money, easy morals, easy love, and, in effect, easy rights. Ostensibly in Venice to find her father's grave, Lina is unafraid of being followed, as she tells her lover Robert, because she after all has "residential rights" and "rights" by virtue of being a defector; she will simply "go to the police and complain."[29] When she is drawn in unknowingly by the long arm of a London private intelligence agency, GESS, and given an attic studio, she insists on her right to keep it, even though Violet de Winter, the proprietor (and agent of GESS for Northern Italy), is nonplussed by Lina's several boatloads of baggage and threatens to deny her the use of the loft. Lina insists flamboyantly on both her Eastern and Western rights:

> I've rented my flat to an Ethiopian student. I've brought my belongings to your house. You gave me the attic studio and I have my civil rights. I fled my country and I got asylum. You have no rights on your side. The student has paid me three months' rent in advance, which is money that I needed, and it is my right to make my profit in a capitalist system. (114)

"Rights," and especially "territorial rights," suggest the potential for the abuse of such rights, particularly the abuse known as trespassing (perhaps the abuse known as sin). Lina and others talk about rights defensively, as though they suspect that they are more or less constantly trespassing on other people's property and rights. Lina, whose right it is to seek out her father's grave, does indeed find it, and trespasses on it, dancing on both halves of it (for her murdered father's body was divided so that each of his lady loves could bury a part of it in her own rose garden). But Lina, the right-claiming trespasser, is ignorant of what lies beneath the gardens. Robert laughs in triumph at her, but Lina is dancing with his father, Arnold Leaver, at the time, and she thinks she has successfully triumphed over her one-time lover.

Such moral guesswork typifies the several missions which the characters undertake. All are guessing (except for a smiling executive of "GESS"), but since they don't know this, most feel by the time they leave Venice that they have indeed successfully protected their rights or the rights of those in whom they take a proprietary interest. Arnold Leaver, for instance, has perhaps the simplest and most conventional motive for being in Venice. Restless after retiring as headmaster of Ambrose College, he gains his doctor's permission to take a vacation without his wife. He gives himself permission to take along his mistress, Mary Tiller, and he frequently defends his "holiday," as though guiltily uncertain whether he has a right to it. Through persistent interruptions he explains that he is on a "holiday" (125, 185, 186), and will not be deterred from this by his son's unexpected appearance in Venice — nor by his son's disappearance from Venice, a disappearance that worries Grace Gregory (Arnold's former mistress), who tries to worry Arnold about it. Arnold is not even moved by the photo of a criminal in the newspaper; the photo, a "photokit" composite put together by witnesses, is quite reminiscent of his son Robert, as Grace points out (231). In fact, the news story does concern his son's successful jewelry heist. Returning to England, Arnold finds his wife in a good humor; he has doggedly pursued his postretirement life-crisis "holiday" as though he had a right to it and also a right to learn absolutely nothing about life, himself, or his family during the entire liminal excursion beyond his home territory. Psychologically, he remains at home.

His wife has remained even more thoroughly at home. Anthea Leaver harbors neither revenge nor passion with regard to her husband's holiday. Her reasons for tracking him down are resolutely petty. As she explains to the smiling "Mr. B." of GESS, "I believe in one man, one vote." When the agent amends, "You mean one man, one woman," Anthea affirms that she said this in the first place (57). Her relationship with her husband is to her a matter of rights, and no more than that. She has, somewhat like Frederick in *The Public Image*, accepted completely "a living part such as many multitudes believe exists," and she describes this part, this "public image," when she describes her reasons for marrying. She married, she says, "for marriage in general, but more specifically for my wedding day, the event, the white dress, the hymns and the flowers, the picture in the papers" (58). She demands the rights and perquisites of an empty image. Yet, though Spark destroyed the cardboard Frederick, she lets the cardboard Anthea and Arnold slip by; she lets them be defined by their own pathetically limited definitions of themselves. In so doing, Spark demonstrates again that there is more than one way to write desegregated art. An author can kill or shock a character who assumes there is breath and life in a mere public image, or in a phantasm of jealousy; yet, for perhaps an even more appalling effect, the author can refuse to kill or shock a character who is a moral automaton. There are worse things than being awakened morally, and one of these is not to be so awakened at all.

Worse than not being awakened to good, however, is to be luminously awakened to evil, to evil as one's true calling. As Frank Kermode notes, Robert has a "vocation for evil."[30] And his vocation transforms him. When he becomes acquainted with Giorgio, the apprentice butcher who helped distribute the remains of Lina's father thirty years earlier, Robert is delighted, and we see him "smiling so openly and sunnily that his mother herself would have been amazed at the transformation" (215). Usually we are not allowed into the consciousness of Spark's characters if they have a genius for evil; they are portrayed mostly from the outside. We are, however, allowed into the interior of Robert's heart as it is taken over by his great "talent" for crime. This occurs as he enters the sun-tight room prepared for him as a supposed kidnap victim (but he participates in the "kidnapping," the aim of which is to blackmail Curran). Several times, as he walks with Anna and her uncle Giorgio, Robert thinks warily: "Am I walking into a trap?" (219, 221) But as he walks into his hideout, he thinks, "with a rush of pleasure: At last I'm home—I'm out of the trap" (221). As he walks into the trap of a life thoroughly insulated from human feelings and responsibilities, he senses the moment as the beginning of "happy days, the first fruition of his youth" (221). His commonplace sulkiness of heart is transformed into a vigorous destiny of evil.

The others are not so secure against shock and guilt: Curran's moral consciousness flickers sporadically. But no one's political consciousness flickers at all. For the people in this novel, "rights" are merely rhetoric. Liminality has become either frozen (a routine life-crisis holiday with a mistress) or completely fluid, completely unrelated to any structure; it is no longer the inversion of anything, because there is no structure to invert. While Elsa, in *The Hothouse by the East River*, could look at the light of "Nothing," which was also the mystical light of a divine reality, the luminous nothing in this novel shines from the opposite metaphysical pole and illuminates Robert's smile during his sunny recognition of his true calling — evil. The levelling seems to be complete, and the only creative energy seems to be on the side of evil.

Yet in the final sentence of the book (Spark's typical location for an image of transformation), there is a hint of an enduring creative process, as though "all things are possible" if human history has the patience to bear with its own mingled corruption, ostentation, and creative persistence. The narrator's eye moves from the two sisters (former lovers of the dead and divided Pancev) and surveys the Venetian landscape, a landscape that none of the characters has bothered to look at: "Katerina and Eufemia were always busy in the Pensione Sofia, whether attending to their guests at all seasons of the year or cultivating their roses in the garden, beyond which the canals lapped on the sides of the banks, the palaces of Venice rode in great state and the mosaics stood with the same patience that had gone into their formation, piece by small piece" (239-40). The characters in the novel may seem to have little in common with this vision of the city. They are impatient and readily vocal about rights. They are very small pieces in a mosaic of petty intrigues, but they think they are big pieces. After most of these off-season, spiritually out-of-season visitors have left, the worldly but luminous city of Venice abides precariously on the water, a mixed image of corruption and grace; a holiday territory, it can still renew the eye that claims it, that claims the "right" to the patience required for transforming the commonplace into goodness rather than evil.

Loitering With Intent

The novel that follows *Territorial Rights* turns our attention in a different direction. *Loitering With Intent* (1981), whose first-person narrator claims to be using autobiographical material, brings us once again into the world of Spark's early novels, the world of sinister, exploitative fanatics and vulnerable coteries who populate *The Comforters*, *The Bachelors*, and *Peckham Rye*. The first-person narrator of the recent novel has a much more vital and tough personality than the only other such narrator in Spark's fiction, the allegorical everywoman, January, of Spark's second novel, *Robinson*. Like the independent and practical Barbara Vaughan, Fleur Talbot in *Loitering With Intent* is quite unsentimental about sex. Fleur shocks Dottie, the wife of one of Fleur's lovers, by receiving nonchalantly Dottie's suspicions that the husband is homosexual. Fleur does not assign to gender and age and class the readiest public image. As a result, she can perceive in the ancient Lady Edwina, whose bladder is as whimsical as her mind, a likeable and useful accessory in Fleur's struggle with Sir Quentin, Edwina's son and founder of the Autobiographical Association. In her capacity as temporary secretary to this group, Fleur, like Caroline in *The Comforters*, is a novelist who is fascinated by the interplay of life and fiction, and especially by the tendency of life to imitate fiction, indeed to plagiarize it. Although evil is potentially as menacing in this novel as in any of Spark's work, it has drawn in its claws and does not seek its "rights" everywhere; its territory is the suburb of Kensington, and its takeovers are provincial rather than thriving operations that seek footholds in Italy, Switzerland, or Brazil.

The novel is interesting though not exciting.[31] I will consider it only briefly, and as a kind of epilogue to Spark's opus so far. The novel is manifestly a throwback to its author's earlier concerns, and intentionally so. It "loiters with intent" among the materials that became the germ of the narrator-novelist's work. Fleur Talbot tells us as much, once she has extricated herself from Sir Quentin's association. She transcribed, edited, and even embellished with her own invented material the otherwise dull autobiographies being written by self-centered people, several of them titled, whose belief in their own importance had drawn them into Sir Quentin's project. Assured that Sir Quentin has added portions of her manuscript, *Warrender Chase*, to the feeble autobiographies of his followers, and convinced of the leader's sinister efforts to demoralize the members of the association, Fleur is delighted when she realizes that she must look for a new job. With the autobiographical works of John Henry Newman and Benvenuto Cellini in mind, she considers the members of Sir Quentin's sect as a subject for the future: "I would write about them one day. In fact, under one form or another, whether I have liked it or not, I have written about them ever since, the straws from which I have made my bricks."[32] Readers of Spark's novels have seen these bricks many times.

The bricks are more interesting than the straws. That is, Spark's other novels are more subtle and complex than this one in which Fleur claims to be giving us the central matter of an author's subsequent fiction. As though giving us the sketch last instead of first, *Loitering With Intent* hints of actions and characters found everywhere in Spark's fiction. Sir Quentin, although his regime of fasting and guilt leads one of his clients to suicide, is a less efficient Seton or Dougal, and he is certainly less bold than Lister or Robert Leaver. Like Jean Brodie, Sir Quentin plays Providence with the lives of others and forms a quasi-religious community around himself. Like Jean Brodie, he is "betrayed" by a young woman who writes and who can envision a "transfiguration of the commonplace," a transformation of real-life straw into the sturdy brick of prose.

If indeed something like Sir Quentin's absurd Autobiographical Association was the germ of Spark's fiction as it was of Fleur Talbot's, we can especially appreciate the satiric vision by which Spark transforms the world in her more typical novels. Sometimes this vision yields the luminous evil conscience confidently enjoyed by the abbess of Crewe and by Robert Leaver, and sometimes it yields the unsettling and invisible "light" which gives Elsa her peculiar but good shadow, her cloud of unknowing. In *Loitering With Intent* Muriel Spark may be announcing a change in the kind of fiction that she proposes to write in the future; perhaps her comedy is to be less harsh, less drastic. Yet, it is the drastic quality of her transforming and satiric vision that gives us her "De-segregated art" at its very best and its most uncomfortable. In her best work, the takeovers are so buoyant or insidious that the values and comfortable assumptions of the normal world totter on the edge of continuing holiday, the reversed world being sometimes a parody, sometimes a bizarre premonition, of what a radically restructured conscience or society might become.

6

Feminist Comedy

In the novel, the most radical affirmations of social or psychological change thrive, I have argued, in a liminal context, especially if the liminality is never resolved. Placed in its natural habitat of liminal imagery — the imagery of inversion, of disguise, of transformed sexual and social identity — a political subject matter becomes much more than rhetoric, special pleading, or stiff polemic. The imagery of life transition or of festivity brings with it a built-in rebellion. Virginia Woolf and Muriel Spark capitalize on this rebellion. When they undertake to transform these commonplace patterns, their comedy mocks established values, and the roots of their mockery go all the way down to myth, that is, to the archetypes expressive of "God," or of our biological and social chemistry. In its starkest "moments" or "transfigurations" the fiction of these authors almost sweeps clean the metaphysical and mythic slate, and the laughter then confronts anything short of the blank world seen without a self, or short of the "Nothing." When Spark and Woolf evaluate relationships between the sexes, and use such an ascetic norm to do so, their laughter is not content to tease follies and flail vices, or to urge a little common sense. Their laughter instead demands a radically "new plot." Woolf and Spark, from different directions, approach the four-thousand-year-old secular scripture and rip the temple curtain from top to bottom.

As we can see from the preceding chapters, liminal imagery does not always mean patently feminist comedy. Feminist comedy, however, when it is saying truly dangerous things obliquely and with a faceted organic complexity, will very likely draw upon liminal imagery. It will mock assumptions rather than ramifications; it will challenge a world view. The feminist comedy of Woolf and Spark celebrates, sometimes, a radically overturned world, a world in which Orlando shrugs off civilization after civilization. At other times the comedy is directed against the presumptions of a society that insists on "proportion," on "human nature" as this or that, on yin as bad and yang as potent; or it is directed against policemen in epaulets and caps, insulated from pity and fear. Without this insulation, Spark's more positive characters see a world in which all things are possible. Woolf's characters perceive, beyond the insulation of daytime roles or notebook phrases, an apparently neutral objective, glowing world, an "it" untouched by human phrases, by human social and mythic "plots." In either case, whether the mysticism is agnostic, almost scientific (as it is for Woolf), or Christian, it serves to inspire and reinforce a very radical politics and a very radical feminist comedy. Indeed, mysticism and politics have similarities. The ascetic searcher for God is like the social reformer, Victor Turner notes, in that both place themselves outside the normal social and intellectual structures; both experience liminality.[1] Theologian Michael Novak and feminist Carol Christ have recently paraphrased Charles Peguy's statement that "everything begins in mysticism and ends in politics."[2] Mediating between this beginning and this ending is the feminist comedy of Virginia Woolf and Muriel Spark.

Can the politics of holiday be found in other writers? Is my critical model for feminist comedy one that will illuminate the fiction of novelists other than Woolf and Spark? Although a thorough testing of this critical context is not possible within the boundaries of the present study, I do want briefly to suggest that the feminist comedy defined and examined here is emerging in the novels of twentieth-century writers and developing in several dimensions.

If we look at the work of Jean Rhys, for instance, we find feminist themes very much linked to the social structures that gave white European males power and money while preventing women, Creoles, blacks, and most colonials from any significant participation in the culture that exploited them. Born in 1894, the daughter of a white Creole mother and a colonial Welsh father, Jean Rhys grew up on the Carribean island of Dominica, acutely aware of the exploited status of the black population, and of her own status as an outsider. As a child, she said "That's not fair" so often that she was known as "Socialist Gwen" (she was born Gwen Williams). As an adult she apparently changed her mind and felt that the European residents of the islands, rather than the black inhabitants, were victims of injustice, and she claimed to be strongly opposed to "women's lib," since she found women untrustworthy, jealous, and ready to hurt the vulnerable.[3] Jean Rhys spent most of her life among the vulnerable, among the economic and cultural outsiders on the Bohemian fringes of London and Paris. She lived in a society of outsiders, although the characters in her novels are more ready than Rhys herself is to express the bitter politics of their status and to mock the white European order that oppresses them.

The most oppressed among the Ryhs heroes, Bertha (Antoinette) Mason in *Wide Sargasso Sea* (1966), is too deeply wounded by her isolated Carribean childhood and by her mad mother to perceive how drastically others, especially her husband, take advantage of her; her final gesture of burning Rochester's home and destroying herself as well — as Charlotte Brontë's character also does — may be a political act, but it is not clear that she perceives it as such. And the novel is hardly comic. In the other four novels, however, the major female character dares to mock. Although she can take no effective action against the white male European lover on whom she usually depends financially and emotionally, she recognizes that the relationship is political, and she often attacks him with mimic, jesting fantasy-dialogues. The middle-age Sasha of *Good Morning, Midnight* (1939), knows she is going to lose her job in Mr. Blank's dress shop, but her thoughts are more political than her vulnerable demeanor is. She inwardly hisses at her emblematic white male employer with satire as unsparing as that directed by Woolf's narrator at Sir William Bradshaw:

> Well, let's argue this out, Mr. Blank. You, who represent Society. . . . There must be the dark background to show up the bright colours. Some must cry so that others may be able to laugh the more heartily. Sacrifices are necessary. . . . Let's say that you have this mystical right to cut my legs off. But the right to ridicule me afterwards because I am a cripple — no, that I think you haven't got. And that's the right you hold most dearly, isn't it? You must be able to despise the people you exploit.[4]

Sacrifices are necessary, and Sasha, like Septimus, feels the pressure to go under. When she does not attempt suicide after all, she is asked, "Why didn't you drown yourself?" Living in cheap hotels in Paris, without a job, and carefully avoiding cafés that might remind her of earlier, happier times during her brief marriage, Sasha recalls and mimics the query about drowning: " 'We consider you as dead. Why didn't you make a hole in the water? Why didn't you drown yourself in the Seine?' These phrases run trippingly off the tongues of the extremely respectable. They think in terms of a sentimental ballad."[5] They think as Sir William thinks; suicide, which they unknowingly encourage, is "their idea of tragedy," as Septimus realized. It is perhaps also their idea of acting their own respectable part well, as the *Hamlet* paraphrase also implies; trippingly they speak the proper lines.

Sometimes the Rhys hero presumes to want a quest, a life adventure, but then begins to suspect the truth which Joseph Campbell, as we saw earlier, noted in passing: that women and slaves were not expected to participate in the Western "miracle" of developing an individual, mature self. In *After Leaving Mr. Mackenzie* (1931), Julia Martin explains to a woman artist why she married (and why her marriage has since collapsed). Julia wanted to get away from England and follow, in effect, the hero pattern of male liminality, of male transition to adulthood. She says, "I wanted to go away with just the same feeling a boy has when he wants to run away to sea — at least, that I imagine a boy has."[6] Although Julia does not get into the driver's seat of male power and adventure, Sasha does get there — accidentally — and proceeds to take a sarcastic and perhaps brutal pleasure in her false position. A gigolo mistakenly assumes, seeing her fur coat, that she truly is wealthy and would generously appreciate his services. In effect Sasha is in disguise. Really a drifter who moves in and out of a floating subculture of outsiders (two Russians, a Jewish painter), Sasha briefly mimes the part of power, sometimes quite evidently relishing the inversion of her status and especially enjoying the possibility of wounding someone who is, she rightly suspects, just sensitive enough to get hurt; indeed, the gigolo is jarred a little when she praises his teeth (73). She identifies herself, during this period of disguise and play-acting, with liminal images of play and mockery. When the gigolo defines a "cérébrale" (a designation Sasha has just playfully claimed for herself) as someone who hates both men and women, Sasha has a brief vision of stagey mockery; she thinks in self-mockery, "So pleased with herself, like a little black boy in a top-hat" (162). The white woman and the black boy appropriately co-alesce into an image that asserts their similarity as outsiders and their shared exploitation as mock human beings, as figures of fun who dress up like real people only in order to entertain real people. Nevertheless the ending of the novel, where Sasha gives herself to a seedy salesman, is ambiguous; we do not know whether she succumbs numbly to oppression or whether she affirms valiantly her status as outsider, her classless solidarity with another human being.

In the next generation of writers, there is both feminism and comedy, the former most notably in Doris Lessing and the latter emerging with a variety of manifestations in the work of Edna O'Brien, Iris Murdoch, Penelope Mortimer, and of course Muriel Spark. The typical paradigm of a Murdoch novel is a character's gradual, often comic, discovery that he or she has been imposing a myth on some other person. Occasionally the puncturing of this myth carries feminist implications, as I have suggested elsewhere.[7] Yet reality is, for Murdoch, essentially a male-defined reality. She considers the male point of view, male culture, to be the normal and "human" one. When asked why she always chooses a male when she writes in the first person, she responded, "I think perhaps I identify with men, because the ordinary human condition still seems to belong more to a man than to a woman." Murdoch favors equality of opportunity and education but quite obviously sees men as the "human race," as the mainstream culture that women should join: "We want to join the human race, not invent a new separatism."[8] nor, the implication is, do we want to change the definition of what the "human race" is.

More radical implications emerge in recent novels by Beryl Bainbridge and Margaret Drabble. We have perhaps a foretaste of this vision in Penelope Mortimer's *The Pumpkin Eater* (1962). The caricature earth mother of this novel, Mrs. Armitage, had assumed that "it was sufficient to be alive, and make love, and have children, and behave as well as possible."[9] We assume she must know how many children she has, but the author never lets us know the exact number. Even their mother thinks of them as a kind of lump sum, once observing that they "cataracted down the stairs" to meet their father (219-20). After submitting herself at last to an abortion and sterilization, she seems both to regret the loss of her identity as maternal hero and at the same time to resent the fact that it took her so long to lose it. She terrifies a journalist who naturally expects that such an obvious mother figure will declare her opposition to the bomb. During their interview, however, Mrs. Armitage is also having a phone conversation with the husband of her husband's current mistress. She is particularly distressed by the uncomfortable news that the mistress is pregnant. The mother of so many children tells the journalist, "I think any child. . .any child. . .would be better off. . .dead" (184; the ellipses are Mortimer's). Shaken by this response, the reporter beats a scrambling and hasty retreat. A mythic mother, or rather a woman who thoroughly and exclusively sacrificed herself to the myth of maternity, looks at the bomb and finds herself thinking, without regret, of the death of children.

Binny Mills in Bainbridge's *Injury Time* (1977) has cataclysmic daydreams, and by the end of the novel she becomes a resigned and even interested, perhaps willing, hostage to urban criminals. Appalled by her verbally abusive, careless, destructive children, the divorced Binny plans to have an evening free of them while she gives a dinner party for her lover, Edward Freeman, and another couple. Her preparations do not go smoothly. While she is at the bank, she experiences a general uneasiness; she meditates on the disgusting, menacing, and alarming world full of hit-and-run drivers and scabby faces. She recalls her typical fantasies. "In her day dreams, usually accompanied by a panic-stricken Edward, she was always being blown up in aeroplanes and going down in ships."[10] On this occasion she is particularly distressed by an odd-looking woman who changes queues at the bank and resembles the shaved misfits in a "home for fallen girls." Mysteriously, however, Binny feels better after taking note of this woman: "Something had pleased her, raised her spirits, though what it was she couldn't be sure" (25).

Later Binny is sure. The images of disaster and of bizarre misfits in banks coalesce when Binny's party is disrupted by the pursued bank robbers; the "woman" Binny had seen in the bank turns out to be one of the robbers, a man named Geoff. Binny's life is subjected to disaster, but she is not nearly as distressed as we might

have expected her to be if her party had been the complete and ful-
filling gesture, the "offering," that the parties of Clarissa or Mrs.
Ramsay were. Binny's identity, particularly her identity as a woman, does not at all merge with her capacity as mother or hostess.
On the contrary, her "moment," her "transfiguration," comes with
the mysterious improvement in her mood as she looks at the disguised criminal in the bank, though she doesn't yet know who he is.
Herself an outsider in her role as mother and mistress, Binny readily
identifies with a criminal subculture and with an "androgynous"
criminal who looks "fallen." Binny thinks, "I knew it would be me,"
when the robbers leave her house and take only her with them as
hostage. In the car, Binny "watched with interest, bent over her
knees, as Harry bundled the wounded Geoff into the passenger
seat" (157). Binny's daydreams in a sense come true, and she
watches with interest while the normal world—which does not feel
normal to her—is left behind.

Like Binny, Janet Bird in Margaret Drabble's *The Realms of
Gold* (1975) can contemplate disaster with some satisfaction. Although she does not, in the course of the novel, leave her immature,
domineering husband nor her baby, she frequently indulges in fantasies of disasters; she tries to imagine something that will improve
her life, something like "a cataclysm, a volcano, a fire, an outbreak
of war, anything to break the unremitting nothingness of her existence."[11] Only a change on the order of a geological revolution will
help her domestic doldrums, so radical is the change she perceives
as necessary. Drabble's narrator ponders the rooted myth of sacrificial domesticity which limits Janet: "Society offers Pyrex dishes
and silver teaspoons as bribes, as bargains, as anesthesia against
self-sacrifice. Stuck about with silver forks and new carving
knives, as in a form of acupuncture, the woman lays herself upon
the altar, upon the couch, half numb" (125). Janet's cousin, Dr.
Frances Wingate, who is both a scientist and a mother, has quite
evidently awakened from her numbness, and literally tossed away
the trappings of bridal sacrifice by divorcing her husband. One
evening she threw all of her coffee cups at his head, one by one,
"and advised him to get out of the house forever. He had done as advised" (153). Frances's comic understatement here expresses her
easy strength and her confidence in her ability to meet a crisis, or

even to perpetrate one. When a situation is intolerable, she can take action — and smile at the action later.

Janet cannot take action so easily; she tries to be content with fantasies of cataclysm. Late one evening she pours hot wax from a candle into an ashtray decorated with a zodiac design. She wonders if people, seeing her, might think her a witch. She sits, "pouring wax onto an ancient symbol, pointlessly. If disinterred as from the ruins of Pompeii, what little rite would it be assumed she had been enacting, what gods would she have been seen to propitiate?" (175). Janet is truly an "underground" figure, playing at swamping the entire zodiac in hot wax from the "hollow green crater in the wide candle" (174). She sees herself as oppressed, buried, interred; naturally, she envisions a volcanic eruption.

She is also drawn to books about military eruptions; she reads novelistic accounts of war and concentration camps. In one novel dealing with these grim subjects, she reads about a Jewish woman who tosses her baby from the window of a train as it moves toward a concentration camp. Janet reflects on the episode:

> She had thrown the baby into the arms of a Polish peasant woman, who was hoeing the turnip field, and as the train moved on inexorably to extinction, the Polish woman and the Jewish woman had exchanged looks of profound significance, and the Polish woman had picked up the baby and had embraced and kissed it with a promise of devotion as the train moved out of sight. (130)

Janet wonders if she likes such stories because of the "death and the destruction? Or the baby salvaged and harvested like a turnip from the field?" (130). The unexpectedness, the inappropriateness almost, of comparing a baby to a turnip, and especially in circumstances so painful and desperate, indicate Janet's wry distance from her own despair. She feels that she would almost like to toss away her own baby, Hugh; she suspects that she is not the best mother for him, but she knows too that there is "no way of getting off this train" (131). She will have to raise her turnip herself.

The imagery of two women and a baby assumes a symbolic aura during Janet's visit to her great Aunt Constance Ollerenshaw's delapidated house on the outskirts of Tockley. After struggling along a path overgrown with tangled foliage, Janet sees the partially boarded-up cottage where her aunt lives. Suddenly Aunt Connie's threatening face appears at a window. Aunt Connie angrily shakes a stick and raps on the window; a dog barks, and Janet fears that it will be let loose. She hastily places a box of Black Magic chocolates on the windowsill, and retreats, remembering that her aunt has the reputation of being a witch. And yet, Aunt Connie apparently wants to see the baby: "And Janet turned again, the last time, human, and she picked up her baby so that Great-Aunt Con could see him. Con stopped rapping, and stared. Hugh slept on, wrapped up in his baby blanket. A curious family group" (282). It is a very ancient family group. This scene in a modern novel is almost an archetypal tableau of the Demeter and Persephone figures whose images recur in the prehistoric art of the Mediterranean area. Often the two female gods (mother and daughter, but essentially one god) were represented in sculpture with a baby between them, an infant passing from one to the other as though from life to death or from death to life.[12] On some antique vases, a baby is portrayed sitting in a cornucopia which is held by Ge ("Earth," the mother of all the gods) as she rises from the ground; she extends the cornucopia and the baby toward Demeter.[13] Interpreted symbolically, the scene between Janet and Aunt Connie, along with the scene from the novel Janet was reading, suggest a psychological regeneration, a passage from death to life. The baby represents not only itself, but Janet's rescuing of herself, we can assume, from psychological collapse or despair. The myth by which this regeneration is implied belongs to an antique female resurrection-fertility myth rather than to a male one.

Margaret Drabble, like Woolf and Spark, brings us some archetypal Stonehenges of female liminality, of the female quest. Along with Rhys, Mortimer, and others, Drabble questions the images of female socialization, of nurturance and submission, which traditionally provide a landscape for the heroic, questing male. The authors whom I have examined at length in this study, and those briefly introduced in this chapter, include as the targets of their comedy certain life patterns deriving from primary socialization. That is, these authors, some of whom consciously identify themselves as outsiders, attack the norm. Instead of satirizing eccentricity and manner (elements of secondary socialization) by way of defending a norm which is a supposedly more hallowed and secure image or behavior (primary socialization), these authors draw upon the festive images of a world overturned. They give structure and narrative substance to the radical laughter of Wittig's guerrilla warriors and Lessing's Kate Brown, who found the concepts of obedience, anatomical destiny, wife, and husband to be extremely funny.

Feminist comedy, to the extent that it makes use of images associated with a literary tradition of festive comedy and of images derived from behavior typical of seasonal and life-transition rituals, is linked by these images to certain radical historical movements which also made use of such behaviors and images. These movements include, as we have seen, renewals within Western Christianity, the Peasant's Revolt, and recent countercultural behavior and ideology. While feminist comedy is not the same as feminist political action, it is not surprising that feminist comedy would use for its imagery the "holiday" actions which have sometimes historically emerged into the everyday, into political action, into revolutionary movements that could envision the possibility of a new world.

For Muriel Spark's awakened characters, "anything is possible." In Spark's fiction possibility is assured, — in effect, guaranteed — by an absolute, eternal openness that judges and shocks any human effort at easy closure. For Woolf as well, the outsider celebrates, offers her gift, and keeps open the possibility of psychological and political change. The jungle laughs; the wild goose of truth flies; the woman in the garden writes, and frightens observers as she does so. Woolf's implied metaphysics are the opposite of Spark's. For Woolf, liminality is a constant only because nothing else — certainly not God — is so. For Drabble's characters the human imagination, sometimes spurred by an uneasy evangelical conscience, is the primary source of new plots, new realms of gold, new myths.

This lack of closure, this lack of resolution, characterizes the feminist comedy of the authors examined here. Even when the imagery suggests myth, the archetypal imagery is in the first place suggestive of a female iconography, not a male one; and secondly, the mythic imagery is treated ironically. It is seen neither as sacred scripture nor as secular scripture. At its best, feminist comedy deals with absolutes, but not absolutely. The novelists discussed here use liminal imagery to mock long-standing social and psychological institutions. These writers violate the usual festive tradition, however, in that they imply no end to the holiday flyting. Such a lack of resolution transforms holiday into politics, and makes celebration the imagination's prelude to action and perhaps to new variations on an open human history in which all things are possible.

Notes

Chapter One

1. For a discussion of comedy as the expression of vitality and healthy balance, see Susan K. Langer, *Feeling and Form* (New York: Charles Scribner's Sons, 1953), pp. 326-50. Other statements about celebrational comedy are discussed below, as are the various approaches to defining "satire" and "norm." Freud elaborates his theory of verbal comedy as censored instinct in *Jokes and Their Relation to the Unconscious*, translated and edited by James Strachey with additional translation and editorial matter by Angela Richards (London: Routledge & Kegan Paul, 1960).

2. Arnold van Gennep, *Rites of Passage*, trans. Monika V. Vizedom and Gabrielle L. Caffee (Chicago: University of Chicago Press, 1960), pp. 10-11, 89-95.

3. Victor Turner, *Dramas, Fields, and Metaphors: Symbolic Action in Human Society* (Ithaca: Cornell University Press, 1974), p. 273.

4. Ibid., pp. 231-71; see also Turner, *The Ritual Process: Structure and Anti-Structure* (Chicago: Aldine Publishing Co., 1969), p. 110.

5. Turner, *The Ritual Process*, p. 95.

6. Northrop Frye, *Anatomy of Criticism* (Princeton: Princeton University Press, 1971), p. 105.

7. See C. L. Barber, *Shakespeare's Festive Comedy* (Cleveland: World Publishing Co., Meridian Books, 1963), pp. 3-10.

8. Annette Kolodny, "Some Notes on Defining a Feminist Literary Criticism," in *Feminist Criticism*, ed. Cheryl L. Brown and Karen Olson (Metuchen, N.J.: Scarecrow Press, 1978), pp. 42-45.

9. See, for instance, Orrin Klapp, "The Fool as a Social Type," *American Journal of Sociology* 55 (September 1949): 157-62; Jacob Levine, "Regression in Primitive Clowning," in *Motivation in Humor*, ed. Jacob Levine (New York: Atherton Press, 1969), pp. 167-78; Max Gluckman, *Custom and Conflict in Africa* (Glencoe, Ill.: Free Press, 1955), pp. 109-36; and C. L. Barber, *Shakespeare's Festive Comedy*, pp. 9-10, 14.

10. Ian Donaldson, *The World Upside Down: Comedy from Jonson to Fielding* (Oxford: Clarendon Press, 1970), pp. 183-206; Mikhail Bakhtin, *Rabelais and His World*, trans. Helene Iswolsky (Cambridge, Mass.: M.I.T. Press, 1968), pp. 268-69,473.

11. See Peter L. Berger, Brigitte Berger, and Hansfried Kellner, *The Homeless Mind: Modernization and Consciousness* (New York: Random House, Vintage Books, 1974), pp. 203-7, 211; Turner, *Dramas, Fields, and Metaphors*, pp. 231-71, 287-88; Turner, *The Ritual Process*, pp. 112-13, 198-99.

12. David Kunzle, "World Upside Down: The Iconography of a European Broadsheet Type," in *The Reversible World: Symbolic Inversion in Art and Society*, ed. Barbara Babcock (Ithaca: Cornell University Press, 1978), pp. 44-47, 61-77, 80.

13. Natalie Davis, "Women on Top: Symbolic Sexual Inversion and Political Disorder in Early Modern Europe," in Babcock, *The Reversible World*, p. 175.

14. Turner, *Dramas, Fields, and Metaphors*, p. 42.

15. Ibid., p. 28.

16. Virginia Woolf, *Contemporary Writers* (New York: Harcourt, Brace and World, 1966), pp. 26-27.

17. Virginia Woolf, *Collected Essays*, 4 vols. (London: Hogarth Press, 1966-67), 2:146. Recent research provides some evidence that men and women do indeed have differing opinions as to what is funny. For instance, Lawrence La Fave reports on an investigation which showed that promale males found antifemale jokes funnier than profemale-antimale jokes; see "Humor Judgments as a Function of Reference Groups and Identification Classes," in *The Psychology of Humor*, ed. Jeffrey H. Goldstein and Paul E. McGhee (New York: Academic Press, 1972), p. 205. See also Donald W. Felker and Dede M. Hunter, "Sex and Age Differences in Response to Cartoons . . . , *The Journal of Psychology* 76 (September 1970):

19-20, and Walter E. O'Connell, "Resignation, Humor, and Wit," *The Psychoanalytic Review* 51 (Spring 1964): 55-56.

18. Joseph Campbell, *The Hero with a Thousand Faces*, 2nd ed. (Princeton: Princeton University Press, 1972), p. 193. Campbell points out that he borrows the word *monomyth* from James Joyce's *Finnegans Wake*; see *The Hero with a Thousand Faces*, p. 30.

19. Monique Wittig, *Les Guérillères*, trans. David Le Vay (New York: Viking Press, 1971), p. 86.

20. Doris Lessing, *The Summer Before the Dark* (New York: Alfred A. Knopf, 1973), p. 168. The ellipsis is Lessing's.

21. Malcolm Bradbury, discussing Huxley's novels of the 1920s, observes: "The novels turn on the emptying out of the centre from any dream, hope, or institution, and hence have an apparent air of cynicism, a suggestion of universal failure." Bradbury, *Possibilities* (London: Oxford University Press, 1973), p. 152. For perspectives on the problematic nature of comedy in a supposedly normless world, see also Nathan A. Scott, Jr., "The Bias of Comedy," in *Comedy: Meaning and Form*, ed. Robert W. Corrigan (San Francisco: Chandler Publishing, 1965), p. 83; Peter Thorpe, "Thinking in Octagons: Further Reflections on Norms in Satire," *Satire Newsletter* 7 (Spring 1970): 91-99; Robert M. Davis, "The Shrinking Garden and New Exits: The Comic-Satiric Novel in the Twentieth Century," *Kansas Quarterly* 1 (Summer 1969): 6.

22. See for instance Richard Duprey, "Whatever Happened to Comedy?" in Corrigan, *Comedy*, pp. 243-49. Matthew Winston argues that "black humor" takes a critical stance, but that satire does not assume a set of norms; Matthew Winston, *"Humour noir* and Black Humor," in *Veins of Humor*, ed. Harry Levin (Cambridge: Harvard University Press, 1972), pp. 274, 279. Richard Hauck, limiting his study to American absurdist fiction, says that writers such as Barth and Vonnegut express a "cheerful nihilism" (borrowing a phrase from Barth); Hauck, *A Cheerful Nihilism: Confidence and "The Absurd" in American Humorous Fiction* (Bloomington: Indiana University Press, 1971), pp. 4-8.

23. Robert Torrance, *The Comic Hero* (Cambridge: Harvard University Press, 1978), pp. 1-7, 259. On the mechanism of classical comedy, see also Maurice Charney, *Comedy High and Low* (New York: Oxford University Press, 1978), pp. 121-22.

24. Peter L. Berger, *Invitation to Sociology: A Humanistic Perspective* (Garden City, N.Y.: Doubleday, Anchor Books, 1963), pp. 72-73; Peter L. Berger and Thomas Luckmann, *The Social Construction of Reality* (Garden City, N.Y. Doubleday, 1966), p. 143.

25. Simone de Beauvoir, *The Second Sex* (New York: Alfred A. Knopf, 1952). See especially Chap. 9, pp. 139-98.

26. D. H. Lawrence, *Women in Love* (New York: Random House, Modern Library, 1950), p. 64.

27. *Values* I identify with concepts, abstractions, such as *love, courage, fidelity; norm,* as I have already indicated in this chapter, is associated with a pattern of action, particularly a stylized mythological paradigm. The two words are related, as sociologist John Finely Scott points out: "What the psychologist calls an expression of 'personality' the sociologist calls an expression of a 'role.' What one calls the expression of 'value,' the other calls 'conformity,' or 'commitment to a norm.' " Scott, *Internalization of Norms: A Sociological Theory of Moral Commitment* (Englewood Cliffs, N.J.: Prentice-Hall, 1971), p. 5.

28. Berger and Luckmann, *The Social Construction of Reality,* p. 124. The classic analysis of the process whereby the child develops a "self" is that of George Herbert Mead, who argues that the child learns an identity first in relation to particular "significant others" (the parents), and secondly in relation to the "generalized other" of society; see *Mind, Self, and Society* (Chicago: University of Chicago Press, 1934), pp. 135-226.

29. Berger and Luckmann, *The Social Construction of Reality,* pp. 127-29.

30. Ibid., pp. 124-25, 127-37.

31. Berger, *Invitation to Sociology,* p. 98.

32. Eleanor Maccoby and Carol Jacklin, *The Psychology of Sex Differences* (Stanford: Stanford University Press, 1974), pp. 349-55.

33. Dorothy Dinnerstein, *The Mermaid and the Minotaur* (New York: Harper & Row, 1976), pp. 95-105, 118.

34. Ibid., pp. 126, 175, and see the entire chapter "The Ruling of the World," pp. 160-97. Nancy Chodorow also makes the point that children accept dependency in relation to fathers and to men generally, as a way of escaping from maternal domination; see her

"Oedipal Asymmetries and Heterosexual Knots," *Social Problems* 23 (April 1976): 462. She elaborates more fully the implications of a mother-reared society in her book *The Reproduction of Mothering: Psychoanalysis and the Sociology of Gender* (Berkeley and Los Angeles: University of California Press, 1978).

35. Sherry B. Ortner, looking at the same issues, argues that the mother-centered early training of children results in the later identification of women with nature and of men with culture, and, especially, results in male control over both nature and women. See "Is Female to Male as Nature Is to Culture?" *Female Studies* 1 (Fall 1972): 5-31.

36. See Raymond Aron, who explicates Durkheim and quotes him extensively, in *Main Currents in Sociological Thought*, trans. Richard Howard and Helen Weaver, 2 vols. (New York: Basic Books, 1967), 2:42, 51, 82-97.

37. Carol Andreas, *Sex and Caste in America* (Englewood Cliffs, N.J.: Prentice-Hall, 1971), p. 67.

38. Ibid., pp. 67-90.

39. Eva Figes, *Patriarchal Attitudes* (London: Faber & Faber, 1970), pp. 35-65.

40. Berger and Luckmann, *The Social Construction of Reality*, pp. 93-94. Bronislaw Malinowski, examining non-Western cultures, confirms this point; see *Magic, Science, and Religion* (Garden City, N.Y.: Doubleday, Anchor Books, n.d.; originally published by Free Press, 1948), pp. 47-53.

41. Berger and Luckmann, *The Social Construction of Reality*, p. 96.

42. See Nancy Chodorow, "Oedipal Asymmetries and Heterosexual Knots," p. 456; and Berger, Berger, and Kellner, *The Homeless Mind*, pp. 81-82, 184-86, 191-97.

43. Berger, *Invitation to Sociology*, p. 149.

44. See, for instance, Charney's discussion of typical objects of attack in the comedy of manners in *Comedy High and Low*, p. 54.

45. Benjamin Lehmann, "Comedy and Laughter," in Corrigan, *Comedy: Meaning and Form*, p. 175.

46. Vivian Gornick, "Woman as Outsider," in *Woman in Sexist Society*, ed. Vivian Gornick and Barbara K. Moran (New York: Basic Books, 1971), pp. 76-78.

47. Frye further suggests that the archetype of the "shadow" is expressed by the villain of a romance. *Anatomy of Criticism*, pp. 304-7.

48. C. G. Jung, *Symbols of Transformation*, trans. R.F.C. Hull (New York: Pantheon Books, for the Bollingen Foundation, 1956), p. 345. Jungian analysts, along with literary critics, have pointed to the considerable masculine bias in much of Jung's work. See Naomi R. Goldenberg, "A Feminist Critique of Jung," *Signs* 2 (Winter 1976): 443-49: Annis Pratt, "Archetypal Approaches to the New Feminist Criticism," *Bucknell Review* 21 (Spring 1973): 3-14; June Singer, *Androgyny* (Garden City, N.Y.: Doubleday, 1976) and Singer, *Boundaries of the Soul* (Garden City, N.Y.: Doubleday, 1972).

49. Frye, *Anatomy of Criticism*, p. 185.

50. Frye, *The Secular Scripture* (Cambridge: Harvard University Press, 1976), p. 79.

51. Charney, *Comedy High and Low*, pp. 89-90.

52. See, for instance, Carolyn Heilbrun's discussion of the female hero, essentially an "androgynous" being, who integrated into her mature and vigorous personality traits that were by convention "masculine"; Heilbrun sees this female hero as having been invented by Henry James and Henrik Ibsen. Heilbrun, *Toward a Recognition of Androgyny* (New York: Alfred A. Knopf, 1973), pp. 49-112.

53. Joseph Campbell, *The Masks of God: Occidental Mythology* (New York: Viking Press, 1964), p. 236.

54. Phyllis Chesler cites studies ranging from 1927 to 1971; see her *Women and Madness* (Garden City, N.Y.: Doubleday, 1972), pp. 18, 335-36, n. 17.

55. Ibid., p. 17.

56. See Campbell, *The Hero with a Thousand Faces*, pp. 105-8, 213-16.

57. Lee Edwards, "The Labors of Psyche: Toward a Theory of Female Heroism," *Critical Inquiry* 6 (Autumn 1979): 33-49.

58. Gail Sheehy, *Passages* (New York: E. P. Dutton, 1976), which discusses the life crises of both women and men; Penelope Washbourn, *Becoming Woman: The Quest for Wholeness in Female Experience* (New York: Harper & Row, 1977); Carol P. Christ, "Margaret Atwood: The Surfacing of Women's Spiritual Quest and Vision," *Signs* 2 (Winter 1976): 316-30; Pratt, "Archetypal Approaches to the New Feminist Criticism," pp. 11-13.

59. Grace Stewart, *A New Mythos: The Novel of the Artist as Heroine, 1877-1977* (St. Albans, Vt.: Eden Press Women's Publications, 1979).

60. N. J. Richardson, ed., *The Homeric Hymn to Demeter* (Oxford: Clarendon Press, 1974), p. 14; Campbell, *The Masks of God*, pp. 48-50.

61. For a description of Eleusinian ritual, see C. Kerenyi, "Kore," in C. G. Jung and C. Kerenyi, *Essays on a Science of Mythology*, trans. R.F.C. Hull (Princeton: Princeton University Press, 1969), pp. 137-47, 153. For Jung's interpretation of Demeter-Persephone imagery and of the Mass, see his "Psychological Aspects of the Kore," in Jung and Kerenyi, *Essays on a Science of Mythology*, pp. 156-77; and Jung, "Transformation Symbolism in the Mass," in *Psyche and Symbol*, ed. Violet S. de Laszlo (Garden City, N.Y.: Doubleday, Anchor Books, 1958), pp. 148-224.

62. Patricia Spacks, *The Female Imagination* (New York: Knopf, 1975) pp. 78-112, 315-17.

63. Sandra M. Gilbert and Susan Gubar, *The Madwoman in the Attic: The Nineteenth-Century Literary Imagination* (New Haven: Yale University Press, 1979), pp. 3-104.

64. Elaine Showalter, *A Literature of Their Own: British Women Novelists from Brontë to Lessing* (Princeton: Princeton University Press, 1977), pp. 160, 180.

65. In *Regionalism and the Female Imagination*, vol. 3 (Fall 1977 and Winter 1977-78), see Emily Toth, "Dorothy Parker, Erica Jong, and New Feminist Humor" (pp. 70-85), and Cathy Davidson, "Canadian Wry: Comic Vision in Atwood's *Lady Oracle* and Laurence's *The Diviners*" (pp. 50-55). This special issue was on "Female Humor." See also five more articles on the subject in *Regionalism and the Female Imagination*, vol. 4 (Fall 1978). Spacks, *The Female Imagination*, pp. 218-21, discusses a very different kind of humor, a quite conservative variety, in books such as MacDonald's *The Egg and I* and Kerr's *Please Don't Eat the Daises;* such humor ultimately supports the "feminine" ideal of cheerful drudgery and incompetence, as Spacks points out.

66. Josephine Hendin, *Vulnerable People: A View of American Fiction since 1945* (New York: Oxford University Press, 1978) pp. 172-90.

67. Lorna Sage draws distinctions between British and Ameri-

can fiction, noting the much greater part women writers played in England as the novel developed as a form. Sage, "Female Fictions: The Women Novelists," in *The Contemporary English Novel*, ed. Malcolm Bradbury and David Palmer (London: E. Arnold, 1979), pp. 67-68. Judith Fetterly argues that British fiction is less sex-biased than American fiction. "American fiction is male," she says. Fetterly, *The Resisting Reader: A Feminist Approach to American Fiction* (Bloomington: Indiana University Press, 1978), pp. xii-xvi. Agate Krouse claims that "feminist comedy" is often attempted by American novelists, but it is "successfully executed by British and Canadian" writers; see "Toward a Definition of Literary Feminism" in Brown and Olson, *Feminist Criticism*, p. 288.

68. Siriol Hugh-Jones, "We Witless Women," *The Twentieth Century* 170 (July 1961): 23.

69. For an illuminating discussion of Lessing's implied theories about humor, see Judith Stitzel, "Humor and Survival in the Works of Doris Lessing," *Regionalism and the Female Imagination* 4 (Fall 1978): 61-68.

70. Pratt, "Archetypal Approaches," p. 11.

71. Hugh-Jones, "We Witless Women," p. 24.

Chapter Two

1. Woolf, *Collected Essays*, 2:106 (hereafter cited in the text as *CE*).

2. On Woolf's style and on stream of consciousness generally, see, for example, Leon Edel, *The Modern Psychological Novel*, rev. ed. (New York: Grosset & Dunlap, 1964); Ralph Freedman, *The Lyrical Novel: Studies in Herman Hesse, Andre Gide, and Virginia Woolf* (Princeton: Princeton University Press, 1962), pp. 185-270; and Harvena Richter, *Virginia Woolf: The Inward Voyage* (Princeton: Princeton University Press, 1970).

Among those who have given at least minimal attention to Woolf's comedy are Jean Guiguet, *Virginia Woolf and Her Works* (New York: Harcourt Brace Jovanovich, Harvest Book, 1976) pp. 438-57; Winifred Holtby, *Virginia Woolf* (1932; rpt. Folcroft, Pa.: Folcroft Press, 1969), pp. 89, 123-24; Hermione Lee, *The Novels of Virginia Woolf* (London: Methuen, 1977); and Aileen D. Lorberg,

"Virginia Woolf, Benevolent Satirist," *The Personalist* 33 (1952): 148-58.

3. Maria DiBattista, *Virginia Woolf's Major Novels* (New Haven: Yale University Press, 1980).

4. Margaret Comstock, " 'The Current Answers Don't Do': The Comic Form of *Night and Day,*" *Women's Studies* 4 (1977): 153-71. See also the unpublished dissertation (Stanford, 1975) by Margaret von Szeliski Comstock, "George Meredith, Virginia Woolf, and Their Feminist Comedy."

5. Virginia Woolf, *The Diary of Virginia Woolf,* ed. Ann Oliver Bell (New York: Harcourt Brace Jovanovich, 1977-), 1:124-25 (9 March 1918). On Woolf's feminist political activities see Jane Marcus, " 'No More Horses': Virginia Woolf on Art and Propaganda," *Women's Studies* 4 (1977): 265-90, and also by Marcus, "*The Years* as Greek Drama, Domestic Novel, and Götterdämmerung," *Bulletin of the New York Public Library* 80 (Winter 1977): 288-93. Herbert Marder looks at Woolf's feminism in *Feminism and Art: A Study of Virginia Woolf* (Chicago: University of Chicago Press, 1968), pp. 18-22, 91-97.

6. Virginia Woolf, *A Room of One's Own* (London: Hogarth Press, 1967), pp. 102-5, 156-57.

7. Among these are C. B. Cox, *The Free Spirit: A Study of Liberal Humanism* . . . (London: Oxford University Press, 1963), pp. 110-13; Elizabeth Monroe, *The Novel and Society* (Chapel Hill: University of North Carolina Press, 1941), pp. 189-224; and Angus Wilson, "Diversity and Depth," *Times Literary Supplement,* 15 August 1958, which is cited in *Virginia Woolf: The Critical Heritage,* ed. R. Majumdar and Allen McLaurin (London: Routledge & Kegan Paul, 1975), p. 40.

8. In an earlier essay Woolf had compared "our novelists" who provide "external appearances — tricks of manner, landscape, dress" with the more spiritual and tumultuous Dostoevsky; see "More Dostoevsky," in *Books and Portraits: Some Further Selections from the Literary and Biographical Writings of Virginia Woolf,* ed. Mary Lyon (London: Hogarth Press, 1977), p. 119. The following scholars discuss in some detail the British enthusiasm for Russian writers, and the effects of this milieu on Virginia Woolf: Dorothy Brewster, *Virginia Woolf* (New York: New York Univer-

sity Press, 1962), pp. 53-62; James Hafley, *The Glass Roof: Virginia Woolf as Novelist* (New York: Russell & Russell, 1963), p. 77.

9. Virginia Woolf, "Modes and Manners of the Nineteenth Century," in *Books and Portraits*, pp. 23-24.

10. Clive Bell, *Old Friends* (New York: Harcourt, Brace and Co., 1957), p. 120.

11. Avrom Fleishman, *Virginia Woolf: A Critical Reading* (Baltimore: Johns Hopkins University Press, 1975), p. 2. Fleishman evidently sees the stylized characterization as effective. So does Jane Novak in *The Razor Edge of Balance: A Study of Virginia Woolf* (Coral Gables, Fla.: University of Miami Press, 1975), p. 74. A. D. Moody, however, feels that these "caricatures" merely contribute to the miscellaneous quality of the novel, to its lack of form; see his *Virginia Woolf* (New York: Grove Press, 1963), pp. 11-12.

12. *The Letters of Virginia Woolf*, ed. Nigel Nicholson and Joanne Trautmann (New York: Harcourt Brace Jovanovich, 1975-), 2:76; *A Room of One's Own*, pp. 110-11.

13. Woolf, *A Room of One's Own*, p. 114.

14. Virginia Woolf, *A Writer's Diary*, ed. Leonard Woolf (London: Hogarth Press, 1975), pp. 243-44 (9 April 1935).

15. Virginia Woolf, *Three Guineas* (London: Hogarth Press, 1947), pp. 192-206; Elaine Showalter, "Literary Criticism," *Signs* 1 (Winter 1975): 445-47; Nina Auerbach, *Communities of Women* (Cambridge: Harvard University Press, 1978) p. 119.

16. Virginia Woolf, *Moments of Being: Unpublished Autobiographical Writings* (New York: Harcourt Brace Jovanovich, 1976, pp. 131-32.

17. Ibid., pp. 126-27.

18. John Maynard Keynes, in *Two Memoirs*, cited by J. K. Johnstone, *The Bloomsbury Group* (London: Secker and Warburg, 1954), p. 30.

19. For an account see Quentin Bell, *Virginia Woolf: A Biography* (New York: Harcourt Brace Jovanovich, 1972), 1: 157-60; and see Woolf's short story, "A Society" which draws upon this event, in *Monday or Tuesday* (New York: Harcourt, Brace and Co., 1921), pp. 9-40.

20. Virginia Woolf, *The Voyage Out* (New York: Harcourt, Brace, and Co., 1926), p. 76 (hereafter cited by page number in the

text). The American edition is being used here because its substantial revisions evidently express Woolf's later decisions about Rachel's character, which is much more reserved in this edition (Doran, 1920) than in the English one (Duckworth, 1915). For an analysis of the differences between the two editions, see Louise De-Salvo, "Virginia Woolf's Revisions for the 1920 American and English Editions of *The Voyage Out,*" *Bulletin of Research in the Humanities* 82 (Autumn 1979): 338-66.

21. Jean Alexander overemphasizes the limiting effects of Rachel's ignorance and focuses on the terrifying distortions of her response; see *The Venture of Form in the Novels of Virginia Woolf* (Port Washington, N.Y.: Kennikat Press, 1974), p. 39.

22. In the several drafts of this scene there is a grassy tussel between Rachel and Helen, Rachel in one draft saying that she loves Terence better than Helen and evidently shifting her love from mentor to future husband. See the reproduced drafts in Mitchell Leaska, *The Novels of Virginia Woolf* (New York: The John Jay Press, City University of New York, 1977), pp. 35-38; see also, for a discussion of the several early drafts, Elizabeth Heine, "The Earlier *Voyage Out:* Virginia Woolf's First Novel," *Bulletin of Research in the Humanities* 82 (Autumn 1979): 294-316.

23. Nancy Bazin suggests that the image of the mermaid here shows that Rachel is unconquerable sexually: "To die a virgin, as she does, is for her a victory." Bazin, *Virginia Woolf and the Androgynous Vision* (New Brunswick, N.J.: Rutgers University Press, 1973), p. 52.

24. Louise A. DeSalvo, *Virginia Woolf's First Voyage: A Novel in the Making* (Totowa, N.J.: Rowman and Littlefield, 1980), pp. 98-102, 155-59.

25. See Bazin, *Virginia Woolf and the Androgynous Vision,* p. 67. Hafley, *The Glass Roof,* pp. 17-19, argues that the ending of the book proves that Terence's greater social responsiveness is morally right and Rachel's reserve is wrong.

26. Annis Pratt, "Women and Nature in Modern Fiction," *Contemporary Literature* 13 (Autumn 1972): 481-88.

27. Virginia Woolf, *Mrs. Dalloway* (London: Hogarth Press, 1947), p. 164 (hereafter cited by page number in the text). There are some minor differences between the English and the American

texts; for a discussion of these see E. F. Shields, "The American Edition of *Mrs. Dalloway,"* *Studies in Bibliography* 27 (Charlottesville: University Press of Virginia, 1974): 157-75.

28. For Woolf's development of the book and its title, see Charles G. Hoffman, "From Lunch to Dinner: Virginia Woolf's Apprenticeship," *Texas Studies in Literature and Language* 10 (Winter 1969): 609-27. Among those who discuss the book's thematic polarities are Fleishman, *Virginia Woolf,* pp. 37-43; Alice van Buren Kelley, *The Novels of Virginia Woolf: Fact and Vision* (Chicago: University of Chicago Press, 1973), pp. 47-62; Jane Marcus, "Enchanted Organs, Magic Bells: *Night and Day* as Comic Opera, in *Virginia Woolf,* ed. Ralph Freedman (Berkeley and Los Angeles: University of California Press, 1980), pp. 97-122.

29. See, for instance, Bazin, *Virginia Woolf and the Androgynous Vision,* pp. 82-83; Guiguet, *Virginia Woolf and Her Works,* pp. 209-10; and Holtby, *Virginia Woolf,* pp. 91, 96-97.

30. Josephine Schaefer, *The Three-Fold Nature of Reality in the Novels of Virginia Woolf* (The Hague: Mouton and Co., 1966), p. 60; Margaret Comstock, " 'The Current Answers Don't Do,' " p. 157.

31. Virginia Woolf, *Night and Day* (London: The Hogarth Press, 1950), p. 357 (hereafter cited by page number in the text).

32. Fleishman, *Virginia Woolf,* p. 28.

33. M.-L. von Franz, "The Process of Individuation," in *Man and His Symbols,* ed. Carl G. Jung (Garden City, N.Y.: Doubleday, 1964), pp. 212-15; Aniela Jaffé, "Symbolism in the Visual Arts, " in *Man and His Symbols,* pp. 240-43.

34. For a positive assessment of Woolf's first experimental novel, see Guiget, *Virginia Woolf and Her Works,* p. 224; Lee, *The Novels of Virginia Woolf,* pp. 74-79; and Schaefer, *The Three-Fold Nature of Reality in the Novels of Virginia Woolf,* pp. 68-77. Among those who say there are serious flaws in the novel are Johnstone, *The Bloomsbury Group,* pp. 333-34, and Novak, *The Razor Edge of Balance,* p. 100.

35. Phyllis Rose, *Woman of Letters: A Life of Virginia Woolf* (New York: Oxford University Press, 1978), pp. 104-5. Others who have taken at least a glance at the social comedy in *Jacob's Room* include T.E. Apter, *Virginia Woolf: A Study of Her Novels* (London: Macmillan, 1979), pp. 34-35; Lee, *The Novels of Virginia*

Woolf, pp. 81-82, 85-88; and Schaefer, *The Three-Fold Nature of Reality in the Novels of Virginia Woolf*, pp. 189-91.

36. Judy Little, *"Jacob's Room* as Comedy: Woolf's Parodic Bildungsroman," in *New Feminist Essays on Virginia Woolf*, ed. Jane Marcus (Lincoln: University of Nebraska Press, 1981), pp. 105-24.

37. Virginia Woolf, *Jacob's Room* (London: The Hogarth Press, 1945), p. 83 (hereafter cited by page number in the text).

38. Aileen Pippett, *The Moth and the Star: A Biography of Virginia Woolf* (Boston: Little, Brown, and Co., 1953), pp. 150-51.

39. H. G. Wells, *Joan and Peter: The Story of an Education* (New York: Macmillan Co., 1918), pp. 19, 549.

40. Carol Ohmann discusses Jacob's relationships with women in connection with feminist themes; see "Culture and Anarchy in *Jacob's Room," Contemporary Literature* 18 (Spring 1977): 164-66.

41. Hafley, *The Glass Roof*, p. 52.

42. See especially Barry S. Morgenstern, "The Self-Conscious Narrator in *Jacob's Room," Modern Fiction Studies*, 18 (Autumn 1972): 351-61. Others who comment on the narrator as a character are Hafley, *The Glass Roof*, pp. 49-50, and Novak, *The Razor Edge of Balance*, pp. 87-88.

43. See, for instance, Bazin, *Virginia Woolf and the Androgynous Vision*, pp. 106-9, 122-23 and A. D. Moody, *Virginia Woolf* (New York: Grove Press, 1963), pp. 21-28. The most negative assessment of Clarissa is argued, mistakenly and reductively, by Mark Spilka, who sees Clarissa's limitations as a presentation of Woolf's failure to grieve at her mother's death. Spilka, "On Mrs. Dalloway's Absent Grief: A Psycho-Literary Speculation," *Contemporary Literature* 20 (Summer 1979): 316-38.

44. *Diary*, 2:272.

45. Woolf's phrase is in *Diary*, 2:248. Alex Zwerdling, "Mrs. Dalloway and the Social System," *PMLA* 92 (January 1977): 69-82. For an analysis of the "system" as essentially masculine and oppressive, see Barbara Rigney, *Madness and Sexual Politics in the Feminist Novel* (Madison: University of Wisconsin Press, 1978), pp. 42-44.

46. Lotus Snow reviews Virginia Woolf's relationship with Kitty, who had been a sort of "foster mother" to her and her sister,

introducing them to society after Julia Stephen's death; see "Clarissa Dalloway Revisited," *Research Studies* 46 (September 1978): 197-202. Woolf's ambiguous responses to Lady Ottoline Morrell, whom she admired in many respects, are expressed frequently in the *Letters* and the *Diary*; on 4 June 1923 Woolf speaks of the "despicableness of people like Ott" (*Diary*, 2:244).

47. Rose, *Woman of Letters*, pp. 126-35.

48. See, for instance, Apter, *Virginia Woolf*, pp. 57-58; Rigney, *Madness and Sexual Politics*, p. 51; Rose, *Woman of Letters*, p. 144.

49. Apter, *Virginia Woolf*, pp. 51-55; Rose, *Woman of Letters*, pp. 135-42; Michael Payne, "Beyond Gender: The Example of *Mrs. Dalloway*," *College Literature* 5 (Winter 1978): 2-3; Morris Philipson, " 'What's the Sense of Your Parties?' " *Critical Inquiry* 1 (September 1974): 134-37. Lee, *The Novels of Virginia Woolf*, p. 106, is an exception in that she sees the party as the final convincing proof of Clarissa's lies and compromisings; it is "hollow, trivial and corrupt, providing satisfaction for the least satisfactory part of her character."

50. Kenneth J. Ames, "Elements of Mock-Heroic in Virginia Woolf's *Mrs. Dalloway*," *Modern Fiction Studies* 18 (Autumn 1972): 363-74; Lee, *Novels of Virginia Woolf*, pp. 103-5; Allen McLaurin comments on the mock-heroic elements in *Virginia Woolf: The Echoes Enslaved* (Cambridge: Cambridge University Press, 1973), pp. 155-56.

51. John Ruskin, *Sesame and Lilies* (London: J. M. Dent and Sons, 1907), p. 57.

52. Some critics would disagree with my reading, but I think they have not listened to the mocking language of these passages; among those who see in this episode a serious, nonironic lyricism are Reuben Brower, *The Fields of Light* (London: Oxford University Press, 1962), p. 135, and Lee, *Novels of Virginia Woolf*, pp. 98-103.

53. Lucio P. Ruotolo, *Six Existential Heroes* (Cambridge: Harvard University Press, 1973), p. 19.

54. Joan Bennett, *Virginia Woolf: Her Art as a Novelist*, 2nd ed. (Cambridge: Cambridge University Press, 1964), p. 100. DiBattista also points out that Woolf refuses to sentimentalize Septimus's rebellion or his madness; see *Virginia Woolf's Major Novels*, p. 55.

55. Richard B. Hauck, "The Comic Christ and the Modern

Reader," *College English* 31 (February 1970): 499. Northrop Frye emphasizes the ironic position of Septimus; he is a random scapegoat, "guilty" only because he is a member of a guilty society. *Anatomy of Criticism* (Princeton: Princeton University Press, 1975), pp. 41-42. On the other hand, Fleishman asserts that Septimus's death is genuinely creative, just as Clarissa's parties are: Fleishman, *Virginia Woolf*, pp. 87-88. Rigney also sees Septimus as a real, renewing scapegoat; see *Madness and Sexual Politics*, p. 60.

56. Lee R. Edwards, "War and Roses: The Politics of *Mrs. Dalloway*," in *The Authority of Experience: Essays in Feminist Criticism*, ed. Arlyn Diamond and Lee R. Edwards (Amherst, Mass.: University of Massachusetts Press, 1977), pp. 175-77.

57. See, for instance, Marder, *Feminism and Art*, pp. 48-50 and Novak, *The Razor Edge of Balance*, p. 124. Among those who praise the characterization of Bradshaw and do not see it as a flaw in the work are Bennett, *Virginia Woolf*, p. 100, and Brewster, *Virginia Woolf*, p. 111.

58. Robert C. Elliott discusses this aspect of comedy in *The Power of Satire: Magic, Ritual, Art* (Princeton: Princeton University Press, 1960), pp. 3-6, 38-47.

59. The following critics build the major portion of their analysis on the resolution (or on the lack of resolution) of the polarities in the novel: Hafley, *The Glass Roof*, p. 82; Bazin, *Virginia Woolf and the Androgynous Vision*, pp. 138, 166-67; John Edward Hardy, *Man in the Modern Novel* (Seattle: University of Washington Press, 1964), pp. 117-22; Novak, *The Razor Edge of Balance*, pp. 128-43; Kelley, *Novels of Virginia Woolf*, pp. 114-29.

60. DiBattista argues that the comedy derives, as in Joyce's *Ulysses*, from the "imperfect coincidence between [Woolf's] literary figures and their mythic ground"; see *Virginia Woolf's Major Novels*, pp. 78, 64-110.

61. Virginia Woolf, *To the Lighthouse* (London: Hogarth Press, 1974), p. 33 (hereafter cited by page number in the text).

62. Freedman, *The Lyrical Novel*, p. 227.

63. See Bernard Blackstone, *Virginia Woolf: A Commentary* (New York: Harcourt, Brace and Co., 1949), pp. 109, 113-14; Hardy, *Man in the Modern Novel*, p. 101; James Naremore, *The World without a Self: Virginia Woolf and the Novel* (New Haven: Yale University Press, 1973), pp. 128-31; Schaefer, *The Three-Fold Na-*

ture of Reality in the Novels of Virginia Woolf, pp. 112-13.

64. Leslie Stephen, *The Science of Ethics,* 2nd ed. (New York: G. P. Putnam's Sons; London: Smith, Elder, and Co., 1907), p. 170.

65. See a letter from Leslie to Julia in which he says she must take the place of the "saints" he doesn't believe in, quoted by Noel Annan, *Leslie Stephen* (London: MacGibbon and Kee, 1951), p. 75. For an analysis of Mrs. Ramsay as a domineering, destructive presence, see Glenn Pederson, "Vision in *To the Lighthouse,*" *PMLA* 73 (December 1958): 585-600.

66. Woolf, *A Writer's Diary,* p. 88 (30 April 1926).

67. This passage varies slightly in the American edition, but the trivialized, tea-conversation tone, is retained: "Prue Ramsay died that summer in some illness connected with childbirth, which was indeed a tragedy, people said, everything, they said, had promised so well." *To the Lighthouse* (New York: Harcourt, Brace and Co., 1927), p. 199. For a discussion of the variations in the American and English editions see J. A. Lavin, "The First Editions of Virginia Woolf's *To the Lighthouse,*" *Proof* 2 (1972): 185-211.

68. Naremore, for instance, says of Mr. Ramsay that "he thinks" the depths are only water, and at this point briefly surrenders his ego; see *The World without a Self,* p. 150.

69. The following argue essentially this view: Bazin, *Virginia Woolf and the Androgynous Vision,* pp. 8-9; Sharon Kaehele and Howard German, "*To the Lighthouse:* Symbol and Vision," *Bucknell Review* 10 (1962): 328-46; Moody, *Virginia Woolf,* pp. 38-42; S. P. Rosenbaum, "The Philosophical Realism of Virginia Woolf," in *English Literature and British Philosophy,* ed. S. P. Rosenbaum (Chicago: University of Chicago Press, 1971), pp. 343-46.

70. Lily's thoughts on this debt differ slightly in the two editions. In the American (Harcourt, Brace, 1927), Lily says, "She owed it all to her" (p. 241); the word "revelation" is used a few sentences earlier and is the probable antecedent of "it." In the English (Hogarth, 1974), Lily says, "She owed this revelation to her" (p. 250).

71. Joseph Blotner, "Mythic Patterns in *To the Lighthouse,*" *PMLA* 71 (September 1956): 547-62; Fleishman, *Virginia Woolf,* pp. 110-12; Grace Stewart, *A New Mythos: The Novel of the Artist as Heroine, 1877-1977* (St. Albans, Vt.: Eden Press Women's Publications, 1979), pp. 69-71.

72. June Singer, *Androgyny: Toward a New Theory of Sexuality* (Garden City, N.Y.: Doubleday, 1976), p. 321; Singer, *Boundaries of the Soul*, p. 262; Carl Jung, "The Psychological Aspects of the Kore," in C. G. Jung and C. Kerenyi, *Essays on a Science of Mythology*, trans. R. F. C. Hull (Princeton: Princeton University Press, 1969), pp. 156-57, 159.

Chapter Three

1. Virginia Woolf, *The Waves* (London: Hogarth Press, 1943), p. 158 (hereafter cited by page number in the text).

2. Woolf, *Moments of Being* pp. 114-15.

3. Virginia Woolf, *A Writer's Diary* (London: Hogarth Press, 1953), p. 86 (27 February 1926) (hereafter cited in the text as *AWD*).

4. See Bazin, *Virginia Woolf and the Androgynous Vision*, pp. 29-30, and Blackstone, *Virginia Woolf*, pp. 154-62. Jeanne Schulkind also discusses the mystical element in Woolf's novels; see "Introduction" to *Moments of Being*, pp. 17-22.

5. Scholars who have discussed the relationship between *Orlando* and the Sackville family include Frank Baldanza, *"Orlando* and the Sackvilles," *PMLA* 70 (March 1955): 274-79; Charles G. Hoffmann, "Fact and Fantasy in *Orlando:* Virginia Woolf's Manuscript Revisions," *Texas Studies in Literature and Language* 10 (1968): 435-39; Naremore, *The World without a Self*, pp. 196-208; Joanne Trautmann, *The Jessamy Brides: The Friendship of Virginia Woolf and Vita Sackville-West*, Pennsylvania State University Studies, no. 36 (University Park, Pa.: Pennsylvania State University, 1973).

6. Frye, *Anatomy of Criticism*, pp. 304-05.

7. Barbara Babcock, " 'Liberty's A Whore': Inversions, Marginalia, and Picaresque Narrative," in Babcock, *The Reversible World*, pp. 105, 114.

8. Fleishman, *Virginia Woolf*, pp. 146-47. Woolf's own image of androgyny, the whole creative mind, is that of the man and woman riding away in the taxi together; see *A Room of One's Own*, pp. 144-48. Others who discuss androgyny in connection with *Orlando* include Marilyn R. Farwell, "Virginia Woolf and Androgyny, *Contemporary Literature* 16 (Autumn 1975): 433-51 and Marder, *Feminism and Art*, pp. 111-16.

9. Lee, *The Novels of Virginia Woolf,* pp. 147-51. The following also emphasize this point: W. R. Irwin, *The Game of the Impossible: A Rhetoric of Fantasy* (Urbana: University of Illinois Press, 1976), pp. 104-5; Ralph Samuelson, "Virginia Woolf: *Orlando* and the Feminist Spirit," *Western Humanities Review* 15 (Winter, 1961): 51-58; Stewart, *A New Mythos,* pp. 129-31.

10. Virginia Woolf, *Orlando* (London: Hogarth Press, 1928), p. 144 (hereafter cited by page number in the text).

11. Alexander, *The Venture of Form,* p. 146.

12. The note, in the margin of the entry for 14 March 1927, was made on 8 July 1933; see *AWD,* p. 105.

13. J. W. Graham notes that Woolf's manuscript indicates "solitude," not "solicitude" (as printed in American and English editions): see "Point of View in *The Waves:* Some Services of the Style," in *Virginia Woolf: A Collection of Criticism,* ed. Thomas S. W. Lewis (New York: McGraw-Hill, 1975), p. 103, n. 9.

14. Robert Richardson, "Point of View in Virginia Woolf's *The Waves,*" *Texas Studies in Literature and Language* 14 (Winter 1973): 703-9.

15. See for instance Graham, "Point of View in *The Waves,*" pp. 107-8; Harold Nicholson, review of *The Waves (Action,* 8 October 1931, in Majumdar and McLaurin, *Virginia Woolf: The Critical Heritage,* p. 266. Most critics agree that *The Waves* is Woolf's masterpiece. A recent dissenter is Naremore, who finds the book a failure and the style "stifling"; see *The World without a Self,* pp. 156-59.

16. Edwin Muir, review of *The Waves (Bookman,* December 1931), in Majumdar and McLaurin, *Virginia Woolf: The Critical Heritage,* p. 291; Hafley, *The Glass Roof,* pp. 123-24.

17. Lee, *The Novels of Virginia Woolf,* p. 169 (in *The Waves,* pp. 88, 97).

18. Virginia Woolf records a very similar event, recalling her own shock, as a child, when she overheard her father tell of a neighbor's suicide. "The next thing I remember is being in the garden at night and walking by the apple tree. . . . I could not pass it." Woolf, *Moments of Being,* p. 71.

19. Susan Gorsky discusses Percival in relation to the grail legends; see " 'The Central Shadow,': Characterization in *The*

Waves," *Modern Fiction Studies* 18 (Autumn 1972): 451-53. Beverly Schlak also looks at Percival's literary analogues, in *Continuing Presences: Virginia Woolf's Use of Literary Allusion* (University Park, Pa.: Pennsylvania State University, 1979), pp. 128-30. For Frye's discussion of "mythos" see *Anatomy of Criticism*, pp. 140, 162-239.

20. See especially the rituals connected with the worship of Attis, to whom violets were sacred, in James Frazer, *The Golden Bough*, abridged, 1-vol. ed. (New York: Macmillan Co., 1922), pp. 347-56 (part IV of 12-vol. ed.). Virginia Woolf's library included an abridged *Golden Bough* (1929). See *Catalogue of Books from the Library of Leonard and Virginia Woolf* (Brighton: Holleyman and Treacher, 1975), Index, p. 27. Woolf cites *The Golden Bough* in *A Room of One's Own*, p. 45.

21. Anais Nin's words are quoted by Tillie Olsen, "Women Who Are Writers in Our Century: One Out of Twelve," *College English* 34 (October 1972): 9. The psychological "Angel," sympathetic and deferential to men, which threatened to sabotage Woolf's critical reviews of men's books (until Woolf "killed" her) is described in "Professions for Women," *CE*, 2:285-86.

22. Carl Jung writes that God-images or God-archetypes always seem numinous, fateful, full of "mana," to the perceiving consciousness; see *Answer to Job* in *Psychology and Religion: West and East*, vol. 11 of Jung's *Collected Works* (New York: Pantheon Books, 1958), pp. 359-63.

23. Richter, *Virginia Woolf: The Inward Voyage*, pp. 125-27.

24. In the early stages of her work on this novel, Woolf asked, "Who thinks it?" *A WD* p. 146 (25 September 1929).

25. For a discussion of the psychological significance, for a woman, of the animus image see M.-L. Franz, "The Process of Individuation," in Jung, *Man and His Symbols*, pp. 189-95. For the significance of the image of the Self see Singer, *Androgyny*, p. 321; Singer, *Boundaries of the Soul*, p. 262; Jung, "The Psychological Aspects of the Kore," pp. 156-57, 159.

26. Harvey Cox, *The Feast of Fools* (Cambridge: Harvard University Press, 1969), p. 154.

27. Nicolson and Trautmann, *Letters of Virginia Woolf*, 1:404.

28. Hafley, *The Glass Roof*, p. 120. Schlak gives several possi-

ble sources for the wave imagery, including Samuel Butler, De Quincy, Meredith, and Joyce; see *Continuing Presences*, pp. 101-2, 177.

29. Jane Harrison, *Epilegomena to the Study of Greek Religion* (Cambridge: Cambridge University Press, 1921), p. 37.

30. Jack Stewart argues that the sun girl is an "anima" image, which is a plausible interpretation if one sees Bernard as the ego, the consciousness. Stewart, "Existence and Symbol in *The Waves*," *Modern Fiction Studies* 18 (Autumn 1972): 445-46. My own interpretation sees the sun girl, and the woman writing, as images of the Self, the deepest god-image of the female psyche. DiBattista also reads the pervasive consciousness (and unconsciousness) of the novel as "She" and as imaged in both the sun girl and the woman in the garden; Percival is merely a "decoy" in the Freudian dream work of Woolf as she writes the novel. DiBattista, *Virginia Woolf's Major Novels*, pp. 159, 149-72.

31. Nicolson and Trautmann, *Letters of Virginia Woolf*, 4:408 (22 November 1931).

32. Among those who look at the interrupted or unfinished statements are Lee, *Novels of Virginia Woolf*, pp. 192-98, and Sally Sears, "Notes on Sexuality: *The Years* and *Three Guineas*," *Bulletin of the New York Public Library* 80 (Winter 1977): 212-13. In the same journal issue, Grace Radin, though she does not comment on this matter, reproduces in her article some sections of earlier drafts; in these drafts Eleanor and Maggie complete sentences which are left unfinished in Woolf's final manuscript. See Radin, " 'Two enormous chunks': Episodes Excluded during the Final Revisions of *The Years*," pp. 223-26.

33. Virginia Woolf, *The Years* (London: Hogarth Press, 1937), p. 395 (hereafter cited by page number in the text). Alexander discusses the hammer imagery as Wagnerian (forging of Siegfried's sword); see *The Venture of Form*, p. 186. John DiGaetani also discusses the Wagnerian imagery in *The Years* in his *Richard Wagner and the Modern British Novel* (Cranbury, N.J.: Associated University Presses, 1978), pp. 124-28. Other critics who offer illuminating discussions of repeated images include Bazin, *Virginia Woolf and the Androgynous Vision*, pp. 187-88; Lee, *Novels of Virginia Woolf*, pp. 191-92; Marcus, "*The Years* as Greek Drama," pp. 280-88; and Marder, *Feminism and Art*, pp. 100-103.

34. Joanna Lipking, "Looking at the Monuments: Woolf's Satiric Eye," *Bulletin of the New York Public Library* 80 (Winter 1977): 143-45. In the same issue see Beverly Schlak's discussion of "scornful humor": "Virginia Woolf's Strategy of Scorn in *The Years* and *Three Guineas*," pp. 147-49.

35. Victoria Middleton, "*The Years:* 'A Deliberate Failure,' " *Bulletin of the New York Public Library* 80 (Winter 1977): 163-64.

36. Schaefer, *The Threefold Nature of Reality*, p. 182.

37. Marcus, "*The Years* as Greek Drama," pp. 278, 285.

38. Frazer, *The Golden Bough*, pp. 632-36 (part VIII of the 12-vol. ed.).

39. Virginia Woolf, *Three Guineas* (London: Hogarth Press, 1947), pp. 192-208. The inspiration for *The Years* evidently grew out of a speech, "Professions for Women," which Woolf delivered to the National Society for Women's Service, 21 January 1931. See *AWD*, pp. 165-66 (20 January 1931). An account of the genesis and metamorphosis of the novel is given in Leaska, *Novels of Virginia Woolf*, pp. 191-94, and in Leaska's introduction to Virginia Woolf, *The Pargiters* (New York: Harcourt Brace Jovanovich, 1977), pp. vii-xxiv.

40. Lipking, "Looking at the Monuments," p. 144.

41. Barber, *Shakespeare's Festive Comedy*, pp. 3-10; Judy Little, "Festive Comedy in Woolf's *Between the Acts*," *Women and Literature* 5 (Spring 1977): 26-37.

42. A. D. Moody gives more attention than most critics to the comedy in the novel; see his *Virginia Woolf* (New York: Grove Press, 1963), pp. 84-87, 108. Others who mention its presence are Joan Bennet, *Virginia Woolf: Her Art as a Novelist*, 2nd ed. (London: Cambridge University Press, 1964), pp. 111-14 et passim, and James Naremore, *The World without a Self*, pp. 228-29. Dorothy Brewster emphasizes the sinister impulses and the passions beneath the "social comedy" in *Virginia Woolf*, pp. 153-54. B. H. Fussell looks at instances of mock-epic and satire; see "Woolf's Peculiar Comic World," in *Virginia Woolf: Revaluation and Continuity*, ed. Ralph Freedman (Berkeley and Los Angeles: University of California Press, 1980), pp. 263-83. DiBattista's reading finds history and the tragic love relationship of Giles and Isa to be a sort of counterpointing reality to the comic form of the pageant; see *Virginia Woolf's Major Novels*, pp. 190-210.

43. Richard Gill finds it a burlesque of the village pageant; see *Happy Rural Seat: The English Country House and the Literary Imagination* (New Haven: Yale University Press, 1972), p. 200.

44. Virginia Woolf, *Between the Acts* (London: Hogarth Press, 1941), pp. 34, 119, 123 (hereafter cited by page number in the text).

45. Jane Harrison, *Ancient Art and Ritual* (New York: Greenwood Press, 1969), pp. 141-52.

46. In several diary entries during 1938 she expresses delight about a good review or concern over an indictment; see *AWD*, pp. 295 (5 June), 298 (16 June), 301 (1 September). On 7 July she speaks of the difficulty of working on Roger Fry's biography "after these violent oscillations, *Three Guineas* and P. H. [*Between the Acts*]." *AWD*, p. 299.

47. William Morris, *News from Nowhere*, in *Three Works by William Morris*, ed. A. L. Morton (New York: International Publishers, 1968), pp. 390-99. Although Virginia Woolf's library did not contain this book, it did include two of Morris's romances (*The Defence of Guenevere* and *The Story of Sigurd the Volsung and the Fall of the Niblungs*), and Woolf was evidently acquainted with his work. In a letter of 22 February 1915 she requests a copy of Morris's "The Pilgrims of Hope" (Nicolson and Trautmann, *Letters of Virginia Woolf*, 2:60), and Sally Seton gives Clarissa a William Morris work "wrapped in brown paper" (38). Woolf's immediate source for the idea of a country festival is probably Forster's *Abinger Harvest*; see Jean Wyatt, "Art and Allusion in *Between the Acts*," *Mosaic* 11 (Summer 1978): 93.

48. Bazin, *Virginia Woolf and the Androgynous Vision*, p. 210.

49. Harrison, *Ancient Art and Ritual*, pp. 61-62.

50. Ibid., pp. 25-26, 204-40. In August 1939 Virginia Woolf records that she is "condensing" Fry's *Vision and Design;* see *AWD* p. 303. For Fry's discussion of emotion and art, see *Vision and Design* (London: Chatto and Windus, 1923), pp. 20-29. Harrison lists Fry's "Essay in Aesthetics" (published in April 1909 in the *New Quarterly* and later incorporated into *Vision and Design*) in the bibliography to her *Ancient Art and Ritual*, praising Fry and noting that her ideas were formulated independently; see *Ancient Art and Ritual*, p. 254.

Chapter Four

1. Muriel Spark, "Edinburgh-Born," *New Statesman*, 10 August 1962, p. 180.

2. Muriel Spark, "The Desegregation of Art," in *Proceedings of the American Academy of Arts and Letters*, 2nd ser., no. 21 (1971), p. 24.

3. See, for instance, James Brockway, "New Spark of Genius," review of *The Takeover* by Muriel Spark, *Books and Bookmen* 22 (November 1976): 60-61; Derek Stanford, "Muriel Spark," in *Contemporary Novelists*, ed. James Vinson (London: St. James Press, 1976), p. 1272. In a collection of sermons to which Spark wrote the Foreword, Newman admonishes all to "aim at seeing things as God sees them." *Cardinal Newman's Best Plain Sermons*, ed. Vincent F. Blehl (New York: Herder and Herder, 1964), p. 82.

4. Muriel Spark, "Foreword" to *Cardinal Newman's Best Plain Sermons*, pp. vii-viii.

5. Muriel Spark, *The Mandelbaum Gate* (New York: Alfred A. Knopf, 1965), p. 194 (hereafter cited by page number in the text).

6. Muriel Spark, "My Conversion," *Twentieth Century* 170 (Autumn 1961): 60.

7. Among the accusers are Richard Mayne, "Fiery Particle: On Muriel Spark," *Encounter* 25 (December 1965): 62-64, and Christopher Ricks, "Extreme Instances," review of *The Public Image, Collected Stories: I* and *Collected Poems I* by Muriel Spark, *New York Review of Books*, 19 December 1968, pp. 31-32. The following point to the neutrality of the Catholic imagery: Frank Baldanza, "Muriel Spark and the Occult," *Wisconsin Studies in Contemporary Literature*, 6 (Summer 1965): 191-202, and Stanford, "Muriel Spark," p. 1272. Joanne Parnell Mongeon looks at several comic devices in relation to Spark's Catholicism in her unpublished dissertation (University of Rhode Island, 1977), "A Theology of Juxtaposition: Muriel Spark as a Catholic Comic Novelist." Brief discussions of Spark's comedy include Allan Massie, *Muriel Spark* (Edinburgh: Ramsay Head Press, 1979), pp. 91-93, and Ruth Whittaker, " 'Angels Dining At the Ritz': The Faith and Fiction of Muriel Spark," in Bradbury and Palmer, *The Contemporary English Novel*, pp. 168-71.

8. Frank Kermode, "The Novel as Jerusalem: Muriel Spark's

The Mandelbaum Gate," The Atlantic Monthly 216 (October 1965): 92.

9. Josephine Jacobsen, "A Catholic Quartet," *The Christian Scholar* 47 (Summer 1964): 141-42; Peter Kemp, *Muriel Spark* (London: Paul Elek, 1974), pp. 14, 27; Alan Kennedy, *The Protean Self: Dramatic Action in Contemporary Fiction* (New York: Columbia University Press, 1974), p. 161.

10. Anthony Paul, "Muriel Spark and *The Prime of Miss Jean Brodie," Dutch Quarterly Review* 7 (1977): 174; Bernard Harrison, "Muriel Spark and Jane Austen," in *The Modern English Novel,* ed. Gabriel Josipovici (London: Open Books, 1976), pp. 228-43.

11. Derek Stanford, *Muriel Spark* (London: Centaur Press, 1963), p. 83; Samuel Hynes, "In the Great Tradition: The Prime of Muriel Spark," *Commonweal,* 23 February 1962, p. 567.

12. Muriel Spark, "Newman as Catholic," in *Letters of John Henry Newman,* ed. Derek Stanford and Muriel Spark (London: Peter Owen, 1957), p. 154.

13. Stanford, *Muriel Spark,* p. 109.

14. *Newman's Best Plain Sermons,* pp. 53,57.

15. Muriel Spark, *Collected Poems I* (London: Macmillan & Co., 1967), p. 9.

16. John Updike, "Creatures of the Air," review of *The Bachelors* by Muriel Spark, *New Yorker* 30 September 1961, p. 165.

17. Muriel Spark, "Keeping It Short," an interview by Ian Gillham, *The Listener* 24 September 1970, p. 411.

18. Unhappily married, and stranded in Africa with her husband, Sybil reads the *Journals.* "She felt like a desert which had not realised its own aridity till the rain began to fall upon it," Spark, "Bang-bang You're Dead," in *Collected Stories: I* (New York: Alfred A. Knopf, 1968), p. 87.

19. Søren Kierkegaard, *Journals and Papers,* ed. and trans. Howard V. Hong and Edna H. Hong, 7 vols. (Bloomington: Indiana University Press, 1967-78), 1:171. On another occasion Spark uses Kierkegaard in a less positive context; the abbess of Crewe, redesigning the Rule for the convent, says "to hell with St. Francis," and announces her preference for Sextus Propertius, Hamlet, Werther, Rousseau, and Kierkegaard; here Kierkegaard is linked to some violent romantics and egotists. See Spark, *The Abbess of Crewe* (New York: Viking Press, 1974), p. 40.

20. Spark, "My Conversion," p. 63; she makes a similar statement about "truth" in an interview with Frank Kermode, "The House of Fiction: Interviews with Seven Novelists," *Partisan Review* 30 (Spring 1963): 80. Peter Kemp gives a thorough analysis of the concept of "economy" in Spark's writing, and of its relation to Newman's enunciation of the idea. See his *Muriel Spark*, pp. 8-13, 35-36.

21. Spark, in Kermode, "The House of Fiction," p. 79.

22. Spark, "My Conversion," p. 61.

23. Muriel Spark, "The Gentile Jewesses," in *Winter's Tales*, ed. A. D. Maclean (London: Macmillan & Co., 1963), pp. 241-42. For a biographical account of Spark's parents and grandparents, see Stanford, *Muriel Spark*, pp. 23, 31-37. Charles Hoyt has pointed to the unusual independence of Spark's women; most of them lack the "traditional feminine fragility and dependency." Hoyt, "Muriel Spark: The Surrealist Jane Austen," in *Contemporary British Novelists*, ed. Charles Shapiro (Carbondale: Southern Illinois University Press, 1965), p. 132. For the biblical account of Miriam, see Exodus 15:20-21 and Numbers 12. Of course, Moses, not Miriam, leads the people through the parted sea, though she and the women dance and sing in praise of God afterwards; when she and Aaron later speak against Moses for marrying a Cushite woman, God punishes Miriam with a plague of leprosy for seven days.

24. Spark also remarks that "castrating men is a bad idea"; see an interview by Victoria Glendinning, "Talk With Muriel Spark," *New York Times Book Review*, 20 May 1979, p. 48.

25. Spark, "My Conversion," p. 59.

26. Muriel Spark, *The Comforters* (Philadelphia and New York: J. B. Lippincott, 1957), p. 150 (hereafter cited by page number in the text).

27. For discussion of the novel's relation to the Job story, see Kemp, *Muriel Spark*, pp. 17-20; Karl Malkoff, *Muriel Spark* (New York: Columbia University Press, 1968), pp. 6-7; Stanford, *Muriel Spark*, p. 126.

28. During her illness, Spark was assisted by a priest who was a student of Jungian analysis. Stanford, *Muriel Spark*, p. 62. She also wrote an article on Jung's *Answer to Job* (London, 1954, in English translation), finding the book's implicit theology too anthropomorphic. Unlike Jung, Spark asserts the value of the "epilogue" in the

Job story, since it gives "that type of anagogical humour which transcends irony, and which is infinitely mysterious." See Spark, "The Mystery of Job's Suffering," *Church of England Newspaper*, 15 April 1955, 7. For a discussion of the "shadow" and the "anima-animus" archetypes, see C. G. Jung, *Aion*, trans. R.F.C. Hull, 2nd ed. (Princeton: Princeton University Press, 1968), pp. 3-22.

29. Spark, *Collected Poems I*, p. 38

30. See, for instance, Baldanza, "Muriel Spark and the Occult," p. 197; Kemp, *Muriel Spark*, pp. 36-37; Harold W. Schneider, "A Writer in Her Prime: The Fiction of Muriel Spark," *Critique* 5 (Fall 1962): 37-38.

31. Muriel Spark, *Robinson* (London: Macmillan & Co., 1958), p. 1 (hereafter cited by page number in the text).

32. For the Freudian interpretations see Kemp, *Muriel Spark*, pp. 30-32; Malkoff, *Muriel Spark*, pp. 12-16; Carol Ohmann, "Muriel Spark's *Robinson*," *Critique* 8 (Fall 1965): 70-84.

33. Kemp, *Muriel Spark*, p. 34.

34. Annis Pratt, "Archetypal Approaches to the New Feminist Criticism," *Bucknell Review* 21 (Spring 1973): 3.

35. Malkoff, *Muriel Spark*, p. 16.

36. Stanford argues otherwise, saying that the island represents paganism, youth, magic, and poetry—all of which are overthrown "at the hands of orthodox thought." Stanford, *Muriel Spark*, pp. 127-28.

37. C. G. Jung, *Answer to Job*, in *Psychology and Religion: West and East*, trans. R.F.C. Hull (New York: Pantheon Books, 1958), pp. 386-89, 397-400, 442. See note 28 above.

38. Ann Belford Ulanov discusses the several occasions in the work of Jung where evil, matter, and the feminine are implicitly or even explicitly linked; see Ulanov, *The Feminine in Jungian Psychology and in Christian Theology* (Evanston, Ill.: Northwestern University Press, 1971), pp. 135-36. Muriel Spark has said that one of the things that interested her in Catholicism was "its acceptance of matter. So much of our world rejects it." She does not imply here a linkage between matter and the feminine. See "My Conversion," p. 63.

39. Jung, *Answer to Job*, p. 458.

40. Malkoff, *Muriel Spark*, p. 18; Kemp, *Muriel Spark*, pp. 40-42.

41. Muriel Spark, *Memento Mori* (Philadelphia and New York: J. B. Lippincott, 1959), p. 128 (hereafter cited by page number in the text).

42. See Berger and Luckmann, *The Social Construction of Reality*, p. 148.

43. For a discussion of this figure, see Charney, *Comedy High and Low*, pp. 62-65.

44. Muriel Spark, *The Ballad of Peckham Rye* (Philadelphia and New York: J. B. Lippincott, 1960), pp. 158-59 (hereafter cited by page number in the text).

45. Kemp, *Muriel Spark*, pp. 52-54. Massie observes that Dougal himself is "the Saturnalia made flesh"; see *Muriel Spark*, p. 30.

46. Barber, *Shakespeare's Festive Comedy*, pp. 6-10.

47. Kemp, *Muriel Spark*, pp. 48-55; Malkoff, *Muriel Spark*, pp. 22-24.

48. Kemp, *Muriel Spark*, pp. 49-50.

49. Muriel Spark, *The Bachelors* (London: Macmillan & Co., 1961), p. 1 (hereafter cited by page number in the text).

50. John Updike, "Creatures of the Air," review of *The Bachelors* by Muriel Spark, *New Yorker*, 30 September 1961, p. 161. For a similar interpretation see Malkoff, *Muriel Spark*, pp. 26-27.

51. Kennedy, *The Protean Self*, p. 182.

52. Spark, in Kermode, "The House of Fiction," p. 80.

53. Kennedy observes that the pun in Ronald's name indicates that he is a better "medium," a better "bridge," to other people than Seton is; see *The Protean Self*, p. 182.

54. Muriel Spark, *The Prime of Miss Jean Brodie* (Philadelphia and New York: J. B. Lippincott, 1962), p. 17 (hereafter cited by page number in the text).

55. Nina Auerbach, *Communities of Women* (Cambridge: Harvard University Press, 1978), p. 185.

56. See Hynes, "In the Great Tradition: The Prime of Muriel Spark," p. 568: Auerbach, *Communities of Women*, pp. 168-69; Kemp, *Muriel Spark*, pp. 73-76; David Lodge, *The Novelist at the Crossroads* (London: Routledge & Kegan Paul, 1971), pp. 135-37.

57. Stanford, *Muriel Spark*, pp. 38-39.

58. Daniel J. Levinson, *The Seasons of a Man's Life* (New York: Alfred A. Knopf, 1978), pp. 97-101, 333-34. In the title of his book, Levinson does not use "man's life" loosely and generically; he limits

his study to men. He points out (p. 98) that mentoring among women is still quite rare: "One of the great problems of women is that female mentors are scarce, especially in the world of work."

59. In the first group see Kennedy, *The Protean Self*, pp. 187-93; Paul, "Muriel Spark and *The Prime of Miss Jean Brodie*," pp. 179-82; Lodge, *The Novelist at the Crossroads*, pp. 140-42. Gary Laffin argues that Sandy is an ironic figure and nearly as deceived as Jean Brodie. Laffin, "Muriel Spark's Portrait of the Artist as a Young Girl," *Renascence* 24 (Summer 1972): 214-21.

60. Muriel Spark, *The Girls of Slender Means* (New York: Alfred A. Knopf, 1963), p. 69 (hereafter cited by page number in the text).

61. Ricks, "Extreme Instances," p. 32.

62. See, for this viewpoint, Warner Berthoff, "Fortunes of the Novel: Muriel Spark and Iris Murdoch," *Massachusetts Review* 3 (Spring 1976): 306-13; Mayne, "Fiery Particle: On Muriel Spark," p. 66.

63. Berthoff, "Fortunes of the Novel: Muriel Spark and Iris Murdoch," pp. 312-13.

Chapter Five

1. Spark, "Edinburgh-Born," p. 180.

2. Spark, "The Desegregation of Art," pp. 23-27.

3. Alan Kennedy examines this theme in Spark's novels (through *Not to Disturb*) from a sociological perspective, in *The Protean Self*, pp. 151-211.

4. Muriel Spark, *The Public Image* (New York: Alfred A. Knopf, 1968), p. 29 (hereafter cited by page number in the text).

5. Velma B. Richmond emphasizes this point, in "The Darkening Vision of Muriel Spark," *Critique* 15 (1973):74.

6. Spark, in Gillham, "Keeping It Short," p. 413.

7. Ibid., pp. 412-13.

8. Richmond, "The Darkening Vision of Muriel Spark," pp. 76-77; Frank Kermode, "Sheerer Spark," review of *The Driver's Seat* by Muriel Spark, *The Listener*, 24 September 1970, p. 425.

9. Kemp, *Muriel Spark*, pp. 126-27; Kennedy, *The Protean Self*, pp. 204-5; Malkoff, *Muriel Spark*, p. 17. Whittaker emphasizes the novel's several oblique hints of a fuller world, a world of

emotion and freedom; see " 'Angels Dining at the Ritz': The Faith and Fiction of Muriel Spark," pp. 174-79.

10. Rosalind Miles, *The Fiction of Sex* (London: Vision Press, 1974), pp. 21-22.

11. Muriel Spark, *The Driver's Seat* (New York: Alfred A. Knopf, 1970), p. 117 (hereafter cited by page number in the text).

12. Muriel Spark, *Not to Disturb* (New York: Viking Press, 1972), p. 29 (hereafter cited by page number in the text).

13. Spark, interviewed by Philip Toynbee, *Observer*, Colour Magazine, 7 November 1971, p. 74.

14. Muriel Spark, *The Hothouse by the East River* (New York: Viking Press, 1973), p. 127 (hereafter cited by page number in the text.)

15. *The Cloud of Unknowing*, trans. Ira Progoff (New York: Julian Press, 1957), p. 82. I have inserted in brackets the words from *The Cloud of Unknowing*, ed. Phyllis Hodgson (London: Oxford University Press, for the Early English Text Society, 1944), 33. 11-15; for further instances of the words "deedly body," see 1.8, 41.2, 42.7. Joanne Mongeon briefly notes Spark's use of *The Cloud of Unknowing;* see "A Theology of Juxtaposition: Muriel Spark as a Catholic Comic Novelist," pp. 182-83.

16. See for instance *Hamlet*, 5. 2. 347-48: "This fell sergeant, Death, / Is strict in his arrest.

17. *The Cloud of Unknowing*, trans. Progoff, pp. 75-76, 133-34.

18. Ibid., p. 224.

19. Kemp, *Muriel Spark*, p. 142; Jonathan Raban, "On Losing the Rabbit: New Novels," *Encounter* 40 (May 1973): 84.

20. *The Cloud of Unknowing*, trans. Progoff, p. 227.

21. Muriel Spark, *The Abbess of Crewe* (New York: Viking Press, 1974), p. 99 (hereafter cited by page number in the text).

22. To Michael Wood, the "joke" is merely "cute," a "thin gag." Wood, "Fiction in Extremis," *New York Review of Books*, 28 November 1974, p. 29. George Stade, however, praises the author's perception of the "farce" in the Watergate materials; see his review of *The Abbess of Crewe*, in the *New York Times Book Review*, 20 October 1974, pp. 4-5.

23. Traherne, from "The Third Century," poem 3 in *Centuries of Meditations*, ed. Bertram Dobell (London: P. J. & A. E. Dobell,

1908) p. 152. Spark quotes the first part of this line in an interview where she speaks of the "unusual" quality of life to a child, and to herself as a child. Spark, in Gillham, "Keeping It Short," p. 411.

24. Muriel Spark, *The Takeover* (London: Macmillan, 1976), pp. 6-7. Further references will be to this edition and will be cited in parentheses in the text.

25. See, for instance, Linda Kuehl, review of *The Takeover* by Muriel Spark, *Saturday Review*, 18 September 1976, p. 32; and Shernaz Mollinger, review of *The Takeover* by Muriel Spark, *World Literature Today* 51 (Summer 1977): 445. See also Massie's good discussion (*Muriel Spark*, pp. 85-88); he finds the major characters surviving because ultimately they do not worship possessions, but trust their own resources instead.

26. James Brockway, "New Spark of Genius," review of *The Takeover* by Muriel Spark, *Books and Bookmen* 22 (November 1976): 60-61.

27. Newman, in *The Arians of the Fourth Century*, praises Saint Paul's and Origen's use of "economy" in conversion; they led converts to Christianity, but through pagan allusions or readings. See *The Essential Newman*, ed. Vincent F. Blehl (New York: New American Library, Mentor-Omega, 1963), pp. 82-86.

28. Anatole Broyard, "Thinking a Novel in Venice," review of *Territorial Rights* by Muriel Spark, in *Books of the Times* 2 (July 1979): 239. Edmund White, on the other hand, finds the many surprise encounters full of meaning and excitement; see his "Fun in Venice," review of *Territorial Rights* by Muriel Spark, in *New York Times Book Review*, 20 May 1979, pp. 1, 46.

29. Muriel Spark, *Territorial Rights* (New York: Coward, McCann and Geoghegan, 1979), p. 66 (hereafter cited by page number in the text).

30. Frank Kermode, "Judgment in Venice," review of *Territorial Rights* by Muriel Spark, *The Listener*, 26 April 1979, p. 584.

31. Reviewers use words like "thin" (Updike) and "too thinly well-wrought" (Treglown) to express their dissatisfaction, which I share, with the texture of this novel. John Updike, "Fresh from the Forties," review of *Loitering With Intent* by Muriel Spark, *The New Yorker*, 8 June 1981, pp. 148-50; Jeremy Treglown, "A Literary Life," review of *Loitering With Intent* by Muriel Spark, *Times Literary Supplement*, 22 May 1981, p. 561.

32. Muriel Spark, *Loitering With Intent* (New York: Coward, McCann and Geoghegan, 1981), p. 196.

Chapter Six

1. Turner, *Dramas, Fields, and Metaphors*, pp. 292-93.

2. See Carol P. Christ, "Spiritual Quest and Women's Experience," in *Womanspirit Rising*, ed. Carol P. Christ and Judith Plaskow (New York: Harper & Row, 1979), pp. 243 and 245, n. 39. And see Michael Novak, *A Theology for Radical Politics* (New York: Herder & Herder, 1969), pp. 125-26.

3. See David Plante, "Jean Rhys: A Remembrance," *Paris Review*, no. 76 (Fall 1979), pp. 279-80, 272.

4. Jean Rhys, *Good Morning, Midnight* (New York: Harper & Row, n.d.) , p. 29. The first ellipses is mine; the second belongs to Rhys.

5. Ibid., pp. 41-42.

6. Jean Rhys, *After Leaving Mr. Mackenzie* (New York: Harper & Row, 1931), p. 51.

7. Judy Little, "Satirizing the Norm: Comedy in Women's Fiction," *Regionalism and the Female Imagination* 3 (Fall 1977 and Winter 1977-78): 39-49. See also Gary Goshgarian, "Feminist Values in the Novels of Iris Murdoch," *Revue des Langues Vivantes* 40, no. 5 (1974): 519-27.

8. Jack I. Biles, "An Interview with Iris Murdoch," *Studies in the Literary Imagination* 11 (Fall 1978): 119.

9. Penelope Mortimer, *The Pumpkin Eater* (Plainfield, Vt.: Daughters, 1975), p. 194 (hereafter cited by page number in the text).

10. Beryl Bainbridge, *Injury Time* (London: Duckworth and Co., 1977), pp. 21-22 (hereafter cited by page number in the text).

11. Margaret Drabble, *The Realms of Gold* (New York: Knopf, 1975), p. 129 (hereafter cited by page number in the text).

12. Campbell, *The Masks of God*, pp. 48-50.

13. Richardson, *The Homeric Hymn to Demeter*, pp. 318-19.

Index